I0760038

TRANSACTIONS

of the

American Philosophical Society

Held at Philadelphia for Promoting Useful Knowledge

VOLUME 76, Part 1, 1986

Prussia in Transition: Society and Politics under the Stein Reform Ministry of 1808

MARION W. GRAY

TRANSACTIONS

of the

American Philosophical Society

Held at Philadelphia for Promoting Useful Knowledge

VOLUME 76, Part 1, 1986

Prussia in Transition:
Society and Politics under the Stein Reform Ministry of 1808

MARION W. GRAY
Associate Professor of History, Kansas State University

THE AMERICAN PHILOSOPHICAL SOCIETY

Independence Square, Philadelphia

1986

Library of Congress Catalog
Card Number 84-45902
International Standard Book Number 0–87169–761–0
US ISSN 0065–9746

To my parents
Mary S. Gray and Marion W. Gray, Sr.
who gave me unquestioning support

ACKNOWLEDGMENTS

The archivists of the collections mentioned in the preface generously assisted me in my search for source material. I am grateful for the opportunity to draw upon their professional expertise. I also received invaluable help from the staffs of several libraries, including: Niedersächische Staats- und Universitätsbibliothek, Göttingen; Universitätsbibliothek, Giessen, Bibliothek des Historischen Seminars, Justus Liebig-Universität Giessen; Farrell Library, Kansas State University; and the Watson and Spencer Libraries, University of Kansas.

A grant from the National Endowment for the Humanities enabled me to conduct the research for the project. The Bureau of General Research of Kansas State University's graduate school provided support for securing materials and preparation of the manuscript.

I am grateful to the Historische Kommission zu Berlin and to the journal, *Central European History,* for permission to reprint, in revised form, passages from articles which represent early stages of my research and conceptualization. The manuscript also contains some sections from an article published by University Microfilms for the *Journal of Modern History.*

Many friends and colleagues lent their scholarly and personal support to this project. Theodore Hamerow first suggested to me that I undertake a reinterpretation of the Stein ministry, and I am indebted to him for this initial stimulus.

Others have contributed through their critical reading and challenging discussions of parts of the work in its many phases. This includes the entire faculty of the history department of Kansas State University, who tore apart two chapters in their infamous departmental seminars, forcing me to reconceptualize many of my early ideas. I am especially grateful, also, for the encouragement and criticism I received from Steve Golin, Herbert Obenaus, Jürgen Schlumbohm, Rudolf Vierhaus, and Arthur Imhof. Richard Raack was very supportive of my project in many ways and over a period of several years. Near the last phase of the writing, he and Konrad Jarausch kindly read the manuscript and rendered substantive suggestions.

I received outstanding editorial assistance from Carole N. Le Faivre, Elizabeth Read Foster, and Eleanor Roach of the American Philosophical Society. I appreciate their careful combing of the manuscript for inconsistencies and stylistic roughness and for their professional suggestions.

Finally, I wish to thank Esther Cappon Gray, who gave me emotional and material support, as well as intellectual stimulation, while I researched and wrote the manuscript.

PREFACE

I first became interested in the society and culture of modern Germany over twenty years ago when I had the opportunity of living for two months with the family of Hein and Bertha Somfleth in the village of Mittelnkirchen near Stade on the Elbe River. Here I encountered traditions which reached back through many centuries of agricultural life. At least since the Thirty Years War, and probably much longer, the Somfleth family, like their neighbors, had raised fruit in a picturesque region called simply, Altesland, the old land.

My association with this family brought me into immediate contact with powerful cultural traditions and close community ties. Being inhabitants of the twentieth century, the Somfleths are, nevertheless, sharply aware of both the costs and the benefits of the rapid social change which we in the western world have sometimes called "progress."

A desire to know more about how modern German society became what it is today, and to understand how it is changing even now, led me to the topic of the Prussian reforms under Baron vom Stein. This, admittedly, is far from the villagers of Mittelnkirchen. However, the general process of social, cultural and political change which they and their forebears have experienced is related to the transitions fostered by the Prussian reformers of 1808. Indeed, both are a part of a constellation of social changes which affect the lives of all of us who live in the modern western world. I hope that my study of the Stein reforms contributes to our understanding of these phenomena.

Like many historians, I found my topic shaped by the availability of source materials. My original intention to analyze the reforms of both the Stein and the Hardenberg administrations could not be realized because I was never able to gain access to essential Prussian archives now located in the German Democratic Republic. I confined my primary research to the Stein ministry, for which adequate source material was available. Fortunately several historians, both of East and West Germany, have recently evaluated the Hardenberg ministry from the vantage point of modern scholarship and with use of the necessary archives.

The outstanding published collection of documents relating to the Stein ministry, edited by Heinrich Scheel and compiled by Doris Schmidt, formed a basis for my research. I was able to lend a unique perspective to the reforms of 1808 with sources from the former provincial archive of East Prussia. During the Second World War this depository was moved from Königsberg to the medieval imperial palace in Goslar in the Harz Mountains in order to protect it from bombing. After the war it was moved to nearby

Göttingen and deposited in the Staatliches Archivlager where I used it. It has since been relocated as a part of the Archivbestände Preussischer Kulturbesitz in West Berlin.

Because the Prussian government was located in Königsberg during the reform year, and because many of the reform activities focused on the province of East Prussia, sources from the former provincial archive bring one especially close to the reformers and their work. They offer a view of the reforms of which historians have not often taken advantage. In addition, three other archives in West Germany house collections useful for my study. The Geheimes Staatsarchiv Preussischer Kulturbesitz, Berlin-Dahlem, contains papers of Auerswald and Gneisenau, who were active in the Stein government. The papers of Ludwig von Vincke, another colleague of Stein, are located in the Staatsarchiv, Münster. And a rich collection of documents from former Prussian archives is contained in the papers of the Weimar Historian, Eckart Kehr in the Bundesarchiv, Koblenz. Kehr collected these documents for a planned publication which he never was able to complete due to the disruptive political events of the 1930s and his untimely death. Only subsequent to the completion of my research has a volume of sources from this valuable collection been published.[1]

My research focuses upon social, political and economic change. It does not include an analysis of the military reforms of the Stein ministry. I leave this topic to those with expertise in military history, although with a plea not to view military reforms in isolation from a broad social context.[2]

This study is an analysis of one phase of Prussia's transition in the modern world. It is grounded upon a close analysis of the short-lived reform government during which Baron vom Stein and his colleagues frantically tried to alter the nature of the state, society and economy. In order to understand the activity of these thirteen months, I have devoted three chapters to conditions prior to and subsequent to the reform ministry. This is in support of my argument that Stein and his co-workers were participants in a process of change which was much more long-lived than their short tenure of activity, and was much more comprehensive than even they were able to realize.

---

[1] Hanna Schissler and Hans-Ulrich Wehler, eds., *Preussische Finanzpolitik 1806–1810: Quellen zur Verwaltung der Ministerien Stein and Altenstein,* collected by Eckart Kehr (Göttingen, 1984).

[2] See my bibliographical essay: Marion W. Gray, "The Rise of German Nationalism and the Wars of Liberation (1803–1814)," in Donald D. Horward, ed., *Napoleonic Military History: A Bibliography,* Military History Bibliographies 9, Garland Reference Library of Social Science 194 (New York and London, 1986), 435–78.

CONTENTS

I. THE STEIN MINISTRY IN HISTORICAL PERSPECTIVE: HERO HISTORY AND BEYOND

THE STEIN MINISTRY OF 1807–1808

In 1806 Napoleon's imperial army inflicted a crushing blow on the Hohenzollern monarchy. The defeat was stunning because only a few years previously Prussia had been universally regarded as one of Europe's great powers. But the once proud kingdom emerged from the Napoleonic war with a shattered military organization, a devastated countryside, a bankrupt treasury, a broken economy, a government in chaos, and with all but a fraction of its territory either annexed or occupied by foreigners. To Prussians it was suddenly apparent that while France had undergone almost two decades of revolutionary change, their state and society had remained relatively static. Prussia seemed hopelessly antiquated.

King Frederick William III summoned Baron Karl vom Stein to head a ministry dedicated to making Prussia as vital and as strong as France. Only months previously Frederick William had dismissed Stein because of the minister's resolute advocacy of reform. But in defeat even the cautious monarch adopted the view that innovation was necessary. From October 1807 to November 1808 Stein and a small group of zealous colleagues labored intensely to make Prussia a modern state by contemporary standards. They sought to transform the rigid aristocratic society into one based on the Enlightenment notion of free citizens. They strove to replace absolute monarchy and bureaucratic inefficiency with a constitutional system. The reformers planned to rid Prussia's economy of a land-bound peasantry, of artisans tied to guilds, and of a rigid barrier restricting the flow of capital between cities and the countryside. The reformers endeavored to give Prussia a mobile society similar to that of England, which was at that time in the midst of its industrial revolution.

Stein's government fell from power after a mere thirteen months of work. The reformers were forced to abandon many of their reform plans only partially enacted, while they left others on the drawing board, some hardly conceptualized. For approximately a decade, successive governments continued to endorse the ideals of reform, especially in the economy. By 1815 a coalition of European powers had defeated Napoleon, removing the external threat to Prussia, and by 1820 "normalcy" reigned again. The rhetoric of reform was heard no more in official circles until the eve of the 1848 revolutions.

The reform year 1807–1808 in Prussia is comparable in significance to 1787 in the history of the United States, the year of the constitutional convention. In North America a small elite succeeded in drawing together ideals of their eighteenth-century world. Their constitution was an expression of emerging social, economic and political patterns, and it gave direction to subsequent historical change. The Founding Fathers helped shape the middle-class democracy which characterized modern America in the two following centuries.

The Prussian leaders performed an analogous task in their own land. Unlike their near contemporaries in the New World, they never wrote a constitution, and they were bitter and disappointed at the outcome of their efforts. They believed their enemies—the conservative aristocracy, the French conquerors, and the inertia of a traditional agrarian society—had destroyed their dreams. But in a more encompassing sense than Stein and his associates comprehended, the year 1808 was a dramatic, eventful episode in Prussia's transformation from a tradition-bound, absolutist system to a commercially oriented, bureaucratically led society. The reform movement should be understood as a dynamic interaction between Enlightenment ideals and forces of social conservatism. Although Stein's fall from power left the reform work incomplete, the patterns his government established became woven into the social and economic fabric of Prussia in succeeding decades. The legacy of the Stein ministry included a strengthened aristocracy, a reinforced bureaucracy, and a hierarchical society. These results are due to the particular context in which the reform movement gained its sustenance. The Prussian reformers, like the American framers of a constitution, accelerated in their land a complex process of social and economic change which was already under way as they set about their work.

Prussia was not alone in experiencing the kinds of changes fostered by the Stein ministry. Everywhere in western and central Europe, and in much of eastern Europe, innovators applied eighteenth-century ideals to existing conditions. Out of this eventually grew nineteenth- and twentieth-century industrial societies. In some states there were visible turning points, such as Prussia's reform year, which itself was a response to the most spectacular event of all, the French Revolution. In other areas one cannot point to a single year or movement to symbolize the transfiguration. But every locale, either with slow, inconspicuous evolution, or with sudden spurts of change, experienced the transition, each with its local variations. Prussia's experience was but a part of a larger process of transformation shared by the western world.

PRAISE AND CRITICISM OF THE REFORMERS IN GERMAN HISTORIOGRAPHY

Among Stein's contemporaries there were many advocates of change who were overwhelmed by enthusiasm when they viewed the reform work. Others, like Adam Müller and F. A. Ludwig von der Marwitz, deplored the reforms, along with much else that was happening in their times. Representing the viewpoint of the conservative aristocracy, they despised innovation.[1] These two patterns are mirrored in the historical literature and popular thought concerning the reforms and their meaning for Germany. On the one hand there are eulogizers who have regarded the reformers as heroes of Prussia's and Germany's past. On the other hand, the critics have assessed the effects of the reforms as negative. The former view is by far the most prevalent.

Stein is one of the few political heroes of the past whom Germans comfortably honor. He usually escapes the criticism aimed at figures like Frederick the Great, Bismarck and William II who are often thought to personify the Prussian traditions of authoritarianism and militarism which are part of Germany's past. Many historians believe Stein stands outside of these traditions. Instead, the Stein era symbolizes for many a struggling heritage of political freedom, egalitarianism, self-government and social progress. "Stein's ministry lasted slightly more than a year . . ." wrote Friedrich Meinecke in the early twentieth century. "But this one year nurtured all of Prussian-German history in the nineteenth century. In this creative epoch originated the institutions and impulses which today still have living consequences."[2]

Politicians of contemporary West Germany look to Stein as an ideal and model.[3] School teachers in both post-war German states use history lessons about Stein to inspire civic virtues in their pupils. In the Federal Republic Stein personifies "freedom," "democracy," and "constitutionalism." His work is used to teach the lesson that reform is healthy change, contrasted to the "dead end" of revolution.[4] Schoolbooks in the German Democratic Republic pay tribute to Stein as the opponent of native aristocracy and foreign oppressors.[5]

Historians, likewise, have praised rather than questioned Stein's work. Georg Pertz published the first scholarly biography of Stein in the mid-

---

[1] Adam Müller, *Vermischte Schriften über Staat, Philosophie und Kunst* (Vienna, 1817). *Friedrich August Ludwig von der Marwitz: Ein märkischer Edelmann im Zeitalter der Befreiungskriege*, ed. Friedrich Meusel (Berlin, 1908–13).

[2] Friedrich Meinecke, *Das Zeitalter der deutschen Erhebung (1795–1815)* (Göttingen, 1963 [1st ed. 1906]), 78.

[3] Peter Meyers, "Unterrichtsversuche zum Thema," *Der Freiherr vom Stein in unserer Zeit: Gedanken und Versuche zur politischen Bildung*, Cappenberger Gespräche der Freiherr-vom-Stein Gesellschaft, V (Cologne and Berlin, 1971), 35.

[4] Hildegard Vellen, "Bericht über eine Unterrichtsstunde," ibid., 43–49. Karl-Friedrich Warner and Bernd Januschke, "Freiherr vom Stein und der preussische Staat," *Der Freiherr vom Stein im Unterricht: Versuche zur historisch-politischen Bildung*, Freiherr-vom-Stein Gesellschaft, V, a (Cologne and Berlin, 1971), 20–22. Hans Heumann, *Unser Weg durch die Geschichte* (Ausgabe für Realschulen), Vol. 3: *Die Grundlagen unserer Gesellschaft* (Frankfurt-am-Main, 1975), 27–29.

[5] Authorcollective, *Geschichte. Lehrbuch für Klasse 7* (Berlin, 1975), 161–63. Authorcollective, *Unterrichtshilfen: Geschichte. 7. Klasse* (Berlin, 1972), 257–61. Veronika Roeder, "Preussische Geschichte in der sozialistischen Schule: Die preussischen Reformen und die Befreiungskriege im Geschichtsunterricht der DDR," *Geschichte in Wissenschaft und Unterricht* 32 (1981): 411–13.

nineteenth century.[6] Pertz was a friend of Stein and collaborated with him on the large project of Stein's later life, a monumental collection of medieval sources in German history. Pertz could find nothing to criticize in the minister's political work, and his six-volume study set the tone of later scholarship. Scholars of the Bismarck era engaged in heated debates about whether Stein was inspired by the radical ideas of the French Revolution or the healthy historical traditions of Prussia. But almost uniformly they saw Stein's reform work as a foundation for what they viewed as the prosperity and progress of their own times.[7]

To those who lived through the first World War, Stein remained a historical leader who commanded veneration. After 1918, scholars intensified their research on the man and his achievements. Many believed Stein's stalwart efforts to rebuild Prussia in 1808 to be instructive for contemporary statesmen of defeated Germany. The deliberate and even heavy-handed liberalism of the reform era seemed to contrast favorably with the stormy political atmosphere of the young Weimar republic. Stein was a favorite of nationalistic and conservative Germans of the early twentieth century.[8]

Under the rule of National Socialism, historians praised Stein because he "raise[d] up the oppressed German *Volk* against the overwhelming French Emperor," freed the peasants and sought to establish national representation. A widely read history of Germany of the late 1930s called Stein "the man of the Prussian rebirth."[9] After the experience of Nazism, many scholars launched a search for the "good" in Germany's seemingly tarnished past. Especially those historians troubled by what they viewed as Prussia's (implying Germany's) failure to adopt "western liberal traditions" have seen the Stein era as a salutory interlude, a small step in the

---

[6] G. H. Pertz, *Das Leben des Ministers Freiherr vom Stein* (Berlin, 1849–1855).

[7] The debate between Max Lehmann and Ernst von Meier over the origin, and hence the ideology, of Stein's thought was bitter. Each claimed Stein for his own side in a political disagreement. But neither questioned the overall positive nature of the reforms. Max Lehmann, *Freiherr vom Stein* (Leipzig, 1902–05); Ernst von Meier, *Französische Einflüsse auf die Staats- und Rechtsentwicklung Preussens im 19. Jahrhundert* (Leipzig, 1907–08), Ernst von Meier, *Der Minister vom Stein, die französische Revolution und der preussische Adel: Eine Streitschrift gegen Max Lehmann* (Leipzig, 1908). For more details on this argument as well as other Stein scholarship of the period see Klaus Epstein, "Stein in German Historiography," *History and Theory* V (1966): 241–74. A recent essay continues the nineteenth-century argument that the reformers were attempting to reestablish ancient German rather than "revolutionary" institutions: Heinrich Bodensieck, *Preussen, Deutschland und der Westen: Auseinandersetzungen und Beziehungen seit 1789. Zum 70. Geburtstag von Oswald Hauser* (Göttingen, 1980), 3–22.

[8] Gerhard Ritter, *Stein: Eine politische Biographie* (Stuttgart and Berlin, 1931). Erich Botzenhart, *Die Staats- und Reformideen des Freiherrn vom Stein: Ihre geistige Grundlagen und ihre praktischen Vorbilder* (Tübingen, 1927). The great interest in Stein in this period is evidenced by the publication of Botzenhart's multivolume edition of the Stein papers: *Freiherr vom Stein: Briefwechsel, Denkschriften und Aufzeichnungen* (Berlin, [1931–37]). Bernd Faulenbach, "Deutsche Geschichtswissenschaft zwischen Kaiserreich und NS-Diktatur," in B. Faulenbach, ed., *Geschichtswissenschaft in Deutschland* (Munich, 1974), 76–77. Hans Schleier, *Die bürgerliche deutsche Geschichtsschreibung der Weimarer Republik*, Akademie der Wissenschaften der DDR, Schriften des Zentralinstituts für Geschichte 40 (Berlin, 1975), 186–88.

[9] Richard Suchenwirth, *Deutsche Geschichte von der germanischen Vorzeit bis zur Gegenwart* (Leipzig, 1938), 427–30.

direction of progress, and a historic model for a healthy society. In 1942, anticipating the end of World War II, an American political scientist called for the military obliteration of Nazism and invoked the name of Stein in advocating the establishment of a federal republic based on historical precedents.[10]

Those who have assessed the Stein ministry positively have uniformly emphasized that the reform era's spark of promise for Germany was snuffed out by overwhelming opposition. Gerhard Ritter's massive Stein biography of 1931 was reissued after World War II and is certainly the most widely read work on the Prussian leader. It portrays the 1808 reform movement as a clear alternative to "Prussian traditions" of militarism and authoritarianism. Ritter believes that with fewer obstacles, Stein might have made "a successful transformation of the . . . authoritarian state into a modern republic."[11] The contemporary historian Golo Mann tells students of German history that Prussia remained "half absolutist" because "Baron vom Stein was less than half successful in his reform work." The reform era was, Mann writes in his textbook, one of those "short moments in history when noble enthusiasm reigns. . . . We should be thankful for every remainder of what was created in such a time."[12] Less emotionally involved, but similar in effect, is the message which historian George Rudé gives to English-speaking students of the Napoleonic age:

> Stein . . . believed in borrowing, though in moderation, from the French principles of 1789; . . . But Napoleon got wind of his intentions and he and the Junkers combined to drive him from office; so that most of his plans came to nothing. After this, the Junkers (whose aims were entirely Prussian) were in control and . . . there was no further talk of social reform.[13]

This type of thinking has roots in the immediate post-reform era, for Prussian liberals were bitter about the raw treatment Stein received from his enemies as well as the disappointing performance of Stein's successors.[14] Stein's foes were indeed numerous. Even some whom he counted among his closest supporters intrigued to precipitate his fall.[15] It has therefore been

---

[10] Hans Mommsen, "Haupttendenzen nach 1945 und in der Ära des Kalten Krieges," in B. Faulenbach, ed., *Geschichtswissenschaft in Deutschland,* 114; James Pollock, "What Shall We Do With Germany?" *Current History* 2 (March 1942): 2; Karl Buchheim, "The *Via Dolorosa* of the Civilian Spirit in Germany," *German History: Some New German Views,* ed. Hans Kohn (London, 1954), 50.

[11] G. Ritter, *Stein,* 3d ed. (Stuttgart, 1958). The book was reissued again in 1981. Quotation from Gerhard Ritter, *Das deutsche Problem: Grundfragen deutschen Staatslebens gestern und heute* (Munich, 1962), 39. In 1966 Klaus Epstein called Ritter's biography "One of the greatest biographies in the German language. . . . It is likely to remain—and deserving to remain—the last work on Stein for a long time to come." K. Epstein, "Stein in Historiography," 265.

[12] Golo Mann, *Deutsche Geschichte des 19. und 20. Jahrhunderts* (Frankfurt, 1969), 80.

[13] George Rudé, *Revolutionary Europe 1783–1815,* Meridian Histories of Modern Europe (Cleveland and New York, 1964), 276.

[14] Caroline von Rochow and Marie de la Motte-Fouqué, *Vom Leben am preussischen Hofe 1815–1852,* ed. Louise von der Marwitz (Berlin, 1908), 231.

[15] R. C. Raack, *The Fall of Stein,* Harvard Historical Monographs, no. 58 (Cambridge, Mass., 1965).

easy to believe that opponents of reform prevented Prussia from developing a healthy, modern society. So thoroughly has this theme implanted itself in historical thought that scholars have devoted entire books to the "failure" of the reform movement.[16] Focusing upon why the reforms did not succeed, many have neglected to question where Stein and his colleagues were actually leading Prussia with their reforms.

There are fundamental reasons why the ministry of 1807–1808 has for nearly two centuries appeared as a positive factor in German history. Stein and his colleagues personify the Enlightenment values that are the ideological basis of modern Western society: personal freedom, individualism, social equality, economic mobility, and self-government. The reformers fought against authoritarianism and hereditary privilege. In the sense that Stein and his co-reformers sought to reshape the state according to liberal ideals, they were Germany's "founding fathers." So thoroughly did they express the ideology and assumptions of the contemporary Western world that German conservatives, liberals, nationalists and Social Democrats have found little to criticize and much to praise in the reform efforts.

The picture of Stein as a hero[17] has served many generations, but it contains deep flaws. Essentially it is ahistorical, and it obscures much that took place in the context of the reform movement. The historians, schoolteachers and politicians who eulogize Stein often identify with the minister and his contemporaries who asserted that their efforts, crushed by opponents, were almost without effect upon Prussian society. It is of course understandable that the reformers themselves lacked historical perspective on their work, but it is not excusable for historians to have shared this shortsightedness.

The heroic assessments of the reform era are based upon the popular notions that men make history and that history consists of politics alone. Kings, prime ministers and their decrees are, in this tradition, thought to shape state and society. Historians who have operated with these assumptions have naturally concluded that the reforms failed because the reform edicts were never completed. The weakness of this reasoning is that it ignores larger ongoing social and economic processes of which the reform decrees were a mere part.

In contrast there stands a less prevalent, yet articulate, tradition in historical scholarship which portrays the reforms in the context of the larger socio-economic process. An early proponent of this perspective is the nineteenth-century historian Georg Friedrich Knapp. Unlike most of his contemporaries, Knapp did not approach history biographically, but rather from the point of view of society's lower classes. His investigation of the

---

[16] Walter M. Simon, *The Failure of the Prussian Reform Movement, 1807–1819* (1955; reprint, New York, 1971).

[17] See, for example, Gunther Ipsen, "Staat aus dem Volk: Scheitern, Wollen, Vollbringen des Freiherrn vom Stein in der preussischen Reform," *Der Staat: Zeitschrift für Staatslehre, öffentliches Recht und Verfassungsgeschichte* 12 (1973): 147, 155.

changing conditions of the rural masses in Prussia's eastern provinces led to an unflattering assessment of the reformers. They appeared as manipulators of peasants rather than as crusaders for progress.[18] Marxist historians and revisionist scholars of recent decades have reached similar conclusions, believing that Stein's work was detrimental to Prussian society. Those who approach history "from the bottom up" are uniformly critical of the Stein reforms.

Marxist scholarship, beginning with Marx's and Engel's own assessments of the Stein government, has traditionally portrayed the reform movement as a factor in the competitive struggle between bourgeois and aristocratic elites. Franz Mehring, an early twentieth-century Marxist, wrote penetrating history for a popular readership. He portrayed Stein as a perpetuator, rather than a destroyer, of aristocratic society, as an exploiter, rather than as a friend, of peasants.[19] Eckart Kehr, a brilliant historian of the Weimar era, rigorously employed the tools of socialist scholarship in a study of Prussian bureaucracy. He discovered in Stein's work an oppressive manipulation of the population for the benefit of the Prussian state and its related economic elites. Kehr's biting analysis frightened established historians. It was ignored until scholars of the 1960s rediscovered Kehr.[20]

In some historical studies produced in the German Democratic Republic the criticism of the Prussian reformers is ambiguous. A standard history of Germany published in the late 1960s, for example, describes Stein's associates as "progressive men," leaders of a "middle-class patriotic" movement. While both "middle class" and "patriotic" can have negative connotations from a Marxist perspective, the assessment remains ambivalent in light of the fact that it depicts the "progressive" reforms as victim to bureaucratic and aristocratic opposition.[21] Several important East German studies of the agrarian reforms have emphasized that the Stein ministry promoted a transition from feudalism to capitalism at the expense of the lower classes. East German researchers often follow Lenin's assessment

---

[18] Georg Friedrich Knapp, *Die Bauern-Befreiung und der Ursprung der Landarbeiter in den älteren Theilen Preussens* (Leipzig, 1887).

[19] Walter Schmidt, "Marx und Engels über den historischen Platz der preussischen Reformen," in Heinrich Scheel, ed., *Preussische Reformen—Wirkungen und Grenzen. Aus Anlass des 150. Todestages des Freiherrn vom und zum Stein,* Sitzungsberichte der Akademie der Wissenschaften der DDR: Gesellschaftswissenschaften, 1982, 1G (Berlin, 1962): 56–70; Franz Mehring, *Gesammelte Schriften und Aufsätze,* vol. 4, *Zur preussischen Geschichte von Tilsit bis zur Reichsgründung* (Berlin, 1930): 21–150.

[20] Eckart Kehr, "Zur Genesis der preussischen Bürokratie und des Rechtsstaats: Ein Beitrag zum Diktaturproblem," in Hans-Ulrich Wehler, ed., *Der Primat der Innenpolitik: Gesammelte Aufsätze zur preussisch- deutschen Sozialgeschichte im 19. und 20. Jahrhundert,* Veröffentlichungen der Historischen Kommission zu Berlin, no. 19 (Berlin, 1970), 31–52. Since the 1970s controversies have raged between "Kehrites" and their opponents. See for example the several articles in Vol. 4 of *Geschichte und Gesellschaft* (1978) and the literature to which they refer. Hans Schleier, an East German historiographer, maintains that Kehr was no Marxist, but rather a "left-liberal" historian: *Bürgerliche Geschichtsschreibung,* 482–530.

[21] Joachim Streisand, "Deutschland von 1789 bis 1815," *Deutsche Geschichte,* author-collective ed. (Berlin, 1967), 2: 78–82.

that in the social collapse caused by military defeat, there was "no alternative except the one leading to the bourgeois state." In recent years a group of historians of the German Democratic Republic have pursued a very articulate debate concerning the essential nature of the reforms, especially with reference to the phrase "revolution from above," which has frequently been used to describe the activities of the Stein administration.[22]

While Marxist interpreters of the reform era differ in their conclusions, they share one important characteristic: an ideological distance from the reformers. Historians in this tradition emphasize that history makes men, rather than that men make history. This allows Marxists a historical perspective not possessed by those who identify with the values of the reform party. In sharp contrast to the popular view of the reformers as personifications of positive factors in Germany's past, historical materialists see them as mere participants in a stage of development.

Sharing this insight are several historians who in the recent past have adopted methodologies of modern social sciences. They employ vocabulary and models developed in disciplines such as economics, political science, and sociology. Having declared an end to the division between social history and political history, they advocate "history of societies" in which economic, demographic, social, cultural and political factors are understood to be but facets of the whole.[23] In this view, political history, for example the Stein reform movement, is an expression of the society which surrounds it.

Bureaucracy is a favored theme among scholars of the new history who have sought a revised understanding of the Prussian reforms. Hans Rosenberg, following the analytical tradition pioneered by Max Weber, por-

---

[22] Rudolf Berthold, "Zur Herausbildung der kapitalistischen Klassenschichtung des Dorfes in Preussen," *Zeitschrift für Geschichtswissenschaft* 25 (1977): 557–74; Gerhard Heitz, "Varianten des preussischen Weges," *Jahrbuch für Wirtschaftsgeschichte*, 1969/3: 99–109; Rudolf Berthold, Hartmut Harnisch, and Hans-Heinrich Müller, "Der preussische Weg der Landwirtschaft und neuere westdeutsche Forschungen," *Jahrbuch für Wirtschaftsgeschichte*, 1970/4: 259–89; Karl Obermann, "Bemerkungen über die soziale und nationale Bedeutung der preussischen Reformbewegung unter dem Ministerium des Freiherrn vom Stein," Hans Joachim Bartmuss et al., eds., *Die Volksmassen: Gestalter der Geschichte. Festgabe für Leo Stern* (Berlin, 1962), 131, quoting Lenin, *Werke* (Berlin, 1960), 27: 149; Heinrich Scheel, "Probleme der deutsch- französischen Beziehungen 1789–1830," *Zeitschrift für Geschichtswissenschaft* 18 (1970), 169; Helmut Bock, "Reform und Revolution: Zur Einordnung des preussischen Reformministeriums Stein in den Kampf zwischen Fortschritt und Reaktion," *Militärgeschichte* 19 (1980): 599–614; Heinrich Scheel, "Eine notwendige Polemik in Sachen Stein," in *Preussische Reformen—Wirkungen und Grenzen. Aus Anlass des 150. Todestages des Freiherrn vom und zum Stein*, Sitzungsberichte der Akademie der Wissenschaften der DDR: Gesellschaftswissenschaften, 1982, 1G (Berlin, 1962): 75–83. See also Hanna Schissler, "Bauernbefreiung oder Entwicklung zur agrarkapitalistischen Gesellschaft?" *Sozialwissenschaftliche Informationen für Unterricht und Studium* 8 (1979): 140–41.

[23] Jürgen Kocka, "Theoretical Approaches to Social and Economic History of Modern Germany: Some Recent Trends, Concepts, and Problems in Western and Eastern Germany," *Journal of Modern History* 47 (1975): 101–19; E. J. Hobsbawm, "From Social History to the History of Society," Felix Gilbert and Stephen R. Graubard, eds., *Historical Studies Today* (New York, 1972), 1–26. Hans-Ulrich Wehler, *Geschichte als historische Sozialwissenschaft* (Frankfurt-am-Main, 1973).

trays the reform era as a culmination of two centuries of bureaucratization in the Hohenzollern monarchy.[24] Reinhard Koselleck published a compelling study of Prussian social and political institutions between 1791 and 1848. He attributes to the reformers the oppressive officialism of the early nineteenth century. The Stein party's emphasis on administrative reorganization at the expense of social change and governmental reform at lower levels, argues Koselleck, resulted in a misshapen society: an eighteenth-century social structure top-heavy with a modern bureaucracy.[25]

Recently Hanna Schissler produced an important study of the transformation of Prussian agriculture from what she termed a "commercial" to a capitalist phase. Writing from a similar perspective, Barbara Vogel has newly assessed the reform policies of the Hardenberg administration. Like others whose research borrows from social science disciplines, Schissler and Vogel believe that the reformers were mere spokesmen for—even products of—a social and economic process which both predated and postdated their work by decades. At most, the reformers accelerated the process. They certainly did not produce it. Moreover, far from standing "outside Prussian traditions" as many scholars have argued, both Stein and Hardenberg were very much bound up in important formative Prussian traditions.[26]

Marxist scholars often portray Stein negatively, as a representative of elites who oppressed the masses. The new historians influenced by social science methodologies imply, if they do not explicitly state, a similar argument: the reformers did not have the interests of all Prussians at heart. Instead, in maneuvering their society through crisis, they favored aristocracy, bureaucracy, and capitalist agriculture at the expense of the populace. Such analyses are much closer to the actual course of events than the older hero history. But they overlook one important aspect of the movement, its optimistic idealism about the potential of reform. The reformers shared an abiding faith that they could transform their eighteenth-century state and society into a world of equality, freedom, self-government and social opportunity.

When one measures the outcome of the reforms against the rhetorical hopes which sustained the reformers, one finds sharp contrasts, even op-

---

[24] Hans Rosenberg, *Bureaucracy, Aristocracy and Autocracy: The Prussian Experience 1660–1815* (Boston, 1968 [1st ed., 1958]). See also Max Weber's analysis, "Capitalism and Rural Society," in which Stein is not mentioned, but a way of viewing the reform work is described: *From Max Weber: Essays in Sociology*, ed. H. H. Gerth and C. Wright Mills (New York, 1970), 363–85.

[25] Reinhard Koselleck, *Preussen zwischen Reform und Revolution: Allgemeines Landrecht, Verwaltung und soziale Bewegung von 1791 bis 1848*, Industrielle Welt 7 (Stuttgart, 1967). See also: Wilhelm Bleek, *Von der Kameralausbildung zum Juristenprivileg: Studium, Prüfung und Ausbildung der höheren Beamten des allgemeinen Verwaltungsdienstes in Deutschland im 18. und 19. Jahrhundert*, Historische und Pädagogische Studien, no. 3 (Berlin, 1972); John R. Gillis, *The Prussian Bureaucracy in Crisis 1840–1860: Origins of an Administrative Ethos* (Stanford, 1971).

[26] Hanna Schissler, *Preussische Agrargesellschaft im Wandel: wirtschaftliche, gesellschaftliche und politische Transformationsprozesse von 1763 bis 1847*, Kritische Studien zur Geschichtswissenschaft, no. 33 (Göttingen, 1978).

posites. For example, the reform party set out to relieve Prussia of bureaucratic oppression, but instead it intensified bureaucracy's strength. The reformers intended to abolish hereditary class with the expressed desire of seeing the aristocracy die away. Yet the Junker class continued to play a predominant role in politics and society throughout the nineteenth century. The Stein ministry emancipated peasants with the hope of establishing social mobility and a free citizenry. But economic realities often robbed the rural lower classes of any mobility except a downward one. For many, "freedom" meant social dislocation and economic deprivation.

Historians of socialist and revisionist traditions have frequently discounted the rhetoric of the reformers, believing it to be less significant than the reality of social and political changes. In focusing upon outcome, such scholars imply an identity between the intentions and the achievements of the reformers. For example, Schissler argues that the Stein government, needing a strong political ally, forged a compromise with the landowning aristocracy which ultimately strengthened Prussia's hereditary elite.[27] Similarly, historian John Gillis draws upon Koselleck's work to assert: "The legal and institutional innovations of the Reform Era . . . *were aimed* not at altering but at perfecting" the corporate social and bureaucratic monarchical institutions in Prussia.[28] It is demonstrably true that the reformers strengthened bureaucracy and aristocracy. However, by failing to stress that Stein and his colleagues believed themselves to be destroying the abuses of one and the very foundations of the other, revisionist historians tell only half of the story. In other words the reformers' undergirding of old-regime institutions, while very real, was unconscious and unintentional.

One can argue, of course, that language is less important than social reality: what the reformers did is more significant than what they said. It is also arguable that if the Stein ministry helped perpetuate aristocratic institutions and reformed agriculture at the expense of the villagers, they must have intended this, given the alternatives which they perceived themselves to have.

Nevertheless the rhetoric of the reformers is crucial to a study of their accomplishments. There is a relationship between intentions, actions, and results, even though this may not always appear to be the case. The reform movement owed its very existence to a set of ideals which can best be

---

[27] Ibid., 130–35, 143–44. In fairness to Schissler it should be pointed out that she asserts on p. 48: "The direct results of the reforms can seriously differ from the intentions of their initiators. . . . In Prussia the unintentional or uncalculated results of the agrarian reforms were unusually great." Another example: Henning Schrimpf, *Herrschaft, Individualinteresse und Richtermacht im Übergang zur bürgerlichen Gesellschaft: Studien zum Rechtschutz gegenüber der Ausübung öffentlicher Gewalt in Preussen 1782–1821,* Minerva-Fachserie, Rechts- und Staatswissenschaften (Munich, 1979), 318, 331 and passim.

[28] Gillis, *Prussian Bureaucracy,* 6. Italics added. Similarly Rosenberg argues in *Bureaucracy:* "Whatever their original hopes, professed intentions, or ultimate objectives, the reformers functioned as the builders and superintendents of a liberalized police state in which the bureaucracy formed the core of the ruling class" (108). Rosenberg's powerful arguments substantiating the second half of this statement encourage oversight of the first half.

described as early Prussian liberalism. Participating in the Enlightenment tradition, devoted to the economic thought of Adam Smith, and inspired by the society of Great Britain, the reformers sought to remake entirely the world in which they lived. They spoke of their goal of abolishing servile relationships as a "holy cause," and they asserted that with the establishment of "freedom" and "national representation" the hereditary aristocracy would "wither away." It was their promise to destroy gradually the absolutism which kept the liberals long ineffective prior to 1807, and this promise brought them to power in the crisis of that year. They believed firmly that they could achieve these goals, and in 1808 they thought they were doing so. Their optimism is part of their ideology. Their belief in the possibility of peaceful, orderly change spurred them to action and sustained them in their work.

The reformers themselves certainly took their rhetoric seriously. Otherwise why would they have proclaimed their goals so loudly in face of the tough opposition they were bound to encounter? They openly espoused a social and political program which was sure to provoke resistance from powerful elements of the old society. It is unlikely they would have done this if they had intended to perfect rather than alter or destroy existing institutions. It is historically unfair to dismiss the rhetoric of the reform party as unimportant.

Viewed in this light, the reformers were less villains acting in selfish class interest than they were participants in a giant tragedy. They themselves were the victims as well as the perpetrators of the tragedy. The reformers' vision was, of course, bound by their class and status. Themselves members of elites, they could not destroy the fabric of their society in order to produce a more just one. But the important fact is that they thought they could. This is especially true of the younger, more zealous members of the reform party such as Theodor von Schön who played a central role in drafting the edict of 8 October 1807, abolishing feudal relationships. Others, like Karl vom Altenstein, were motivated in part by personal selfishness. While sharing the rhetorical optimism of the reforms with Schön, Altenstein participated in an intrigue that helped precipitate the fall of the Stein government, a development from which Altenstein stood to gain. There were still others in the reform ministry like Leopold von Schroetter who sought to help steer Prussia through its crisis with as few losses to the old regime as possible. But taken as a whole, the members of the Stein government represent a dedication to the ideal that a planned, deliberate reform program could totally transform their society. They were liberals—heirs of the Enlightenment—in a time when liberalism was young. The new political philosophy had hardly been tried, and its potential seemed boundless to the Prussian reformers. Following their intense reform year they learned the bitter lessons of liberalism's limitations: aristocracies do not fade away as a result of governmental edicts; in periods of innovation bureaucracies take root and thrive; and peasants suffer when agriculture is streamlined without social revolution.

Many reformers themselves were surprised and embittered about the result of their efforts. They often blamed their opponents rather than looking inward to discover their own inadequacies. After the fall of Stein's government, some of his colleagues became paranoid, seeing enemies where there were none, and suspecting their friends of sabotaging their work. This scapegoatism became part of the historical tradition, and it led historians, as it had led contemporaries, to focus on the foes of change rather than to examine the reformers' philosophy and their methodologies.

In contrast, I have emphasized in this study the language of the reformers and the process through which they attempted to apply their ideals. The reform movement cannot be understood except as a product of the optimistic pronouncements of the Prussian leaders of 1808 that they would transform their land in ways never before attempted. The reformers believed that their agrarian edicts would not only increase productivity, but would also create a more equitable society. They were convinced that administrative reorganization would bring Prussia closer to a situation in which citizens governed themselves. Any assessment of the reform movement must take this into consideration.

At the same time it is imperative to ask why the reformers' optimism was ill-founded, rather than to sidestep this question by emphasizing the short tenure of the Stein ministry. The method I have employed is twofold. First, I have analyzed the content of the official correspondence, memoranda and drafted edicts of 1807–1808, assessing these documents against the backdrop of existing conditions. I have sought to project the probable effects of the intended social, political, and economic reforms, given the entrenched conditions in Prussia, the process of change under way, and the methods the reformers chose to employ. My conclusion is that if Stein had remained in office long enough to carry his plans to fruition, a post-reform Prussia would not have had a significantly different complexion from the one we know. The second aspect of my evaluation of the reform activity is a close look at the short-term policy decisions of the Stein ministry. This examination leads to the conclusion that the reformers' own day-to-day activity established patterns that conflicted with their long-range goals. For example, while planning representative institutions which they hoped would minimize the strength of the traditional nobility, the reformers reactivated dormant aristocratic assemblies, giving a renewed political life to the very class whose influence they wanted to diminish.

Given this approach, it is easy to see that the reformers produced results they did not expect: a heavy-handed bureaucracy, a dislocated rural laboring class, and a perpetuated aristocracy. The reformers' ideology of early liberalism was inadequate for the tasks to which they hoped to set it to work. Furthermore, their methods, ultimately linked to their view of the world, stood in the way of their goals. Having said this, one should not make the mistake of believing the reform ministry was without effect upon society. Indeed, its impact was profound.

THE REFORMS IN A EUROPEAN-WIDE CONTEXT

Many students of Prussia and Germany have been preoccupied, especially since World War II, with what they consider Germany's "separate path" into the twentieth century. What they often mean is that Germany did not produce middle-class democracies like those of the French and Anglo-Saxons. Germany, especially influenced by its Prussian heritage, retained old-regime institutions and values most dramatically epitomized by authoritarianism in state and society.[29] This interpretation both mirrors and reinforces the prevalent notion that Stein was unable, early in the nineteenth century, to overcome the powerful conservatism of Prussian people and institutions in order to turn the state down a healthy path of change. As Friedrich Meinecke expressed it, the Prussian reform era was one of the three "turning points" of the nineteenth century at which Germany failed to turn.[30] This led to the evil consequences of militarism and war in the twentieth century.

This comparison of Germany with the French and English-speaking world is narrow. It distorts the degree to which Central European society was undergoing profound transformations in the eighteenth and nineteenth centuries. It identifies western European patterns as the norm by which to judge all others, when in fact they possess much that is unique to themselves. The "separate path" theory's greatest inadequacy is that it singles out parliamentary government as the identifying mark of healthy contemporary societies. This ignores the complex, interwoven nature of social, economic, and political change that took place in Europe. When one looks at Prussia and its neighboring states from perspectives such as bureaucratic development or commercialization of the economy, it is apparent that Prussia participated in a transition experienced by the entire western world. The Prussian experience, with its own local stamp, was more like than unlike that of France and England.

To avoid the pitfalls of the "separate path" interpretation, it is tempting to employ the concept "modernization," coined and made current by social scientists in recent years. Scholars who have studied change in cross-cultural settings have used this term to describe a course of social, political and economic changes which they believe took root in Western Europe in the sixteenth and seventeenth centuries, blossomed in North America and other European areas by the nineteenth century and became world-wide in the twentieth. Included in the notion of modernization are many factors such as industrialization, revolution, bureaucratization, democratization, and westernization. Proponents of the modernization model point to common processes in societies which over time rid themselves of binding traditions,

---

[29] Mommsen, "Haupttendenzen nach 1945," 114. Schissler, *Preussische Agrargesellschaft,* 31.

[30] Friedrich Meinecke, "1848: Eine Säkularbetrachtung," in *Werke* vol. 9, *Brandenburg, Preussen, Deutschland,* (Stuttgart, 1979), 347. Barbara Vogel, ed., *Preussische Reformen 1807–1820,* Neue Wissenschaftliche Bibliothek, no. 96: Geschichte (Königstein/Ts., 1980), 18.

autocratic rule, and localized, pre-market economies. These are replaced by the spread of political power to increasingly large groups in society, growing permeation of government to more and more spheres of human activity, acceleration of economic activity, and growing social and economic mobility.[31]

The Stein reforms fit the patterns generally described by modernization theorists. The ministry of 1808 was intent upon replacing a slow-moving hierarchical society with a fast-paced one of increasing social mobility. The reformers sought to destroy old feudal patterns and replace them with new structures based upon the concepts of individualism and citizenship. They increased the role of governmental authority, while at the same time fostering the development of a free market economy.[32]

While the modernization concept is helpful in emphasizing the cross-cultural nature of such changes, it is also misleading. Those who employ this term often distort the character of regional and cultural variations. The term is ethnocentric, since it is frequently used in ways which imply that non-European societies not only do, but also should, follow a western model.[33]

Because of the distortion fostered by the modernization concept, I have not used it in this study. I have sought rather to describe a particular local process in a specific chronological setting. At the same time, I have emphasized that the Prussian experience of 1808 was not an isolated, provincial occurrence. Indeed its cosmopolitanism is one of its most striking characteristics. Stein's colleagues were educated in the setting of the European-wide Enlightenment. They borrowed intentionally from British and French experiences. Moreover, the society they hoped to reform from top to bottom was already undergoing extensive change as a part of the transition from aristocratic and absolutist rule to middle-class domination. Strongly colored by regional conditions, the East Elbian middle class, nevertheless, was clashing with old, landed aristocratic traditions, just as non-noble entrepreneurs and property owners in Western Europe and North America sought supremacy in their own settings. Stein and his community of reformers accelerated this process. In so doing, they helped indelibly to coin a Prussian variation of a European process.

---

[31] C. E. Black, *The Dynamics of Modernization: A Study in Comparative History* (New York, 1966); S. N. Eisenstadt, *Modernization: Protest and Change* (Englewood Cliffs, N.J., 1966); Joseph LaPalombara, ed. *Bureaucracy and Political Development*, Studies in Political Development, 2 (Princeton, N.J., 1963, 1967). Hans-Ulrich Wehler, *Modernisierungstheorie und Geschichte* (Göttingen, 1975); Barrington Moore, Jr., *Social Origins of Dictatorship and Democracy: Lord and Peasant in the Making of the Modern World* (Boston, 1967). The literature is extensive. See Schissler's discussion concerning modernization of Prussia's agrarian society, as well as her citations: *Preussische Agrargeschichte*, 20–22.

[32] Vogel, *Preussische Reformen*, 18.

[33] Dean C. Tipps, "Modernization Theory and the Comparative Study of Societies: A Critical Perspective," *Comparative Studies in Society and History* 15 (1973): 199–226; Quentin Skinner, "Taking Off," *New York Review of Books* 26, no. 4 (22 March 1979): 15–16. M. M. Postan, *Fact and Relevance: Essays on Historical Method* (Cambridge, 1971), 103–18. Schissler, *Preussische Agrargesellschaft*, 208.

II. SOCIAL CHANGE AND A NEW IDEOLOGY CONFRONT PRUSSIA'S OLD REGIME

The second half of the eighteenth century was a time of profound change in all of Europe. An industrial revolution was transforming England. France was undergoing a social and political revolution of such significance that it has come to symbolize the beginning of the contemporary era. North Americans were struggling to establish their modern nation state. Feudal institutions, wherever they existed in the West, were in a state of transition, if they were not under outright attack. A new middle class was fighting to supersede the hereditary aristocracy.

German-speaking Europe's experience in this process was perhaps less dramatic than that of neighbors to the west. Nevertheless, even Prussia, a patchwork of territories with its heart in northeastern Europe, evidenced signs of strain on account of changes in social structures, economic institutions, and value systems. It is correct to characterize the Hohenzollern monarchy around 1800 as absolutist, tradition-bound, and aristocratic. But the foundations of state and society were eroding. Before considering the changes undermining Prussian institutions, it is useful to clarify the basic social organization of the old regime.

CORPORATE SOCIETY IN ABSOLUTIST PRUSSIA

Like that of other German Protestant lands, Prussian society consisted of three Estates:[1] the aristocracy, the peasantry, and the townspeople or burghers. Social status was hereditary and fixed by law and custom. Social mobility within Estates was limited, although each was internally very complex. Movement between classes rarely occurred except in cases of nonaristocratic families who were granted noble status by a king, usually as a reward for loyal service to the monarchy.

The aristocracy, or Junkers as they were called east of the Elbe, were the elite of society, comprising less than 2 percent of the total population.[2] Eighteenth-century families still recognized two ranks within their class,

[1] Two concepts, both of which are vital to this study, are translated with the English word, "estate." To avoid confusion, I shall employ the following usage: capitalized, "Estate" means a pre-industrial social class (*Stand*). In this sense it can also refer to a political body, as in the French Estates General of 1789. Without capitalization, "estate" means a large agricultural property (*Gut, Rittergut*) which in pre-industrial times was a source of aristocratic status. "Plantation" is a rough translation but it is not appropriate because of its colonial and American connotations.

[2] Schissler, *Preussische Agrargesellschaft*, 73.

the upper nobility (*Herrn*) and the lesser nobility (*Ritter*). This distinction is less important from a historical perspective than it was to contemporaries. Nobles perceived themselves to be a class divinely ordained to stand above the rest of the people. In a time when hierarchy was thought to be the natural order, society regarded Junker families as a superior race.

Aristocrats gained their status from land. (The coveted "von" in family names meant simply "of" the estate.) In the traditional view of the world, an estate was not an investment or source of income so much as it was a mark of rank. Nobles disdained thinking of themselves as business-people interested in money. By law they were limited to careers in agriculture, the military or government, and they were forbidden to enter merchant professions. Status was not synonymous with wealth, and there were aristocratic families who were genuinely impoverished. Nevertheless, as a class, the nobility commanded a highly disproportionate amount of wealth by virtue of their dominance of agriculture. Landholding patterns varied from province to province, but on the average this numerically insignificant group held direct dominion over 11 percent of the agricultural property in the Hohenzollern territories. Eighty percent of the land was designated "peasant property," but much of this—perhaps 50 percent—was within noble estates, so that the upper class enjoyed jurisdiction over, and profits from, as much as half of the total productive ground.[3]

The Junkers' unique type of seigniory over the land and people of their estates, called *Gutsherrschaft,* was found only in Germany's eastern provinces in the eighteenth century. Estate owners were masters of human and economic affairs on their lands. To the lower classes, aristocratic landlords were the government: collectors of taxes, police, judges and administrators. Junkers were furthermore the personal masters of unfree peasants, dictating marriage partners, working conditions and the distribution of resources.[4]

Gutsherrschaft existed in an intense form in the seventeenth and eighteenth centuries as a result of an extended compromise between monarchs and the nobles. After the feudal system of the Middle Ages had decayed, princes had shared governing responsibilities with the Estates in the so-called *Ständestaat* system. But since the sixteenth century the first Estate had given up much of its power to a centralized royal bureaucracy. In return the Hohenzollerns had left the nobility extensive privileges on their estates. In the early modern period when European feudal relations were

---

[3] Statistics from ibid., 74. For comparison see the statistical breakdown for East Prussia given by Friedrich-Wilhelm Henning, *Herrschaft und Bauernuntertänigkeit: Beiträge zur Geschichte der Herrschaftsverhältnisse in den ländlichen Bereichen Ostpreussens und des Fürstentums Paderborn vor 1800,* Beihefte zum Jahrbuch der Albertus-Universität Königsberg/Pr., no. 25 (Würzburg, 1964), 111.

[4] For this and the following paragraph: Hans Rosenberg, "The Rise of the Junkers in Brandenburg-Prussia, 1410–1653," *American Historical Review* 49 (1943–44): 228–39; Rosenberg, *Bureaucracy,* 7–8, 28–30; Friedrich Lütge, *Geschichte der deutschen Agrarverfassung vom frühen Mittelalter bis zum 19. Jahrhundert,* Deutsche Agrargeschichte, no. 3, ed. Günther Franz (Stuttgart, 1967): 119–58, passim.

generally loosening, Junkers maintained, and even tightened, their control over villagers.

In some less absolutist German states of the eighteenth century, noblemen met periodically to assert their right of sharing with princes the responsibilities for foreign, domestic and fiscal affairs.[5] Prussia's assemblies, however, had practically ceased to convene, except for the obligatory homage ceremonies which occurred when new kings took the throne. This was by royal design, for the monarchs had purposefully neglected calling the aristocrats together in order to centralize their own power at the expense of the Estates system. One vestige of ancient governing authority which the kings had been unable to wrest from the Junkers was control of land taxes (although the nobles themselves were largely exempt from taxation). The Hohenzollerns, however, had devised a bypass of this noble control of the purse by levying the excise, a duty on commerce, which fell upon traders and townspeople. Much of the strength of the monarchy rested on the excise revenue.[6] This arrangement made Junkers absolute lords over the populace and the property in the vast plains of the east, but it limited their participation in interregional or foreign affairs.

Where the king's political power met that of the Junkers was in the office of *Landrat*, or county councillor. The Landräte were powerful bureaucrats whose job was to represent the central government's interests in rural areas. However, they were named at periodically held county assemblies (*Kreisversammlungen*) composed of estate owners. In all but one province, custom dictated that the Landrat be a member of the local nobility, and the councillors were at least as loyal to their peers as to the monarch in Berlin. By the end of the eighteenth century they had begun to develop interests and ambitions of their own, forming a bureaucratic buffer between kings and Estates. Although there were obvious conflicts between the nobility and crown, the heavy-handed state bureaucracy of Prussian absolutism generally defended the interests of the hereditary nobles, for the king and the Junkers shared a mutual dependence.[7]

The lower classes of the countryside totaled 70 percent of the monarchy's people. In the late eighteenth century roughly half of these claimed the status of belonging to the peasant Estate (*Bauerntum*). These people occupied and worked farms, often by right of hereditary tenure. In the feudal

---

[5] G. Benecke, *Society and Politics in Germany 1500–1750* (London, 1974), 51–158, 181–225.

[6] Günther Birtsch, "Der preussische Hochabsolutismus und die Stände," Peter Baumgart, ed., *Ständetum und Staatsbildung in Brandenburg-Preussen: Ergebnisse einer internationalen Fachtagung,* Veröffentlichung der Historischen Kommission zu Berlin, no. 55: Forschungen zur preussischen Geschichte (Berlin and New York, 1983), 389–408; Gustav Schmoller, "Die Epochen der preussischen Finanzpolitik bis zur Gründung des deutschen Reiches," *Umrisse und Untersuchen zur Verfassungs- Verwaltungs- und Wirtschaftsgeschichte, besonders des preussischen Staates im 17. und 18. Jahrhundert* (Leipzig, 1898), 147–55.

[7] Rosenberg, *Bureaucracy,* 39, 165–67. Birtsch, "Der preussische Hochabsolutismus," 399–400. Alf Lüdtke, *"Gemeinwohl," Polizei und "Festungspraxis": Staatliche Gewaltsamkeit und innere Verwaltung in Preussen, 1815–1850,* Veröffentlichungen des Max-Planck-Instituts für Geschichte 73 (Göttingen, 1982), 41–55.

landholding scheme, their land was contained within larger estates. The remainder of the rural classes, the so-called "free" people, were only indirectly a part of the prevailing semi-feudal pattern.

Among the peasants,[8] there were both well-off and poverty-stricken families. For the class as a whole, subsistence farming was the norm. Peasants hoped to be able to raise enough to provide their households with food, clothing and fuel through the winter, and they had to count on their lords for help in times of insufficient harvest. When this help was not forthcoming, peasants might face starvation. Consistent with the hierarchy of society, peasants often employed on a contractual basis one or more fieldhands, maids or gardeners. These were persons not attached to land and were of lesser status than the family for whom they worked. But they usually resided in the same household. They were sometimes peasants' children, waiting to inherit their fathers' status and farm.

If the landlord was the peasants' government, the village was their economic and social community. In many parts of Prussia, collectivist agriculture (*Flurzwang*) prevailed. This meant that although families "owned" specific strips of land in the fields, the entire village plowed, sowed and harvested in common. Furthermore, villages owned common lands, usually pasture and forest.[9] Peasants' lives were governed by centuries of tradition.

With respect to legal status and property rights, peasants were serfs (*Untertanen*). In the words of an eighteenth-century writer, this meant that "peasants with their children are regarded as a part of the estate to which they belong."[10] (The most extreme form of serfdom, ownership of persons without regard to land, *Leibeigenschaft,* had been legally abolished in Prussia in the eighteenth century.)[11] Serfs were obligated to uncompensated labor

---

[8] Although some authors use the word "peasant" to refer to all non-noble rural people, I have retained the eighteenth-century distinction. Only those who remained in a feudal or semi-feudal relationship were, technically speaking, peasants.

[9] Schissler, *Preussische Agrargesellschaft,* 74. On communal orientation of villages: Rudolf Berthold, "Einige Bemerkungen über den Entwicklungsstand des bäuerlichen Ackerbaus vor den Agrarreformen des 19. Jahrhunderts," Deutsche Akademie der Wissenschaften zu Berlin, *Beiträge zur deutschen Wirtschafts- und Sozialgeschichte des 18. und 19. Jahrhunderts,* Schriften des Instituts für Geschichte, Reihe I: Allgemeine und deutsche Geschichte, no. 10 (Berlin, 1962), 88. On collective agriculture see Karl Böhme, *Gutsherrlich-bäuerliche Verhältnisse in Ostpreussen während der Reformzeit von 1770 bis 1830,* Staats- und sozialwissenschaftliche Forschungen, no. 20/3 (Leipzig, 1902), 7–16. On the significance of *Flurzwang* to the peasants, see Moore, *Social Origins,* 71–72.

[10] F. G. Leonhardi, *Erdbeschreibung der preussischen Monarchie* (Halle, 1791–1799) 1: 347, 359; August von Haxthausen, *Die ländliche Verfassung in den einzelnen Provinzen der preussischen Monarchie* (Königsberg, 1839), 106–109; Schrimpf, *Herrschaft, Individualinteresse und Richtermacht,* 101–46.

[11] Walther Hubatsch argues that "it is well-known that there were no more [serfs] in Prussia" in 1807. *Die Stein-Hardenbergschen Reformen,* Erträge der Forschung 65 (Darmstadt, 1977), 125–26. While it is true that Leibeigenschaft had been legally abolished, Untertänigkeit, properly translated as "serfdom," still existed. On the legal abolition of Leibeigenschaft, see, "Allgemeines Landrecht: vom Bauernstande," Werner Conze, ed., *Quellen zur Geschichte der deutschen Bauernbefreiung,* Quellensammlung zur Kulturgeschichte 12 (Göttingen, 1957), 99–100 (no. 19). Nevertheless, Leibeigenschaft was still a word in current vocabulary at the end of the

(*Scharwerk* or *Frondienst*) for the lord on a stipulated number of days a week. This could be as many as six in harvest seasons, although it was sometimes as low as two. A percentage of the harvest from "their" land also went to the lord as rent, except in cases where such dues had been converted to monetary payments. There was the possibility that peasants might buy themselves out of servitude if their lord were willing. One writer mentions a standard fee of ten *Thaler*, about half of an average peasant family's yearly income, but a lord might also grant a patent of freedom without compensation. In only one other case could serfs leave the estate: military conscription. The landlord could not evict them against their will.[12]

In contrast to the peasants, the "free" lower classes were not attached permanently to estates. They often bound themselves by contract to work for aristocrats, peasants, or town dwellers. There were many categories of such people in Prussia, including gardeners (*Gärtner*), handworkers (*Handwerker*), cottagers (*Instleute* or *Einlieger*) and servants (*Gesinde*). The latter term was frequently employed generically, referring to any of the numerous classifications of non-peasant lower classes who contracted their labor. A typical agreement might be that of a cottager family which, in return for living quarters and a garden, performed labor without pay for the landlord and worked a specified number of days a week for an established wage. The family had to pay taxes and rent as well. Such contracts, often of a three-year duration, were regulated by complex "master-servant codes" (*Gesindeordnungen*) which varied from province to province. When they expired, both parties would have to agree to a renewal if one were to be reached. A contemporary source emphasizes that such people were, "in regard to their property as well as their person, totally free [and] could leave the estate."[13]

This freedom was limited by the informal authority of powerful lords and by economic circumstances. There were few possibilities for Gesinde who left their estates. If they possessed freedom, they lacked security, which may have been more important in a corporate society of subsistence agriculture. The free people actually belonged to none of society's three Estates. In the eighteenth-century view, since they were propertyless (*eigentumslos*), they were also classless (*standlos*). From a twentieth-century

---

century when Leopold Krug published his *Über Leibeigenschaft oder Erbuntertänigkeit der Landbewohner der preussischen Staaten* (Halle, 1798). The critics of serfdom frequently used the two words interchangeably, perhaps employing the more offensive term, Leibeigenschaft, for the polemical effect.

[12] Leonhardi, *Erdbeschreibung*, 1: 347–48. I used Schissler's figures on peasant income, *Preussische Agrargesellschaft*, 74. Otto Büsch, *Militärsystem und Sozialleben im alten Preussen 1713–1807: Die Anfänge der sozialen Militarisierung der preussisch-deutschen Gesellschaft*, Veröffentlichungen der Berliner Historischen Kommission beim Friedrich-Meinecke-Institut, no. 7 (Berlin, 1962), 51–67. See the critique of this book in Hans-Heinrich Müller, "Bauern, Pächter und Adel im alten Preussen," *Jahrbuch für Wirtschaftsgeschichte* 1966/1: 260–77.

[13] *Allgemeines Landrecht für die Preussischen Staaten von 1794*, ed. Hans Hattenhauer (Frankfurt/M, 1970), 1: 419–25, 438–52; Leonardi, *Erdbeschreibung*, 1: 347.

perspective they were Prussia's rural proletariat. People who practiced petty trades often were counted among this class, including smiths, joiners, tailors, herdsmen, and even schoolmasters. They wandered from village to village, finding work where they could and, where possible, forming contracts with families and communities to provide services. Many were day laborers.[14]

Of the free families, there was one group, the renters (*Zinsleute*), who had a relatively enviable position. They paid a higher rate of rent than the Instleute, gardeners, and others, implying that they had more resources. And they were not required to provide uncompensated labor for the landlord. Like peasants, the renters frequently employed fieldhands on a contractual basis. Many of the Zinsleute also had secure tenure, unlike the cottagers who possessed short-term contracts. They could bequeath their farms to their heirs or they could sell them and leave at will, but they could not be evicted. Their security was limited only by economics. An animal plague or a series of bad harvests in consecutive years could force a renter family to turn to an estate owner for help. In return for supplies to get them through the hard times, they would have to submit to a contract, turning themselves into Instleute, which meant they lost their secure tenure and had to take on the onerous burden of Scharwerk.[15]

Both peasants and free villagers, then, were dependent upon masters. Being born a member of the non-aristocratic rural populace meant living in a condition of political, personal or economic servitude, and often a combination of the three.

Not all rural people served Junkers as lords. Municipalities, ecclesiastical institutions, the king, middle-class proprietors, and as we have seen, peasants themselves were landlords and masters. An important group of such proprietors were the *Kölmer* who were peculiar to the province of East Prussia. Strictly speaking, the Kölmer were prosperous free peasants (*Grossbauern*). However, they were a distinct and unique subgroup of the lower Estate because of their independent status and their importance in the economy. Due to a set of legal protective provisions, the Kölmer owned estates on which peasants and free workers comprised the labor force. They possessed approximately half as much land as the nobility, but they greatly outnumbered the upper class in the province, making up about 12

---

[14] Ritter, *Stein*, 217–18. Koselleck, *Preussen zwischen Reform und Revolution*, 132–42; Werner Conze, "Vom 'Pöbel' zum 'Proletariat': Sozialgeschichtliche Voraussetzungen für den Sozialismus in Deutschland," *Vierteljahrsschrift für Sozial- und Wirtschaftsgeschichte* 41 (1954): 335–37; Anthony J. LaVopa, *Prussian Schoolteachers: Profession and Office, 1763–1848* (Chapel Hill, 1980), 14–16.

[15] Böhme, *Gutsherrlich-bäuerliche Verhältnisse*, 12. Haxthausen, *Ländliche Verfassung*, 1: 224. Gerhard Czybulka, *Die Lage der ländlichen Klassen Ostdeutschlands im 18. Jahrhundert*, Beiträge zum Geschichtsunterricht, no. 15 (Braunschweig, 1949), 47–48.

percent of the population. In spite of their economic status, the Kölmer were excluded from the privileges of nobility.[16]

The largest proprietor in Prussia was the king, or to be more exact, the state. Approximately 4.5 percent of the total agricultural land belonged in the royal domain farms. In some provinces as much as half of the rural populace inhabited the domains, while in others as few as 7 percent were *Immediateinsassen,* direct subjects of the crown. In a series of reforms in the eighteenth century the Hohenzollern kings had abolished personal servitude on the domanial estates. This meant in effect that the villagers who lived there were free tenants such as Instleute and Gärtner. Because the royal reforms had not been uniformly applied, in 1804, on the eve of the Stein ministry, Frederick William III summarized and reiterated the crown's previous reforms, once and for all abolishing personal servitude on the domains of the provinces of East Prussia and Lithuania.[17]

The king's workers, of course, never dealt directly with their lord. Instead their actual overseers were the royally appointed tenant managers of the domains (*Domänenpächter*). They, along with the tenant managers on some noble estates, comprised an important segment of the agrarian populace because as a group they were the most active Prussians in fostering innovative agricultural techniques. Since they lacked the security of aristocratic status, the domain and estate managers were forced to be good administrators and good farmers. If they did not bring in profits, they were likely to lose their positions. This group of 27,800 families enjoyed a social status between the aristocracy and peasantry. They were a prosperous, well-educated but very heterogeneous group, stemming from merchant families, from the bureaucracy, and from well-to-do peasants. Society on domain farms was semi-feudal, but the royal estates were among Prussia's most fertile grounds for social and economic change.[18]

Prussia lived from agriculture. Nevertheless one-fourth of its population dwelled in cities and towns, segregated from the landlords and laborers of the countryside. Townsfolk were an Estate unto themselves, and like rural people, they had little opportunity to alter their inherited place in society. Berlin, Prussia's largest city, had 172,000 inhabitants, while the important export center, Königsberg, had only 50,000. The majority of the urban Estate resided in small market towns, with populations of a few hundred. To modern eyes, cities and towns—Berlin and Königsberg not excepted—

[16] Leonhardi, *Erdbeschreibung,* 1: 350–52. Wilhelm von Brünneck, *Zur Geschichte des Grundeigentums in Ost- und Westpreussen* (Berlin, 1891–1896) 1, passim. On the amount of land the Kölmer held, see Henning, *Herrschaft,* 112. Schissler, *Preussische Agrargesellschaft,* 74, 81.

[17] Hans-Heinrich Müller, "Domänen und Domänenpächter in Brandenburg-Preussen im 18. Jahrhundert," *Jahrbuch für Wirtschaftsgeschichte* 1954/4: 152–92. Verordnung vom 29. 12. 1804 betr. die persönliche Freiheit der Königlichen Untertanen in den ostpreussischen und litauischen Domänen, in Conze, *Quellen,* 100–01 (no. 20).

[18] Müller, "Domänen," 154–65. Müller, "Bauern, Pächter und Adel," 266–76; Schissler, *Preussische Agrargeschichte,* 87–89.

would have had a decidedly agrarian appearance, with animals and fowl in the streets as well as orchards and fields between buildings. However, townspeople lived from trade or from crafts, and agriculture as a profession was legally forbidden to them. This was their distinguishing characteristic.[19]

Townspeople were Prussia's "middle class" in the sense that they belonged neither to the upper, aristocratic, nor the lower, peasant Estate. They were burghers (*Bürger*) because they lived inside the *Burg*, the walls or fortress of the town. In reality towns were complex societies unto themselves. Well-to-do patrician families often rivaled the rural aristocracy in wealth and power, though they lacked the prestige of the Junker estate owners. Urban lower classes were technically not citizens (Bürger) who enjoyed privileges, but belonged to the legal class of "protected members of the corporation" (*Schutzverwandte*). They might be free or unfree, depending on the conditions of their birth. As was typical in a preindustrial society, most lived in meager circumstances, but wealth and property did not determine status.[20]

In their corporate society, burghers played no role as individuals in politics and economics. Only as members of guilds could they participate. These corporations, organized around trades, were medieval in origin. They fostered order and security in society. Economically they regulated business and supervised craftsmanship. It was not normally possible to carry on a trade outside a guild. Socially the corporations provided cohesion and welfare for their membership. Guilds took care of their sick, their poor, their orphans and their widows. Politically, guilds represented their members in government, sometimes with seats on city councils, and sometimes in less formal ways. Guilds even exercised religious functions, being entrusted with the care of souls of living and deceased members. Civic rights, property ownership, and profession were all bound together and expressed through guild membership. To be a burgher was to live a corporate existence identified by birth, guild and social hierarchy.[21]

In the age of absolutism, Prussian cities had lost much of their traditional independence. Hohenzollern princes had compromised with the nobility in order to build a powerful state and a strong army. But the cities had possessed less power to resist. Town councils, made up of senators from the patrician families and representatives from the guilds, still existed. However, they were under the strict supervision of the king's tax councillors

---

[19] Ibid., 72. Fritz Gause, *Die Geschichte der Stadt Königsberg in Preussen*, Osteuropa in Vergangenheit und Gegenwart, no. 10 (Köln, 1968), 2: 293; Johannes Ziekursch, *Das Ergebnis der friderizianischen Städteverwaltung und die Städteordnung Steins, am Beispiel der schlesischen Städte dargestellt* (Jena, 1908), 20–21; W. H. Bruford, *Germany in the Eighteenth Century: The Social Background of the Literary Revival* (Cambridge, 1935), 187–234.

[20] Koselleck, *Preussen zwischen Reform und Revolution*, 87–89.

[21] Friedrich Lütge, *Deutsche Sozial- und Wirtschaftsgeschichte* (Berlin and Heidelberg, 1966), 174–78, 256–57; Mack Walker, *German Home Towns: Community, State and General Estates 1648–1871* (Ithaca, 1971), 98–107; Jürgen Bergmann, *Das berliner Handwerk in den Frühphasen der Industrialisierung*, Einzelveröffentlichungen der Historischen Kommission zu Berlin, no. 11: Publikationen zur Geschichte der Industrialisierung (Berlin, 1973), 15–25.

(*Steuerräte*). These officials originally had the task of collecting the excise tax, but by the end of the eighteenth century they supervised to a large degree the economic and political life of towns.[22]

This bureaucratic governance was consistent with the prevailing theory of mercantilism which shaped national economic policies in Europe in the early modern era. Governments, perceiving themselves to be in competition with one another for the world's wealth, sought to foster manufacture through direct intervention in the economy. In order to secure favorable trade balances, and hence increase the supply of wealth in their treasuries, they strictly regulated economic activity such as imports and exports. They granted monopolies to favored individuals and corporations whom they considered capable of furthering the state's interests. The state itself was proprietor of some monopolies. While many of the patrician families of Prussia's cities profited from this system, as a class they sacrificed control over their traditional realm, business activity. Because economic affairs were strictly regulated by the government, so were many aspects of the social and political life of Prussia's second Estate.[23]

A group in society which belonged formally to none of the three traditional Estates was the "exempt citizens," so called because it stood under the jurisdiction of neither the provincial courts of the aristocracy nor the municipal courts serving the middle class. Instead, because of their special service to state and society, they were subject only to the highest royal courts. To this semi-corporate group belonged such professions as the high-ranking civil service, the clergy, academicians, military officers, justices who served courts of high jurisdiction, and tenant managers of aristocratic estates and royal domains. The exempt citizenry, an elite whose prestige rivaled that of the nobility, had been created by the absolutist state they served. The exempt citizens foreshadowed the direction of change in future decades. By virtue of the fact that they alone stood above the legal and economic separation of rural and urban society, they were the most modern of all Prussia's citizens. Yet the absolutist tradition of the eighteenth century gave them a strict corporate existence.[24]

Prussia's society was based on the remnants of a medieval value system. In the scheme of earlier centuries, community was more important than individuality. Stability was valued over change. Hierarchy was unquestioned. Social mobility existed to a limited extent in practice, but in theory it was only rarely permissible. In government, the idea of absolutism had

---

[22] Theodor Winkler, *Johann Gottfried Frey und die Entstehung der preussischen Selbstverwaltung*, Einzelschriften des Kommunalwissenschaftlichen Instituts an der Universität Berlin, no. 3 (Stuttgart and Berlin, 1936), 21–25; Ziekursch, *Ergebnis der friderizianischen Städteverwaltung*, 20–21, 80–83; Rosenberg, *Bureaucracy*, 39; Horst Krüger, *Zur Geschichte der Manufakturen und der Manufakturarbeiter in Preussen: Die mittleren Provinzen in der zweiten Hälfte des 18. Jahrhunderts*, Schriftenreihe des Instituts für Allgemeine Geschichte an der Humboldt-Universität Berlin, no. 3 (Berlin, 1958), 69–72.

[23] Ibid., 63–111.

[24] Koselleck, *Preussen zwischen Reform und Revolution*, 89–105.

superseded both the medieval ideal of feudalism and the early modern pattern, Ständestaat, or cogovernance by the monarch and the Estates. Yet like these two earlier formulas, absolutism presupposed little interplay between rulers and the populace. The mercantilist economy was government-directed, but this had not destroyed the corporate pattern typified by villages, guilds and provincial estates. Barely perceptible changes had been undercutting the structure of society for centuries. They accelerated in the eighteenth century.

SOCIAL AND ECONOMIC CHANGE

In the eighteenth century demographic growth was beginning to alter the face of Prussia's countryside, as it was in many other areas of Europe. Since the devastating Thirty Years War which ended in 1648, German lands had been inhabited by a population smaller than that of the Middle Ages. But by 1750, earlier levels had been reached, and an increasingly dramatic rise in numbers was becoming disruptive in the slowly moving agrarian society. In the half century before the reform year, the population of the eastern provinces of Prussia increased an average of 50 percent.[25] Accompanying this demographic expansion, and in part as a result of it, was a more important development which threatened the social fabric of the old regime: new forms of business and commerce. As early as the sixteenth century a market economy had slowly begun to replace the manorial agriculture and the guild system of handicraft production. This transformation, which took different forms in various areas, increased in speed in the eighteenth century along with the population rise. The new economy with its emphasis on regional and transregional markets began to undermine the hierarchical basis on which the agrarian economy rested.

Most of Europe—with majors parts of Prussia excepted—experienced these changes in a form which economic historians now call "proto-industrialization." This is a refinement over the older concepts, "domestic industry" and "putting-out system." The central characteristic of proto-industrialization was the growth of manufacture in rural areas, fostered by a flow of capital from cities into the countryside. The twin factors which underlay this development were the urban guilds' restraint of new business activity and the potential new rural work force provided by demographic expansion. Early industry was undermining many features of the old-regime society including landlord-peasant relationships, family life and rural community organizations. Proto-industrialization encouraged a commercial mentality, and it demanded a new type of social mobility to provide labor

---

[25] Ernst Kirsten, Ernst Wolfgang Buchholz and Wolfgang Köllmann, *Raum und Bevölkerung in der Weltgeschichte: Bevölkerungs-Ploetz* (Würzburg, 1955–1956) 2: 157; Krüger, *Zur Geschichte der Manufakturen*, 31–32, 274; Bruford, *Germany*, 157; Wilhelm Abel, *Agrarkrisen und Agrarkonjunktur: Eine Geschichte der Land- und Ernährungswirtschaft Mitteleuropas seit dem hohen Mittelalter* (Hamburg and Berlin, 1978), 201; Czybulka, *Die Lage der ländlichen Klassen*, 51; Conze, "Vom 'Pöbel' zum 'Proletariat,'" *Vierteljahrsschrift für Sozial- und Wirtschaftsgeschichte* 41 (1954): 336–37.

where it was needed. Though it weakened them, it did not completely destroy feudal institutions. In some cases, as in the Silesian textile industry, it transformed feudal relations from an agricultural to a manufacturing setting. The paths from this early type of manufacture to industrial society were very diverse, but proto-industry, based upon a market, and hence an expanding economy, as a rule spurred further change.[26]

While early industrialization transformed other parts of Europe, much of Prussia retained its agricultural orientation. This was especially true of the relatively sparsely populated provinces east of the Elbe where the reformers would center their activities in 1807–1808. Silesia, the province with the greatest population growth, was an exception. It developed a thriving textile industry with European-wide markets. Elsewhere, Junker estate owners maintained a tight control over the village populace, aided by their rigid manorial jurisdiction, Gutsherrschaft. Prussia's eastern regions remained traditional in social structure and thoroughly agricultural. Compared with western provinces and other parts of Germany, eastern Prussia retained a rigid separation of town and countryside at the beginning of the nineteenth century.[27]

Nevertheless, Prussia was far from immune to Europe's new emphasis on commercial activity. In the final third of the eighteenth century an increased foreign demand for grain made East Elbia with its great farms one of Europe's major export centers. England, in its initial phase of industrialization, and increasingly dependent upon imported foodstuffs, became Prussia's best customer. Between 1777 and 1784 the number of ships leaving the harbor of Königsberg approximately tripled, rising in number from 690 to 1989. By 1805 Prussia supplied nearly half of Britain's imported grain. This stimulated, as never before, an intense exploitation of the soil on Prussian estates. Between 1796 and 1805, wrote the contemporary economist J. G. Hoffmann,

> commerce thrived. Every year England received great deliveries of wheat and . . . timber from the Baltic and paid high prices for them. Annually Holland and Sweden needed rye, and southern Spain needed wood. Exports from the previous Polish provinces were considerable. . . . It was often said in Prussia: "We manufacture wheat for England and England manufactures cotton products for us."

---

[26] Charles and Richard Tilly, "An Agenda for European Economic History in the 1970s," *Journal of Economic History* 31 (1971): 184–98; Franklin F. Mendels, "Proto-Industrialization: The First Phase of the Industrialization Process," *Journal of Economic History* 32 (1972): 241–61; Peter Kriedte, Hans Medick and Jürgen Schlumbohm, *Industrialisierung vor der Industrialisierung: Gewerbliche Warenproduktion auf dem Land in der Formationsperiode des Kapitalismus,* Veröffentlichungen des Max-Planck-Instituts für Geschichte, 53 (Göttingen, 1977) pp. 13–271, passim. Herbert D. Kisch, "The Textile Industries in Silesia and the Rhineland: A Comparative Study in Industrialization," *Journal of Economic History* 19 (1959): 541–64 (reprinted in translation with a *Postscriptum* in Kriedte, *Industrialisierung,* 350–86).

[27] Schissler, *Preussische Agrargesellschaft,* 51–52, 69–70; Rosenberg, *Bureaucracy,* 29–32; Rosenberg, "Rise of the Junkers," 1–22, 228–42; Karl Heinrich Kaufhold, "Umfang und Gliederung des deutschen Handwerks um 1800," in Wilhelm Abel, ed., *Handwerksgeschichte in neuer Sicht,* Göttinger Beiträge zur Wirtschafts- und Sozialgeschichte, no. 1 (Göttingen, 1978), 27–63; Ziekursch, *Ergebnis der friderizianischen Städteverwaltung,* 20–44.

Ironically, Britain's industrial revolution was transforming Prussia's rural society.[28]

The commercialization of agriculture resulted in new burdens for the lower classes. Junker proprietors, as well as estate and domain managers, seeking expanded output, frequently increased the work required from their tenants. They shifted the relationships between themselves and their peasants. By the end of the eighteenth century, proprietors were used to converting tenants' dues to money or services, as well as to shortening and lengthening tenure rights to suit their own needs under changing conditions. A Königsberg University economist observed at the turn of the century that

> the innovations which have taken place in the conditions of the peasantry in the course of time, but especially in the last 15 or 20 years, threaten to become greater and greater. This is especially so for the upcoming generation. . . . There is no doubt that their fate is harder [than in earlier times]. More is demanded of them.[29]

In sum, large agriculturalists of the eastern provinces expanded their output in response to new market demands created by England's changing economy. They did so at the expense of the rural laboring population.

Eighteenth-century economic transformation, such as the development of rural industry, often blurred the distinctions between the urban and rural Estates.[30] In contrast, Prussia's commercialization of agriculture magnified them. Not only the Junkers, but also kings such as Frederick the Great, favored retention of the traditional class system. They reinforced the nobility's control over agrarian affairs.

Many Junkers needed capital in order to expand their enterprises to take advantage of new markets. For others, in a time of economic flux, loans were necessary simply to maintain their operations. In general, agriculture could profit from increased investment, but the money was in the cities. Middle-class investors could not loan to Junkers because the merchants of the cities, prohibited from possessing aristocratic properties, would have no way to foreclose on mortgages. In the 1780s Frederick the Great established provincial aristocratic credit associations (*Landschaftliche Kreditsysteme* or *Landschaften*). The Landschaften negotiated loans and provided

---

[28] Schissler, *Preussische Agrargesellschaft*, 59–75, 89; Bruno Schumacher, *Geschichte Ost- und Westpreussens* (Würzburg, 1959), 235; Walter Görlitz, *Die Junker: Adel und Bauern im deutschen Osten. Geschichtliche Bilanz von 7 Jahrhunderten* (Glücksburg/Ostsee, 1957), 129–38; J[ohann] G[ottfried] Hoffmann, "Nekrolog des Staats-Sekretärs und Chef-Präsidenten der Königlichen Bank Friese," *Nachlass kleiner Schriften staatswirthschaftlichen Inhalts* (Berlin, 1847), 695–96.

[29] Hermann Mauer, *Das Landschaftliche Kreditwesen Preussens agrargeschichtlich und volkswirtschaftlich betrachtet: Ein Beitrag zur Geschichte der Bodenkreditspolitik des preussischen Staates*, Abhandlungen aus dem Staatswirtschaftlichen Seminar zu Strassburg 22 (Strassburg, 1907), 24–31; Christian Jakob Kraus, Gutachten über die Aufhebung der Privatuntertänigkeit in Ost- und Westpreussen, 1802, in Conze, *Quellen*, 73 (no. 12).

[30] Peter Kriedte, "Genesis, agrarischer Kontext und Weltmarktbedingungen," in Kriedte et al., *Industrialisierung*, 36–39.

collective security for their members, thus opening the way for urban capital to flow into rural improvements without the potential involvement of the middle class in agriculture. This encouraged the commercialization of aristocratic farming but reinforced the walls between urban and rural elites.[31]

Such developments must have been a frustration to merchants and bankers of Danzig, Berlin and other cities, who saw their peers elsewhere in Europe moving middle-class enterprise into the countryside. They were already restricted in sharing the profits of the new grain trade because of the state's monopolistic control. Berlin merchants, for example, reaped nothing from the market activity in their city resulting from the flow of products from Silesia to Hamburg.[32]

In other ways the urban population suffered from commercialization of agriculture. Inflated prices, resulting in part from speculative agricultural commerce, decreased the living standard of the laboring population. "There is proof," wrote Professor Kraus of Königsberg, "that wages, which have remained stable, have in reality fallen because of the continually increasing grain prices." Between 1750 and 1800 the cost of consumer goods in Prussia rose by 50 to 100 percent. As in pre-revolutionary France, lower classes complained that even in time of poor harvests and scarcity of food at home, massive cereal shipments were sent overseas for foreign consumption. City folk often struck out at bakers and butchers, believing them to be the cause of increasingly expensive food. During the two years before the military crisis of 1806, prices rose so dramatically that the poor in Silesian towns were forced to consume horses and cats. Artisans dismissed their apprentices, and beggars and wanderers increased in numbers daily.[33] This explosive situation threatened the fabric of the old society.

Some agriculturalists, foremost among them managers on domain and noble estates, deviated from the pattern of increased exploitation of peasants for the sake of short-term profits. Market fluctuations made the negative features of hereditary servitude apparent, for in off years the estates were obliged to support workers as well as in times of economic expansion. Realizing the potential incompatibility of an iron-clad social system and an expanding market economy, some managers began to free their peasants from personal bondage and utilize them instead as contractual labor. The record shows that some emancipations were motivated by overpopulation. The landlord of the estate, Angerapp, issued the following declaration in

---

[31] Mauer, *Landschaftliches Kreditwesen*, 9–11; Wilhelm von Brünneck, *Die Pfandbriefsysteme der preussischen Landschaften* (Berlin, 1910), 37; Rosenberg, *Bureaucracy*, 169–70; Büsch, *Militärsystem und Sozialleben*, 107–08, 141–42, 147–48; Leonhardi, *Erdbeschreibung* 1: 349, 360–62; Haxthausen, *Ländliche Verfassung* 1: 182–83; Schissler, *Preussische Agrargesellschaft*, 81–83.

[32] Krüger, *Zur Geschichte der Manufakturen*, 28, 55.

[33] Ibid., 93, 328–43, 351–62; Schissler, *Preussische Agrargesellschaft*, 62–63; C. J. Kraus, Gutachten über die Aufhebung der Privatuntertänigkeit in Ost- und Westpreussen, 1802, in Conze, *Quellen*, 73 (no. 12); Ziekursch, *Ergebnis der friderizianischen Städtevewaltung*, 137; Abel, *Agrarkrisen*, 199.

1793: "If there are more than four able-bodied persons on a hereditary peasant farm, or more than three on a small farm, the rest shall be placed on a daily wage basis." By 1800 free rural laborers—those without security of hereditary contracts—outnumbered serfs on East Prussian noble estates. In Silesia the landless class grew between 1778 and 1786 at the rate of 1,000 per year, from 34,000 to 42,000. Population growth, combined with the reluctance of landlords to support more people than was profitable, led to increasing numbers of rural families with minute plots or with no land at all. It is no exaggeration to speak of pauperization in the countryside by 1800.[34]

But if economic transition was forcing many rural people into precarious existence, other were adapting to, and even fostering, the process. In the province of Brandenburg many peasants, especially those with secure tenure and sufficient property, were converting from subsistence farming to market-oriented agriculture. New demands from urban centers, as well as the increasing size of rural families, induced many to introduce new crops, enlarge their landholdings, expand their output, and sell their produce in cities. Some were successful enough to take advantage of noblemen in financial difficulty and rent the latter's estates. So unusual were the circumstances of the late eighteenth-century that a few peasant villagers were even able to buy out their landlords.[35]

Widening markets and commercialization of agriculture threatened the traditional social structure in other ways. Both as a result of the credit institutions and through acts of royal permission granted in individual cases, middle-class entrepreneurs were beginning to find ways to invest in agriculture. The credit associations had been designed to safeguard upper-class interest in the countryside. But the blurring of distinctions between urban and rural wealth represented a potential threat to noble estates. Agricultural economist Albrecht Thaer predicted an "explosion" of middle-class investment in the realm formerly restricted to the nobility. Furthermore, heightened economic activity in rural areas led to price speculation on noble estates. On the eve of the war of 1806, Junker lands were entering the real estate market with great rapidity, denoting a crisis in the old system. In 1805 a startling 561 noble estates changed hands in Hohenzollern territory. Entrepreneurship sought to replace hereditary privilege in determining the shape of Prussia's large-scale farming operations. Understandably, this caused alarm among the noble families of Prussia.[36]

---

[34] Berthold, "Zur Herausbildung der Klassenschichtung," 559. Schissler, *Preussische Agrargesellschaft,* 71. Quote from Angerapp: Böhme, *Gutsherrlich-bäuerliche Verhältnisse,* 11. Berthold, "Bemerkungen," 87. Koselleck, *Preussen,* 128. Johannes Ziekursch, *Hundert Jahre schlesische Agrargeschichte, vom Hubertusburger Frieden bis zum Abschluss der Bauernbefreiung,* Verein für Geschichte und Altertum Schlesiens, Darstellungen und Quellen zur schlesischen Geschichte, no. 20 (Breslau, 1915), 153–58. Hoffmann describes the dissolution of feudal bonds as a self-evident consequence of increased commercialization. Hoffmann, "Nekrolog Friese," 695.

[35] Hans-Heinrich Müller, "Der agrarische Fortschritt und die Bauern in Brandenburg vor den Reformen von 1807," *Zeitschrift für Geschichtswissenschaft* 12 (1964): 636–48.

[36] Schissler, *Preussische Agrargesellschaft,* 84–85.

The state and the aristocracy were in many ways allied to prevent the development of a new social and economic structure. However, a combination of new market conditions and of population growth was gradually undermining the semi-feudal production system and the corporate structure of society. While a contemporary observer would hardly have been able to perceive it, the stress of economic and social innovation was weakening many features of the existing order. Simultaneously there was growing a new set of ideas and presuppositions whose adherents had little patience with the traditional social structure. They hoped to influence the direction of social, political and economic change.

A NEW IDEOLOGY

Prussia's urban middle class was less active than those of western Europe in fostering the growth of rural industry because of the interwoven factors which favored agriculture east of the Elbe River. Nevertheless, educated nonaristocratic Prussians participated in the development of a new middle-class ideology which was spreading throughout Europe. Historians call the eighteenth century the Age of Enlightenment, meaning that the ideals of modern, post-feudal society were formulated in this period. The most famous expositors of Enlightenment thought are the French philosophes such as Montesquieu, Voltaire, and Rousseau. Locke is better known among English-speaking people.

Many political thinkers of the early Enlightenment criticized absolute royal power. Mid-century writers condemned the arbitrary government of kings, and they formulated the idea of "balance of powers" as a device to check the abuse of governmental authority. Proponents of change such as Montesquieu in France and Schlözer in Germany advocated that royal power be limited by enhancing the role of the Estates in government. Such thinking was not hostile to the idea of monarchy, or to corporate aristocratic society.

By the end of the eighteenth century, however, many writers had begun to criticize hereditary aristocratic privilege as well as monarchical absolutism. Modern concepts such as freedom, equality and individualism began to form the foundations of a new middle-class ideology which was increasingly hostile to corporate society.

Enlightenment ideas did not confine themselves to literary and philosophical elites. Neither did they recognize political boundaries. They filtered down to literate Europeans everywhere. Literacy was a property of the urban Estate, especially its upper layers. Wealthy and informed citizens of Königsberg, Danzig, Stettin, Breslau, Berlin and other Prussian towns gained many of their views of the world through a rapidly expanding literature and political journalism in the eighteenth century. The publication of new books in Germany nearly tripled between 1764 and 1800, while republication of older works also added to the circulation of literature. The number of newly founded magazines and journals grew from 411 in the 1750s to 1,125 in the 1770s. Newspaper circulation showed a comparable increase.

Berlin, which Madame de Staël called "the true capital of the new, the enlightened Germany," boasted the publication of at least five periodicals whose editors represented the growing middle-class ideology. These included the influential *Berlinische Monatsschrift* and the *Berlinisches Journal für Aufklärung*. These and other papers' criticisms of royal absolutism and aristocratic dominance appealed to the townspeople of Prussia who were frustrated by their lack of economic and political freedom and their second-class social status. Dozens of new newspapers which sprang up in the cities of Prussia after 1750 attacked the exercise and abuse of noble prerogative. Moreover, educated Prussians heard increasingly loud denouncements of caste and privilege in much of Germany's classical literature, characterized by giants such as Goethe, Schiller and Lessing.[37]

One symbolic feature of the middle-class mentality which arose in the closing decades of the eighteenth century is a profound alteration of the meaning of the word "freedom" in popular understanding. Originally a term denoting "privilege," "freedom" was used until the 1750s to defend the status quo of corporate society. The word had significance only in specific applied situations, such as the "freedom"—meaning right or privilege—of an Estate to assemble regularly, the "freedom" of a guild to engage in a trade, or the "freedom" of a village to elect its elders. Such freedoms were granted by an authority, purchased, or won in contest. However, within only a few decades journalists, jurists and political thinkers in the Enlightenment tradition had given the word a new definition. They maintained that freedom was universal, not limited to groups or corporations. By right of natural law, freedom belonged to humanity. Since all people, including even peasants, Jews and women, were entitled to freedom, society was egalitarian, not hierarchical. By the nineteenth century, freedom was an important slogan for innovators who fought to destroy privilege.[38]

This is but one example of ways in which eighteenth-century thinkers in Prussia, as in other parts of Europe, applied philosophical concepts of

---

[37] Henri Braunschwig, *Enlightenment and Romanticism in Eighteenth-Century Prussia*, tr. Frank Jellinek (Chicago and London, 1974), 61–66 and passim; quotation from Madame de Staël, *De l'Allemagne*, (1803), 62; Jürgen Schlumbohm, *Freiheit: Die Anfänge der bürgerlichen Emanzipationsbewegung in Deutschland im Spiegel ihres Leitwortes*, Geschichte und Gesellschaft: Bochumer Historische Studien 12 (Düsseldorf, 1975), 39; Adelheid Bues, *Adelskritik—Adelsreform: Ein Versuch zur Kritik der öffentlichen Meinung in den letzten beiden Jahrzehnten des 18. Jahrhunderts an Hand der politischen Journale und der Auseinandersetzungen des Freiherrn vom Stein* (diss., Göttingen, 1948), passim; Otto Tschirch, *Geschichte der öffentlichen Meinung in Preussen im Friedensjahrzehnt vom Baseler Frieden bis zum Zusammenbruch des Staates* (Weimar, 1933–1934), 1: 182–97; Bruford, *Germany* 271–90; Jacques Droz, "Europa-Ideen der deutschen Demokraten und Antidemokraten am Ende des 18. und zu Beginn des 19. Jahrhunderts," in Otto Büsch and Walter Grab, eds., *Die demokratische Bewegung in Mitteleuropa im ausgehenden 18. und frühen 19. Jahrhundert*, Einzelveröffentlichungen der Historischen Kommission zu Berlin, no. 29 (Berlin, 1980), 353–59; Rudolf Vierhaus, "Politisches Bewusstsein in Deutschland vor 1789," in *Deutschland zwischen Revolution und Restauration*, ed. Helmut Berding and Hans-Peter Ullmann (Athenäum/Droste Taschenbücher, Geschichte, no. 7240 [Königsstein/Ts, 1981]), 161–83.

[38] Schlumbohm, *Freiheit*, passim.

the Enlightenment to specific social situations and everyday life. It was in this period that the political vocabulary of the modern western world was born. Profound transformations occurred, for example, in the meanings of terms like "equality," "nation," "society," and "industry." Such shifts were nothing less than a middle-class revolution in ideology. The mentality of society was undergoing a metamorphosis. "Industry," for instance, had previously been a term used to describe the individual personality traits of diligence and hard work. In the late Enlightenment period it became associated with the ideas of moral, cultural and economic progress. By the nineteenth century, those who favored industry advocated a business-oriented society. Industry, or industriousness, moreover, became a moral quality by which people of all social strata were judged. Of course, neither serfs nor guild-bound artisans could be industrious in the modern sense of the term. Those who favored "industry" were advocates of a society based on individual freedom as opposed to corporate privilege.[39]

When one looks at the new vocabulary, one finds some of the internal contradictions which still exist today in the western world's political and social rhetoric. For example, late eighteenth-century advocates of "freedom" claimed universality for their ideal, and this had egalitarian implications. Yet they often emphasized freedom of trade, freedom of the press, and freedom to enter certain professions, concepts which helped establish a middle-class capitalist, but heavily stratified society.[40] Nevertheless to eighteenth-century crusaders, the cause of freedom was a sacred one. They had faith in its power to create a new and just social order.

Königsberg, the capital of the province of East Prussia and its thriving grain export harbor, was a center of the German Enlightenment. One of its most renowned citizens, Immanuel Kant (1724–1804), was Prussia's foremost philosophical interpreter of the new concept, "freedom." Kant was a faculty member at the University of Königsberg from 1755 to 1804. Basic to his philosophical and political writings are several corollaries of the concept freedom: rationality, worth of the individual, natural law, constitutionalism, political equality, independence, citizenship and republicanism. Kant, Germany's famous philosopher of the Enlightenment, rejoiced over the early phases of the French Revolution emphasizing the concept of popular sovereignty. He abhorred its Jacobin and Bonapartist stages, symbolizing terror, oppression and dictatorial power.[41]

---

[39] Werner Conze, "Nation und Gesellschaft: Zwei Grundbegriffe der revolutionären Epoche," *Historische Zeitschrift* 198 (1964): 1–43; Otto Dann, "Gleichheit," in *Geschichtliche Grundbegriffe: Historisches Lexikon zur politisch-sozialen Sprache in Deutschland,* ed. Otto Brunner, Werner Conze and Reinhard Koselleck (Stuttgart, 1972–) 2: 1006–26. In general, see the numerous terms of political vocabulary whose modern meanings developed in the eighteenth century in this useful reference work. On this, see: Helmut Berding, "Neue historische Literatur: Begriffsgeschichte und Sozialgeschichte," *Historische Zeitschrift* 223 (1976): 98–110; Foko Eulen, *Vom Gewerbefleiss zur Industrie: Ein Beitrag zur Wirtschaftsgeschichte des 18. Jahrhunderts,* Schriften zur Wirtschafts- und Sozialgeschichte, no. 12 (Berlin, 1967).

[40] Schlumbohm, *Freiheit* pp. 111–126.

[41] Several important works for understanding Kant as an early political liberal thinker are: *Metaphysics of Ethics* (1785), "National Principle of the Political Order" (1784), "Principles

Kant was a symbol for the eighteenth-century's new way of looking at the world. One need not have read or even known of Kant to have participated in the revolution of ideas which he personified. Businessmen, governmental administrators, literary artists, journalists, schoolteachers, university professors, and enlightened aristocrats all had their own reasons for adhering to the revolution in ideas typified by Kant's new concept of humanity and society.

One of the most important ways in which Prussians participated in the eighteenth-century revolution of ideas was through the work of Adam Smith (1723–1790). The Scottish philosopher and economist had a number of enthusiastic interpreters throughout Germany, especially among the professors of cameral science at the universities. These include Georg Sartorius (1765–1828) at Göttingen, Ludwig Heinrich von Jakob (1759–1827) at Halle, and Christian Jakob Kraus (1753–1807) at Königsberg. By 1800 there existed several German translations of *The Wealth of Nations* which Smith had published in 1776. Modern cameralists reorganized their lectures according to Smith's ideas. Sartorius, for example, published in 1796 his *Handbook of Political Economy for Use with Academic Lectures Developed According to Adam Smith's Principles.* Kraus, teacher and consultant to many of the men who would participate in the Stein reform ministry of 1807–1808, took much of his lecture material directly from Smith's *Wealth of Nations.* His five-volume *Staatswirthschaft* is a conscious adaptation of Smith's work to Prussian conditions. Significantly, whereas Smith derived his thinking from examples of early manufacture in his homeland, Kraus applied the concepts of Smith to agricultural conditions, as was appropriate for Prussia.[42]

Smith is the world's best-known exponent of the principles of free trade and market economy. He is the prophet of the modern capitalist system. Those who disseminated Smith's ideas in Germany were eclectics. They drew inspiration from the French philosophes, from the physiocratic school of economic thought and from a variety of other writers. Smith's thought

---

of Political Right" (1793), and "Perpetual Peace" (1795), *Gesammelte Schriften* (Berlin and Leipzig, 1910–55). There are numerous editions and translations. See Schlumbohm, *Freiheit,* 88–89, 114, 149, 159–60, 165–66; Massimo Salvadori, ed., *European Liberalism,* Major Issues in History (New York, etc., 1972), 83–92; Leonard Krieger, *The German Idea of Freedom: History of a Political Tradition from the Reformation to 1871* (Chicago, 1957), 86–125.

[42] Wilhelm Treue, "Adam Smith in Deutschland: Zum Problem des 'politischen Professors' zwischen 1776 und 1810," in *Deutschland und Europa: Historische Studien zur Völker- und Staatenordnung des Abendlandes. Festschrift für Hans Rothfels,* ed. Werner Conze (Düsseldorf, 1951), 101–133; Wilhelm Treue, *Wirtschafts- und Technikgeschichte Preussens,* Veröffentlichungen der Historischen Kommission zu Berlin, no. 56 (Berlin and New York, 1984), 213–18. Carl William Hasek, *The Introduction of Adam Smith's Doctrines into Germany,* Studies in History, Economics and Public Law, no. 117/2 (New York, 1925), passim; Fritz Milkowski, "Christian Jacob Kraus: Eine längst fällige Korrektur zur Geschichte der Volkswirtschaftlehre," *Schmollers Jahrbuch für Wirtschafts- und Sozialwissenschaften* 88 (1968): 257–97; John G. Gagliardo, *From Pariah to Patriot: The Changing Image of the German Peasant 1770–1840* (Lexington, Ky., 1969), 123–35; Christian Jakob Kraus, *Staatswirthschaft,* ed. Hans von Auerswald (Königsberg, 1808–1811); *Allgemeine Deutsche Biographie* 13: 689–90.

was one of several ideological tools used to challenge the Prussian system of absolutist government, mercantilist economy and hierarchical society. Smith's interpreters called for the application of natural economic laws, by which they meant a society based upon individual self-interest and competition. A market system could not function where land was held by right of hereditary tenure or privilege. Unfree labor conditions stifled economic development. Guilds prohibited market growth and restricted the labor force.

Application of Smith's ideas to Prussia would mean not only economic, but also political change. Subjects of landlords and of kings would have to become citizens in order to lay the groundwork for a market economy in Hohenzollern lands. This meshed with the Enlightenment notion of dignity of the individual, an idea that could not flourish on a soil which supported economic and personal servitude. At a time when increasing commercialization of agriculture in Prussia was beginning to transform the relationships between people and the land, new ideals called for acceleration of this process.

The economic concept of market economy and the political-philosophical notions associated with the Enlightenment merged to form the basis of a new *Weltanschauung*, liberalism. Liberalism is the loose constellation of ideas which underlies capitalist democracy as it developed in the nineteenth and twentieth centuries in Europe. Neither the word "liberalism" nor any notion of a liberal party appeared before the second decade of the nineteenth century, but the underlying ideas, though in an early stage of development, circulated vibrantly in the late eighteenth.[43]

One of the difficulties with identifying the proponents of liberal philosophy is the fact that every exponent of it has applied it in a peculiar or

---

[43] Sheehan describes liberalism as a party movement emerging in the 1820s but also characterizes liberalism as an "ideology and movement" existing in the 1770s. (James J. Sheehan, *German Liberalism in the Nineteenth Century* [Chicago and London, 1978], 7–48; James J. Sheehan, "Partei, Volk und Staat: Some Reflections on the Relationship between Liberal Thought and Action in Vormärz," in Hans Ulrich Wehler, ed., *Sozialgeschichte heute. Festschrift für Hans Rosenberg*, Kritische Studien zur Geschichtswissenschaft, no. 11 [1974]: 162–74.) In a reprinted 1930 essay, Rosenberg distinguishes between pre-nineteenth-century liberalism which he describes as a value orientation and later liberalism which was a political movement. (Hans Rosenberg, "Theologischer Rationalismus und vormärzlicher Vulgarliberalismus," in *Politische Denkströmmungen im deutschen Vormärz*, Kritische Studien zur Geschichtswissenschaft, no. 3 [Göttingen, 1972]: 26–32.) Gall believes that early German liberalism was not oriented to industrial values. (Lothar Gall, "Liberalismus und 'bürgerliche Gesellschaft': Zu Charakter und Entwicklung der liberalen Bewegung in Deutschland," *Historische Zeitschrift* 220 [1975]: 324–56.) On the coining of the word "liberalism," see G. de Bertier de Sauvigny, "Liberalism, Nationalism, Socialism: The Birth of Three Words," *Review of Politics* 32 (1970): 147–55; Eric Voegelin, "Liberalism and its History," *Review of Politics* 36 (1974): 504–20. I believe that many have overlooked the significant combination of sources of early liberal thinking: laissez-faire economics and philosophical commitment to freedom, equality and natural law. Concerning recent literature on German liberalism, see Wolfgang J. Mommsen, "Der deutsche Liberalismus zwischen 'klassenloser Bürgergesellschaft' und 'organisiertem Kapitalismus': Zu einigen neueren Liberalismusinterpretationen," *Geschichte und Gesellschaft: Zeitschrift für historische Sozialwissenschaft* 4 (1978): 77–90.

personal way. This is also true of other "isms." However, adherents of most political ideologies, for example, socialism, have perceived themselves as members of a particular movement. Liberals have not always done so, for the values in which they believe, progress, justice and freedom, are thought by many in the modern Western world to be universal, the basic elements of a well-functioning society. This ahistorical notion grows out of the Enlightenment concept that there is a natural law of humanity, to which all societies should strive to orient themselves.

While the ideology of liberalism was in a pre party stage in Kant's and Kraus's Prussia, it is clear that there existed a community of interests among people who saw themselves as opposed to the old order and favoring a new one. This embryonic liberalism was molded by its historical setting: corporate society and absolute government. Eighteenth-century Europeans believed almost universally in social hierarchy. Hence when statesmen and social innovators sought to apply their ideals of equality and freedom, they usually arrived at solutions which replaced one kind of social ranking with another. Hereditary status, thought to be unnatural, would give way to a new, "natural" rank, one based, for example, on wealth or talent.

One of the most perplexing dilemmas of early liberalism is the conflict between the doctrine of self interest, central to Adam Smith's market economy, and the notions of equality and human dignity. This is illustrated in the pre reform peasant emancipations which, as we have seen, were often the acts of landlords and estate managers who stood to gain economically while their peasants forfeited security and economic welfare. It would be easy to argue that such actions had little to do with the Enlightenment or liberalism.[44] Such was often not the case, however. Peasant emancipation was consistent with the egalitarian and humanitarian ideas of Smith and the philosophes. Abolition of servile duties on both private and domain estates was frequently accompanied by the new rhetoric of freedom. Many saw destruction of medieval bondage as a moral issue, equivalent to the anti-slavery movement in England.[45]

Professor Kraus of Königsberg published a tract in 1802 in which he appealed for the abolition of serfdom on the private estates of Prussia's eastern provinces. He carefully outlined the economic advantages to the landlord of free labor over work performed in a servile relationship. Yet he thought simultaneously in terms of morality and natural rights, decrying

---

[44] For example, Schissler, *Preussische Agrargesellschaft*, 93: "The pre-1806 private peasant emancipations, frequently praised as purely humane deeds, were generally motivated by strong economic interests." While I agree with this, I believe it overlooks vital, ideological considerations.

[45] See, for example, the exposition by the Schlewig-Holstein nobleman, Christian von Rantzau, in relation to peasant emancipation in that state: "Darstellung der Leibeigenschaft," in Conze, *Quellen*, 63–66 (no. 11). For background on the anti-slavery campaign in the British Empire, from which German opponents of serfdom drew inspiration, see Michael Craton, James Walvin, and David Wright, eds., *Slavery, Abolition and Emancipation: Black Slaves and the British Empire* (London and New York, 1976), 195–321.

with passion the "oppression and the misery of the unfree people." Kraus would have had no understanding for the modern analysts' view that the gardeners and cottagers of Prussia were a rural proletariat, having been robbed of their security. In Kraus's view their position was infinitely better than that of the serfs who would, he said,

> feel that their fate is even more cruel . . . when they observe the contrast between themselves and the free people on domains and other estates. This is not to mention the contempt in which they see themselves perpetually held on account of their bondage. . . . This sours their existence and crushes their spirit.

What was to be done about this? "Laws against these sufferings cannot help the serf. To whom shall he appeal?" To a patrimonial court presided over by his lord? To a court of the government, two or more days' journey away? "Nothing can help him but the right to be master of his own affairs." For the sake of justice, peasants must be emancipated and feudal relationships destroyed.[46]

Being on one's own, being personally free was in everyone's interest, believed the early liberals. Those who stressed economics and those who favored change for moral or philosophical reasons were united in their conviction that corporate feudalism should be replaced by a society of individualism and equality. The proponents of these goals represented a strong undercurrent in Prussia at the end of the eighteenth century. Their movement would express itself energetically in the reform year 1807–1808.

That many of their ideals were inconsistent with one another, was not clear to early liberals. It is obvious to many today, after two centuries of practice, that market capitalism embodies a notion of inequality. In its nineteenth-century application it benefitted the propertied classes disproportionately, and it sometimes brought misery to the masses. But eighteenth-century reformers did not foresee this. Early liberals in Prussia believed themselves to represent the underprivileged fighting for a chance to share in society's fruits. The philosophy of universal freedom was their tool. They did not look critically at its implications. If they knew that the middle class would gain, they were also aware of liberalism's promise that everyone stood to benefit from freedom and social mobility.

CONSERVATIVE POLITICS CLASH WITH THE REFORM IDEOLOGY

King Frederick the Great (1740–1786) was famous for his intercourse with French philosophers. He was a self-declared enlightened absolutist, and he even claimed the title philosophe for himself. It would be easy to

---

[46] C. J. Kraus, Gutachten über die Aufhebung der Privatuntertänigkeit, 1802, in Conze, *Quellen,* 73 (no. 12). See also Kraus, "Über die Aufhebung der Erbuntertänigkeit," *Vermischte Schriften über staatswirthschaftliche, philosophische und andere wissenschaftliche Gegenstände,* ed. Hans von Auerswald (Königsberg, 1808–1817) 1: 173–202. "Über die Freiheit des Willens," ibid., 5: 415–34.

believe that his applications of Enlightenment thought initiated a liberalizing movement which culminated in the reform year of 1808. Though events have often been interpreted in this way, such an assumption is unwarranted. On the contrary, the philosophy of early liberalism found itself in a standoff with the state between the reign of Frederick the Great and the military collapse of 1806.

Most of the domestic policies of this powerful king had the result of solidifying corporate institutions. One example is the already-mentioned Landschaften, the aristocratic credit institutions. They helped Junker estate owners enhance their economic and social positions. Another is Frederick's well-known consolidation of the peasant protection edicts (*Bauernschutz*) which prevented landlords from incorporating peasant farms into their estates through enclosure. This policy had the effect of maintaining the dependent peasantry, and hence the rigid class system, under the threat of impending social change. In addition, Frederick favored the nobility with bureaucratic appointments, in contrast to his predecessors who had often preferred the middle class. This gave official recognition to the importance of hereditary status.[47] When Frederick died in 1786, Prussia's aristocracy was entrenched, and from the state's point of view, social change was something to be held in check.

Three years later the French Revolution erupted. Liberal thinkers all over Germany greeted it with great enthusiasm, but Prussia's government under Frederick William II (1786–1797) and Frederick William III (1797–1840) hardened its stance against innovators. It established a heavy-handed censorship commission whose work forced the closing of many middle-class newspapers, drove some liberal publishers out of Prussia and involved Immanuel Kant in a bitter, sad controversy over his right to freedom of expression. Fearful of the French events' shattering implications to themselves, both Frederick Williams united successively with fellow monarchs in a series of political and military alliances against France and revolution. Their fears seemed justified when southern and western German lands experienced "Jacobin" upheavals and violent rural rebellions. Ten to twenty thousand peasants of Saxony, Prussia's neighbor to the south, drove landlords off their estates, looted, burned and pillaged. Across the border in Silesia, Prussia's province with a developed textile industry but rigid feudal conditions, rural lower classes intensified their lawless protests, which had been sporadically erupting since 1779. Under the influence of the French Revolution, Prussian society threatened to explode, but Prussian monarchs stiffened their opposition to change.[48]

---

[47] Vogel, *Preussische Reformen,* 10; Rosenberg, *Bureaucracy,* 146–74; Büsch, *Militärsystem und Sozialleben,* 6, 25, 51, 56–61; Ziekursch, *Hundert Jahre Agrargeschichte,* 158–68; Müller, "Bauern, Pächter und Adel," 262.

[48] Klaus Epstein, *The Genesis of German Conservatism* (Princeton, 1966), 364–69, 434–41; Bues, *Adelskritik—Adelsreform,* 12; Schissler, *Preussische Agrargesellschaft,* 54; Ziekursch, *Hundert Jahre Agrargeschichte,* 226–41.

Even before the threat of 1789, royal conservatism had characterized Hohenzollern policies. In 1780 Frederick the Great had ordered the codification of the extremely unsystematic Prussian laws and judicial procedures. After fourteen years, in the reign of Frederick William II, the task was completed with the publication of the famous General Lawcode of Prussia (*Allgemeines Landrecht*). Spokesmen for the conservative aristocracy fought it bitterly, for they correctly perceived that codification itself was threatening to their authority which was based upon decentralization. But when published, the code turned out to be a mere reflection of existing conditions, and hence a conservative instrument. It placed the power of law in a centralizing monarchy behind the status quo of corporate society and political absolutism.[49]

Frederick William III's reign opened in 1798 with a traditional homage ceremony of the Estates in which the middle class represented its views, vociferously calling for reform and voicing hopes for a liberalization of the society. Nothing significant came of this meeting on which liberals had placed high hopes. Instead, Frederick William III surrounded himself with men of rigid mentality. The upper bureaucracy from 1798 to 1806 was one of the most conservative influences in the monarchy.[50]

As the state became more resolutely opposed to innovation, those who favored it intensified their campaign, in spite of, or perhaps because of, the obstacles they faced. When newspapers were stifled by censorship, there developed an outpouring of political leaflets aimed above all at encouraging the abolition of serfdom. This caused the state to tighten its censorship laws.[51]

The discussion over the enactment of the *Allgemeines Landrecht* itself provoked the expression of a flood of liberal sentiment, especially when judicial chancellor von Carmer surprisingly brought the debate into the open. He offered gold and silver prizes for constructive, critical commentaries of the proposed lawcode. He received a mass of criticism from bureaucrats and academicians. Most condemned the draft for its failure to abolish feudalism and serfdom. The document's authors replied that it was not intended to change society's laws, but to codify them.[52]

The controversy raged on, even after the enactment of the *Allgemeines*

---

[49] Uwe-Jens Heuer, *Allgemeines Landrecht und Klassenkampf: Die Auseinandersetzungen um die Prinzipien des Allgemeinen Landrechts Ende des 18. Jahrhunderts als Ausdruck der Krise des Feudalsystems in Preussen* (Berlin, 1960); Koselleck, *Preussen,* 23–149, passim; Epstein, *Genesis,* 372–87; Günther Birtsch, "Zum konstitutionellen Charakter des preussischen Allgemeinen Landrechts von 1794," *Politische Ideologien und nationalstaatliche Ordnung: Studien zur Geschichte des 19. und 20. Jahrhunderts. Festschrift für Theodor Schieder,* ed. Kurt Kluxen and Wolfgang J. Mommsen (Munich and Vienna, 1968), 97–115.

[50] Hermann Eicke, *Der ostpreussische Landtag von 1798* (Göttingen, 1910); Schissler, *Preussische Agrargeschichte,* 53–56; Marie Rumler, "Die Bestrebungen zur Befreiung der Privatbauern in Preussen, 1797–1806, *Forschungen zur brandenburgischen und preussischen Geschichte* 34 (1922): 265–96.

[51] Bues, *Adelskritik—Adelsreform,* 11–12, 24–25.

[52] Heuer, *Allgemeines Landrecht,* 149–61.

Landrecht. In 1800 the anonymous *Commentaries on the Republican Lawbook Contained in the Notes to the General Lawcode* appeared through the liberal Nicolovius publishing house of Königsberg. Its author was a middle-class jurist of that city, Ernst Gottlob Morgenbesser (1755–1824). Morgenbesser would later play a significant role in the drafting of many reform edicts in the Stein administration. His critique had a radical tone, given the circumstances in which it appeared. Opening with an argument against those who considered a republican form of government too idealistic and unworkable, he replied: "Since the republican constitution is the only one which is in harmony with the nature of mankind, . . . it must be feasible." He called for complete abolition of Estates, maintaining that "the citizenry (*Bürgerstand*) includes all . . . who live in the state. . . . Noble birth ceases to exist in the republic." This is so because "people are free and are born to freedom. Hence they are their own lawmakers." Elected representatives would form a legislature. "Everyone is subject to the law; all other specific forms of subjugation are abolished." Finally, Morgenbesser saw market freedom and private property as the only possible economic system of a republic: private ownership would replace common lands of villages, and "guilds cannot be tolerated."[53]

Morgenbesser was in good company. Theodor Anton Schmalz (1760–1831), professor of jurisprudence at the University of Königsberg, colleague of Kraus and Kant, had written similar works published by the Nicolovius firm in the preceding years. His *Pure Natural Law* (1792) and his *Declaration of the Rights of People and Citizens* (1798) were Kantian in spirit, reformist in tone, although not as extreme as Morgenbesser's commentary. Several members of the future Stein government were students and friends of Schmalz. Like many early Prussian liberals, he had a great admiration for British ideas and institutions. His *Constitution of Great Britain* published in 1806 is laudatory and presented as a model for Germans. For example, Schmalz argued that Great Britain was to be admired for having avoided "more than Germany the evil practice of subjecting various classes to different judicial courts." Society, constitution and economics were all bound together, Schmalz believed. If continental Europeans were envious of England, they should not consider war against her, but rather should

> wage another battle, one for the commerce of this land. Let your soldiers and your customs inspectors return from the shore to the plow. Condemn communal property; abolish that disgrace, forced labor. Abolish serfdom, the shame of mankind. Do not let monopolies lame the industriousness of your manufacturers, and your commerce will flower; factories will . . . rise up of themselves. . . . Riches and blessings

---

[53] [Ernst Gottlob Morgenbesser], *Beyträge zum republikanischen Gesetzbuche enthalten in Anmerkungen zum Allgemeinen Landrechte und zur Allgemeinen Gerichtsordnung für die preussischen Staaten* (Königsberg, 1800); quotes from the following pages in this order: vii, 93, 91, 9, 90, 92, 95; Heuer, *Allgemeines Landrecht*, 259–70.

will favor your fields, and the British will have to envy you when your welfare is secured by greater justice and freedom than they have.[54]

Liberals in Prussia shared a hopeful vision about the future of politics and society. A related source of their inspiration was the movement for scientific agriculture. The figure who personifies this development is economist and agriculturalist Albrecht Thaer (1752–1828). A Hanoverian, Thaer studied medicine at Göttingen, the university in Germany most alive with English ideas and practices. Instead of entering the medical profession, he devoted himself to the dissemination of scientific agricultural practices in Germany. Inspired by English techniques, he advocated the use of fertilizer, the chemical testing of soil, the implementation of modern plows and harvest equipment and the use of planned crop rotation. Equally important to him, however, was the introduction into Germany of social and economic conditions which would favor agricultural progress. Drawing upon the writings of Arthur Young, England's public champion of the enclosure movement, Thaer argued that "gentlemen farmers" were responsible for the impressive improvement in British agriculture. He echoed a dilemma expressed by Young: while the lifestyle of the small peasant family had a desirable, rustic, romantic quality, there was no denying that large farms were more productive than small ones.[55]

Thaer wrote profusely, producing scientific tracts, handbooks for farmers, and agricultural journals. In addition he carried on experimentation on his model farm in Celle, Hanover, and later in Prussia at the invitation of King Frederick William III. In 1804 he set up an agricultural school on land provided by the king. In 1807 he advised the Stein government on matters of agrarian reform. Thaer epitomizes one facet of the Enlightenment tradition with his belief in science, rationality and progress.

Like early political liberals, Thaer believed it was necessary to rearrange society in order to benefit humanity. More food and better living conditions would result, he believed, from the application of Adam Smith's ideas to agriculture. Hence Thaer strongly advocated termination of serfdom, consolidation of small landholdings, and abolition of communal property in

---

[54] Fritz Gause, "Theodor von Schmalz," in *Altpreussische Biographie* ed. Christian Krollmann, Kurt Forstreuter and Fritz Gause (Königsberg and Marburg, 1941–1969) 2: 619. Theodor Schmalz, *Das reine Naturrecht* (Königsberg, 1792); Theodor Schmalz, *Erklärung der Rechte des Menschen und des Bürgers: Ein Commentar über das reine Natur- und natürliche Staatsrecht* (Königsberg, 1798); [Theodor] Schmalz, *Staatsverfassung Grossbritanniens* (Halle, 1806), quotations from 143, 213–14.

[55] For this and the following paragraphs: Treue, "Adam Smith in Deutschland;" *Allgemeine Deutsche Biographie* 37: 636–41; Gagliardo, *Pariah to Patriot*, 130–31; Albrecht Thaer, *Einleitung zur Kenntniss der englischen Landwirtschaft und ihrer neuen praktischen und theoretischen Fortschritte in Rücksicht auf Vervollkommung deutscher Landwirtschaft für denkende Landwirthe und Cameralisten* (Hanover, 1798); Rudolf Stadelmann, *Preussens Könige in ihrer Thätigkeit für die Landeskultur*, Part 4: *Friedrich Wilhelm III*, Publikationen aus den Königlichen Preussischen Staatsarchiven, no. 30 (Leipzig, 1887), 102–06.

villages. In short he championed a modern landholding system and capitalist agriculture. Once a free market existed, the best farmers would thrive while the less efficient would seek a sector of the economy in which they made the greatest contribution.

Thaer represents a characteristic common to many early Prussian liberals. While his ideals were consistent with the abolition of corporate society, he was not especially critical of either royal or aristocratic power. He looked, in fact, to estate owners and kings to improve agriculture and society. He may well have felt justified in doing so when he saw that the government of Prussia introduced some of his recommendations on the royal domains and invited him to become Prussia's expert on agrarian matters. Furthermore, if he was observant, he noticed that Prussia's agriculture was increasing its productivity under the leadership of estate owners and domain managers. Thaer's optimism, humanitarianism, and belief in orderly, scientific progress characterize at least one side of Prussian liberalism on the eve of the reform year.

Many advocates of change in Prussia did not feel as optimistic as Thaer at the turn of the century about the prospect that the government and the nobility would favor their cause. These were people like Morgenbesser and his publisher Nicolovius who had come directly into confrontation with the government and experienced the bureaucracy's resistance to innovation. They found the times frustrating. They were not radicals who advocated violence. They did not seek to destroy society, for they had a stake in it, but they were resolute devotees of change, embittered by the rigid circumstances surrounding them. They pinned their hopes on more favorable times.

THE GROWTH OF PROFESSIONAL BUREAUCRACY

One striking feature of the clash between government conservatism and the forces of change in the pre reform era is the degree to which the advocates of innovation were themselves part of the government. Some of the harshest criticism of absolutism and hierarchy came from the civil service, which was in theory responsible for carrying out the wishes of the monarch. The king's administrators often were allied with the middle classes who stood to gain from change. Indeed, in Prussia civil servants (along with journalists and university professors) seemed to be the primary group who articulated the views of the entrepreneurial class, which in comparison with the French bourgeoisie of the eighteenth century was relatively quiet.[56] The fact that impulses for reform came from within the government can be attributed to an embryonic, but fast-growing sense of professionalism

[56] Ulrich K. Preuss, "Bildung und Büreaukratie: Sozialhistorische Bedingungen in den ersten Hälfte des 19. Jahrhunderts," *Der Staat: Zeitschrift für Staatslehre, öffentliches Recht und Verfassungsgeschichte* 14 (1975): 375.

among state employees. The growth of professional bureaucracy was beginning to transform government all over Europe.

In the era of absolutism, kings had sought to increase their own power in relation to the entrenched aristocracy by recruiting their secretaries, tax collectors, and ministers from the non-noble classes. The primary qualification which could distinguish middle-class aspirants from their aristocratic competitors was education. Like members of the incipient medical, legal, and journalistic professions, civil servants began to perceive themselves as products of education. University training was becoming the key to establishing professional identity. There was a philosophical as well as a practical side to this development. In the age of the Enlightenment, education gained increasing importance as Europeans began to see the solution to the world's problems in science and learning. Governmental administration should be based upon knowledge and expertise, not hereditary status. By the end of the eighteenth century, a primary function of universities had become the training of governmental officials. Governments, moreover, had begun a drive to establish objective criteria for entry into public posts, primarily in the form of civil service examinations.[57]

In Prussia a bureaucratic ethos had been developing since the seventeenth century. This was due in part to the increasing size and function of government. It was necessary for kings to have ever larger staffs of specialized professionals to carry out the state's policies and oversee its many activities. Frederick the Great, however, slowed the development of professional bureaucracy in several respects during his reign from 1740 to 1786. We have seen already that the famous king was interested in maintaining the status quo rather than fostering social change. With regard to the bureaucracy, he temporarily reversed an established trend when he recruited civil servants heavily from the landed aristocracy rather than the middle class. This did not prevent an increase in numbers and duties in the bureaucracy, but it did, for the time being, slow the development of professionalism. The sons of estate owners who served in state offices identified with the interests of their class and their provinces rather than with a profession. It was their hereditary status which they could thank for their jobs, hence they did not entertain notions that would foster the growth of a more independent, self-conscious civil service.[58]

Frederick II was able to curb the increase of bureaucratic professionalism, furthermore, by the sheer power of his managerial ability. The king ruled personally, overseeing details which other monarchs would have delegated to subordinates. He deliberately kept administrative units small so that his

[57] Bernd Wunder, *Privilegierung und Disziplinierung: Die Entstehung des Berufsbeamtentums in Bayern und Württemberg (1780–1825)*, Studien zur modernen Geschichte, no. 21 (Munich and Vienna, 1978); Carl J. Friedrich, "The Continental Tradition of Training Administrators in Law and Jurisprudence," *Journal of Modern History* 11 (1939): 133–42; LaVopa, *Prussian Schoolteachers*, 32.

[58] Rosenberg, *Bureaucracy*, 146–74.

appointees could report directly to him, rather than to bureaucratic intermediaries. This meant that while Frederick was using the technical expertise of his ever-growing staff, he did not allow them the freedom to make decisions or determine policy. This changed after 1786.[59]

Even during Frederick's reign, however, the bureaucracy won significant gains in establishing professional autonomy. In 1770 Frederick's minister, Ludwig Philipp von Hagen, was able to establish required examinations (*Staatsexamen*) to determine applicants' competence, as well as the Civil Service Examination Commission (*Oberexaminationkommission*) which established entrance criteria and checked credentials. This did not prevent Frederick and subsequent kings from appointing prestigious noblemen at their discretion, but it established the principle, which would be more and more systematically applied, that the civil service regulated itself and was not subject to the whims of royal power.[60]

In 1794 under Frederick William II, the civil bureaucracy won another concrete step toward independence with the promulgation of the General Lawcode. It provided protection for state employees against arbitrary dismissal or disciplinary action. It recognized specific privileges of the bureaucracy which came to be called "well-earned rights" (*wohlerworbene Rechte*). Among these were the qualified legal guarantee of permanent tenure for the upper levels of civil service and the unqualified right to due process in cases of questionable conduct. ("Political" ministers, those at the top of the bureaucracy, were not protected in this way. Just as a modern cabinet is responsible to an electorate or parliament, they had to maintain the good will of the king in order to keep their positions.) These measures on the whole limited the powers of the monarch, placing him under the law, while it elevated the independence and prerogative of the bureaucracy. A significant shift in terminology accompanied this transition. No longer did appointees call themselves "royal servants." Now they referred to themselves as state servants or "professional officials of the state" (*Beamten des Staats*).[61]

The development of the independent bureaucracy helps explain the phenomenon of governmental administrators taking a leading role in criticizing the institutions of government and society. Perceiving themselves as loyal to the state rather than to the ruler, they sought to effect such changes as would be beneficial, in their eyes, to the welfare of Prussia. This resulted in clashes between kings and their officials which are exemplified by the activities of the Law Commission, established in 1781. Its

---

[59] Ibid., 192; Kehr, "Genesis der preussischen Bürokratie," 38. Preuss, "Bildung und Büreaukratie," 316. Schmoller, "Die Epochen der preussischen Finanzpolitik," 184–85; Walter Hubatsch, *Frederick the Great of Prussia: Absolutism and Administration*, trans. Patrick Doran (London, 1973), 223.

[60] Bleek, *Von der Kameralausbildung zum Juristenprivileg*, 58–59, 73–79; Rosenberg, *Bureaucracy*, 178–82; Preuss, "Bildung und Büreaukratie," 377.

[61] Ibid.; Rosenberg, *Bureaucracy*, 190–91.

function was to advise upon all edicts, decrees and other legislative matters prior to their enactment. While this body did not eliminate the royal prerogative of issuing laws by arbitrary fiat, it did bind the monarch to seek the advice of experts. Early in the reign of Frederick William III, the Law Commission ran into deep conflict with the king and his closest advisors. Its membership included several young professionals who would later serve in the reform government of 1807–1808. Schooled in the ideals of the late Enlightenment, they were eager to stimulate social and political change. The commission moved beyond its originally intended realm when it embarked upon an extensive campaign to prepare (not review) an agrarian reform abolishing feudal landlord-peasant relations. Although the state's top bureaucracy, the ministers, suppressed the effort in its final stages, it exemplifies the mentality and self-assuredness of the people who would lead the reform efforts a few years hence.[62]

The politics of Prussia in the period between Frederick the Great's death and the formation of the Stein ministry can be characterized by tension between two groups. On the one hand there were the professional bureaucrats who were impatient with the inertia and conservatism of their times and anxious to effect changes. On the other, there were the monarchs and members of the bureaucracy who had reason to fear change. This group included not only those ideologically and socially committed to conservatism, but also civil servants who lacked strong convictions and found it more comfortable to shore up a status quo than to join a crusade which would produce unknown results. In the two decades between 1786 and 1806 the proponents of reform experienced frustration after frustration. Though they represented a significant power group, they were clearly the outsiders. They learned to bide their time waiting for more favorable auspices, but their disappointments, such as the suppression of the Law Commission's agrarian reform, increased their impatience and their determination to fight.

---

[62] Eicke, *Landtag von 1789*, 19–20. Epstein, *Genesis of German Conservatism*, 374, 376, 381, 384.

III. OPTIMISM SPRINGS FROM CRISIS: THE REFORM PARTY

"Serfdom will be abolished, everyone will be able to purchase aristocratic lands, compulsory guilds will be destroyed, and all foreign products will become importable!" rejoiced a Prussian administrator, Friedrich Staegemann in the summer of 1807.[1] What was the cause of this excitement? Why did Staegemann, a veteran of seventeen years in Prussian service, suddenly believe that century-old institutions and practices would be destroyed? Why did the same sentiment of enthusiasm suddenly explode from the lips and pens of Prussian liberals everywhere?

The cause was a catastrophe of greatest magnitude: Prussia's shattering defeat in the war of 1806–1807 against Napoleon's imperial army. As the French emperor methodically extended military and political dominance throughout central Europe after 1799, Prussia's Frederick William III wavered in his anti-French alliances with other monarchs. Opposed to everything that Napoleon stood for, Frederick William nevertheless strove to avoid conflict. It was as if he sensed that by meeting the French on the battlefield, he would have to deal with the forces of revolution and change. Finally he stumbled into war, feeling himself pushed by circumstances: the French poised on Prussia's western borders, and the king, insulted, issued an ultimatum demanding that they withdraw. Instead Napoleon replied by calling for demobilization of the Prussian army. On 9 October 1806, Frederick William issued a war manifesto.[2]

With Prussia's army barely assembled, the French attacked at Jena in northern Thuringia and simultaneously at nearby Auerstädt. Napoleon won both battles almost as they began. In sudden defeat, Prussian morale, discipline and leadership broke down. The battles turned into catastrophe for the monarchy. The French troops marched across Prussian territories, hardly halting at most fortresses they met. The court and the state's ministry,

---

[1] Staegemann to Elisabeth von Staegemann, 20 Aug. 1807, Franz Rühl, ed., *Aus der Franzosenzeit: Ergänzungen zu den Briefen und Aktenstücken zur Geschichte Preussens unter Friedrich Wilhelm III., vorzugsweise aus dem Nachlass von F. A. von Stägemann* (Leipzig, 1904), 30 (no. 25).

[2] For this and the following paragraphs: Streisand, "Deutschland von 1780 bis 1815," 65–72; Kurt von Raumer, *Deutschland um 1800: Krise und Neugestaltung 1789–1815*, ed. Leo Just, *Handbuch der Deutschen Geschichte* 3 (Konstanz, 1965), 225–33; Herbert A. L. Fisher, *Studies in Napoleonic Statesmanship: Germany* (Oxford, 1903), 124–42; Heinz Gerold, "Militärisches Debakel eines überlebten Systems: zum 175. Jahrestag der Schlacht bei Jena und Auerstedt," *Militärgeschichte*, 20 (1981): 587–89.

hastily grabbing records, crown jewels, and parts of the treasury, fled Berlin as the conquerers approached. The French entered the capital city on 27 October 1806, less than two weeks after the campaign had begun. Napoleon victoriously demanded loyalty oaths from the officials who had not evacuated Berlin, and he extracted large payments from the city's citizens as well as from the Brandenburg Estates.

Seeing Prussia's complete demoralization, the French emperor pushed deeper into Hohenzollern lands and forced the court from its first place of retreat, Königsberg, to the small seacoast town of Memel, located at Prussia's easternmost tip. Allied with Russia, the Prussians made one credible military stand at Eylau in the province of East Prussia, and the two eastern powers resolved to drive the French back over the Rhine. The hopes of Frederick William and Tsar Alexander were premature. In the Battle of Friedland (14 June) Napoleon soundly defeated the Russians, driving them further east, beyond the Niemen river. Alexander, without consulting his ally, Frederick William, hastily agreed to conclude a peace with Napoleon. In the Peace of Tilsit the Russian and the French emperors divided Europe into two parts, leaving a helpless, carved up Prussia in the middle. Napoleon could have ended the existence of the Hohenzollern state with the stroke of a pen, as he had done with many other German-speaking principalities. But instead, probably due to the intercession of Alexander, he allowed a remnant of the state to exist. It would serve as a buffer between the two big empires.

The Peace of Tilsit of 9 July 1807 stripped Prussia of all its territories west of the Elbe, most of which went into the new kingdom of Westphalia under the rule of Napoleon's brother, Jerome. The Tilsit agreement gave the city of Magdeburg to Westphalia and most Polish provinces of Prussia to the new duchy of Warsaw. A small area, the county Bialystock, went to Prussia's former ally, Russia. In all, Prussia lost more than half its territory and almost 50 percent of its five million inhabitants. The convention of Königsberg a few days later stipulated that French troops would occupy the remaining Prussian provinces until "war contributions"—or reparations in modern terminology—were made, but the amounts had yet to be established. Humiliated, bankrupt, and in ruins, Prussia was at the mercy of its conquerers. "Wherever one looked," wrote the poet Varnhagen von Ense, "one saw destruction, disruptions and in every direction an uncertain future."[3]

The war of 1806 not only produced a grave political crisis; it also inflicted crippling physical and economic damage on Prussia. In the Napoleonic style of warfare, villages, estates and towns were often the scenes of battle, and many were completely devastated. When they were not, they suffered from foreign troops living off the land, and after cessation of hostilities, from soldiers being quartered in local houses. In the province of East Prussia

---

[3] Fisher, *Studies,* 143–49; Streisand, "Deutschland von 1780 bis 1815," 72–73; K. A. Varnhagen von Ense, *Denkwürdigkeiten des eigenen Lebens,* ed. Joachim Kühn (Berlin, 1922) 1: 245.

alone, damage to buildings and other properties amounted to 75 million thaler. Twenty-two percent of the horses and twenty-seven percent of the cattle of that province were lost. As a contemporary, Heinrich von Beguelin, graphically pictured the situation:

> The results of the war of 1806, the occupation of the land by the French, the contributions which they exacted . . . destroyed a great part of the available capital. . . . Buildings and other real estate properties sank to half their value. There is no city which is not sunk deeply in debt. When [the court] fled Berlin, they took the capital of the state bank and the department of overseas commerce and used it to pay for the war, although it belonged to private individuals. . . . Treasury notes, whose value had no other basis than the solemn promise of the king to redeem them, were not accepted at royal banks. . . . What a terrible indebtedness! . . . The situation of private people was . . . miserable. . . . The holders of state securities received no interest and feared the loss of the capital itself, for which they were offered 50%.

Before the fighting was over, requests poured in to local and provincial authorities for assistance in relieving the suffering and restoring the destruction. In early July provincial minister von Schroetter received the following message from Königsberg: "If there are no supplies of grain remaining after . . . peace and departure of the French troops, the countryside and the city are in greatest danger of massive famine. . . . Already people and whole families are dying daily of hunger."[4]

This was the cause of Staegemann's rejoicing? Yes, for he and other reform-minded officials believed that out of the old, destroyed state of Prussia, a new one could be built. For years they had worked in vain for a new society. They had seen their efforts stifled by bureaucratic conservatism. Suddenly changes had become possible, they felt. Restoration after destruction rendered the opportunity of creating modern social, economic and governmental institutions. Requests for state assistance opened the way for government planning according to the latest theories. Finance Councilor Theodor von Schön pondered the meaning of the destruction around him as the French bludgeoned their way through his home province of East Prussia. "It must all be for the best," he affirmed. "The French advances are at least weakening aristocratic judicial prerogative, compulsory servitude, the nobility [and] limitations in the use of private property. The foundation is being laid for the overthrow of [these institutions]."[5]

---

[4] Schmoller, "Epochen der Finanzpolitik," 192; Gottlieb Krause, *Der preussische Provinzialminister Freiherr von Schroetter und sein Anteil an der Steinschen Reformgesetzgebung* (Königsberg, 1898), 60–66; Ziekursch, *Das Ergebnis der friderizianischen Städteverwaltung*, 137–40; Heinrich and Amalie von Beguelin, *Denkwürdigkeiten aus den Jahren 1807-1813 nebst Briefen von Gneisenau und Hardenberg*, ed. Adolf Ernst (Berlin, 1892), 170–71; Auerswald to Schroetter, Königsberg, July 1807, Auerswald Nachlass, Rep. 92, I, 2, Geheimes Staatsarchiv Preussischer Kulturbesitz, Berlin-Dahlem; Schroetter to Auerswald, Memel, 8 (?) July 1807, ibid; Bock, "Reform und Revolution," 600–02.

[5] Schön to Altenstein, Königsberg, 13 Mar. 1807, Georg Winter, ed., *Die Reorganisation des preussischen Staates unter Stein und Hardenberg*, Publikationen aus den Preussischen Staatsarchiven, 93, Part 1: Allgemeine Verwaltungs- und Behördenreformen, Vol. 1: *Vom Beginn des Kampfs gegen die Kabinettsregierung bis zum Wiedereintritt des Ministers vom Stein* (Leipzig, 1931), 144 (no. 105).

In historical retrospect, the military-economic crisis, as well as the flowering of the new optimism of reform proponents were all lightning-fast events. But the contemporaries who lived through the happenings, while experiencing them with shock and disbelief, also saw time dragging. They were never sure whether the outcome would be favorable or detrimental to their cause.

TWO SOLUTIONS TO PRUSSIA'S PROBLEMS: THE PEACE PARTY AND THE PATRIOTS

From the beginning of the crisis, even prior to the startling defeats of Jena and Auerstädt, there had existed among those in and near the government two answers about the future direction of Prussia. They were represented by two very loosely formed coalitions of officials, each of which held strikingly uniform views on both foreign and domestic affairs. The electric issues of Prussia's diplomatic situation took immediate precedence and gave each group its name: "peace party" and "patriots." But the division went deeper than disagreement over foreign alliances. Christian L. E. von Zeiten, a Brandenburg nobleman who followed the court to Memel, observed that "the King's advisors are clearly divided into two camps." One stands "for the old Prussian leadership and form of government" and the other for "complete renovation of each and every institution."[6] The military crisis brought into the open the smoldering conflict between the young, Enlightenment-educated civil service professionals and the representatives of an old-regime mentality.

Members of the peace party were advocates of a nonaggressive policy toward the French. Their group included Foreign Minister Count Christian August von Haugwitz (1752–1831) and Legation Councilor Johann Wilhelm Lombard (1767–1812), both of whom had urged the noncombative stance of the Prussians prior to 1806. After their tactics of neutrality were discredited by the disasters of Jena and Auerstädt, they advocated joining Napoleon in his offensive against the Russians. Above all they wanted to terminate the conflict. Conservative in mentality, the peace party recognized the potential disruption which an extended French war could bring to their society.[7]

Foreign Minister Haugwitz resigned after his foreign policy was proven thoroughly untenable. Frederick William transferred responsibility for foreign affairs to two others associated with the peace party: Friedrich Wilhelm von Zastrow (1758–1830) and Karl Friedrich Beyme (1765–1838). Zastrow, a general, desired peace with the French, hoping to save his own vast

---

[6] Carl Brinkmann, "Eine neue Quelle zur preussischen Geschichte nach dem Tilsiter Frieden," *Forschungen zur Brandenburgischen und Preussischen Geschichte* 24 (1911), 438.

[7] Leopold von Ranke, *Hardenberg und die Geschichte des preussischen Staates von 1793–1813,* Sämmtliche Werke 46–48 (Leipzig, 1879–1881) 2: 251–69; Peter G. Thielen, *Karl August von Hardenberg 1750–1822: Eine Biographie* (Köln and Berlin, 1967), 119–61 passim, 167–72; Hermann Hüffer, *Die Kabinetsregierung in Preussen und Johann Wilhelm Lombard: Ein Beitrag zur Geschichte des preussischen Staates, vornehmlich in den Jahren 1797 bis 1810* (Leipzig, 1891), 266–300; H. v. Sybel, "Haugwitz," *Allgemeine Deutsche Biographie* 11: 57–66.

estates in Eastern Prussia. As Zeiten observed, the peace advocates feared "total confusion and also the abolition of some institutions which would naturally ruin many [noble] families."[8]

Beyme was a more complex personality. His closeness to the king dated back to Frederick William's days as crown prince. Since February 1798, three months after the monarch ascended the throne, Beyme had held the title, "privy councilor of the cabinet." This made him one of Frederick William's closest advisors. His enemies called him the "invisible prime minister" because of his immediate access to the king on all issues as head of the shadowy cabinet government. Beyme had not previously played a formal role in foreign policy, but he, like the other members of the peace party, advocated an agreement with the French rather than a contest with them. Unlike Zastrow, Beyme had no estates or aristocratic status at stake, and he was not opposed to social and political reform. But he was identified with the old regime. Beyme hoped to pull Prussia out of its crisis by gradual means. An abrupt change of direction might cost him his own position.[9]

In conflict with the peace party on both internal affairs and diplomacy, the informal group who called themselves "patriots" represented an opposition within the government. They advocated a strong Russian alliance and a tough anti-French policy. They were the faction of the upper bureaucracy which stood resolutely for reform of the structure of Prussia's government and society. They openly denounced the king's favorites, Zastrow, Haugwitz and Beyme. The two recognized leaders of the patriot party, Karl August von Hardenberg (1750–1822) and Baron Karl vom und zum Stein (1757–1831) deliberately sharpened the controversy in the crisis of 1806.

The cabinet government, dominated by Beyme, was the most immediate focus of conflict between the king and the patriots. "Government from the cabinet," that is from the king's chamber, was an expression dating from the early eighteenth century. It signified the personal rule of the monarch under the system of absolutism: all ministers were answerable directly to the ruler. By the time of the Napoleonic wars, the role of government had grown to such dimensions that total supervision by the monarch was hardly possible. This was especially true in the case of Prussia, whose rulers had

---

[8] B. Posten, "Zastrow," ibid. 44: 721–23; Raack, *Fall of Stein,* 29–30. Quotation from Brinkmann, "Eine neue Quelle," 438.

[9] There is a tradition in historical literature of portraying Beyme as a liberal who was unjustly pushed aside by the reform party. See Hans Haussherr, "Beyme," *Neue Deutsche Biographie* 2: 208; Ludwig Dehio, "Eine Reformdenkschrift Beymes aus dem Sommer 1806," *Forschungen zur brandenburgischen und preussischen Geschichte* 38 (1926): 321–28; Thielen, *Hardenberg,* 120; Ritter, *Stein,* 206–07. Beyme had participated in drafting the General Lawcode, and he had been a major figure in the campaign to terminate serfdom on domain properties. This culminated in 1804. Neither of these measures, it should be noted, were designed to alter the corporate nature of society. Beyme was a representative of the old regime and he appears to have been an opportunist. His personal position at court depended upon maintaining the cabinet government system, whereas the patriots saw administrative reform and social reform as linked.

added tremendous new acquisitions to their patchwork of territories. The unwieldy bureaucratic structure of the Prussian monarchy also complicated the cabinet government system. The vast General Directory was the monarchy's chief administrative body. It was an organization consisting of several ministries whose responsibilities were illogically divided between territorial and administrative duties. The royal privy council (*Geheimer Staatsrat*), composed of all the king's ministers, no longer functioned in all practicality. Thus each minister communicated individually with the king about matters of his own department. The top administrators had no official means of serving or understanding an overall administrative policy, when indeed there was one.[10]

Meanwhile, "cabinet government" had evolved into an institution more than a system. Under Frederick William III it was a small council of royal advisors who did not necessarily hold ministerial titles. Its members were primarily the king's courtiers and friends rather than experienced or trained administrators. To a large degree they determined state policy. As the contemporary critic, Friedrich Buchholz, wrote in 1808: "What had been the top administrative office under [Frederick the Great's] leadership degenerated into an oligarchy under his successors."[11] During the 1806 crisis, Beyme, Haugwitz and Zastrow were the most important members of Frederick William III's cabinet. In 1806 the cabinet government represented a final endeavor to preserve absolutism, or personal rule, in an age when it was becoming hard to maintain.

The campaign against the cabinet government was a continuation of the lengthy struggle to establish an efficient, professional bureaucracy. Both Stein and Hardenberg, veteran administrators of ministerial rank, had long fought for simplification of the Prussian administrative system. Frustrated by the overlapping and often conflicting responsibilities of various agencies, they had argued for organizational streamlining and strong leadership. But the growing role of the cabinet government especially vexed them in their fulfillment of ministerial responsibilities. Under Frederick William III ministers were often prevented from participating in the formation of policy. They sometimes even found it impossible to present their views to the king. Yet they were responsible for executing royal policies which often had been shaped by a clique of ambitious courtiers. It was unacceptable to trained professionals like Hardenberg and Stein to have to take a back seat to the king's friends in an inefficient bureaucratic web.

As early as 1797 Hardenberg recommended in a lengthy memorandum

---

[10] For this and following paragraph: Hüffer, *Kabinetsregierung*, 266–300; Fritz Hartung, *Deutsche Verfassungsgeschichte vom 15. Jahrhundert bis zur Gegenwart* (Stuttgart, 1965), 116–26, 131–34; Ernst von Meier, *Die Reform der Verwaltungsorganisation unter Stein und Hardenberg* (Leipzig, 1881), 1–69; Walter E. Dorn, "The Prussian Bureaucracy in the Eighteenth Century," *Political Science Quarterly*, 46 (1931): 403–23; 47 (1932): 75–94, 259–73; Paul Wittichen, "Das preussische Kabinet und Friedrich von Gentz: Eine Denkschrift aus dem Jahre 1800," *Historische Zeitschrift*, 89 (1902): 239–73; E. Kehr, "Zur Genesis der preussischen Bürokratie," 31–38.

[11] [Friedrich Buchholz], *Gallerie Preussischer Charaktere* (Germanien [*sic*], 1808), 256.

that the unwieldy administration be replaced by a simple council of ministers. This plan fell on deaf ears, and so did Hardenberg's subsequent proposals of 1800, 1801 and 1806. So frustrated was he that by December 1806 he considered leaving Prussia altogether and entering the service of Tsar Alexander. Stein had come into the chief administration later than Hardenberg. By 1806 he had gained a reputation as the archenemy of the cabinet system. His well-known reform memorandum of April 1806 spares no words in indicting the institution of cabinet government as well as its members. Stein complained that the state totally lacked a constitution in a modern form. The outmoded government of Prussia was being exploited by the king's favorites. Like Hardenberg, Stein advocated the building of a ministerial council (*Staatsrat*) of five members who would work as a unit in shaping a coordinated governmental policy.[12]

Stein and Hardenberg saw the issues of foreign affairs and bureaucratic reform as intertwined. Convinced of the necessity of a strong opposition to the French, they argued that a coherent foreign policy would be impossible until Frederick William dismissed his clique of personal advisors. "Should the king fail to implement the proposed reforms," Stein declared, "it can be expected that the state will either disintegrate or lose its independence and that the monarch will never again gain the respect and love of his subjects." Hardenberg agreed that the existing system contained the "fast ripening seeds of destruction."[13]

Stein's and Hardenberg's reform proposals dealt with a serious constitutional issue. The practical situation in the government precipitated a climax. Stein's memorandum reached the king in May. Its blunt denunciation of the king's favorites, and implicitly of Frederick William himself, offended the monarch terribly. Nevertheless, the disasters following Jena and Auerstädt seemed to justify Stein's and Hardenberg's criticisms of the cabinet government, whose foreign policies were proving counterproductive. Unwilling to consider abolition of his council of advisors, Frederick William, however, attempted to bring both Stein and Hardenberg into the ministry of foreign affairs. This compromise proved disastrous. Hardenberg, a veteran of conflict with Haugwitz and Lombard, refused to work with the peace men, although he retained his ministerial responsibilities in internal affairs. Stein, in response to the king's offer, intensified his attack on the cabinet government with a new memorandum. He again bitterly denounced

---

[12] Hardenberg, Ideen zur Einrichtung eines Conseils, 25 July 1797, synopsis in Winter, *Reorganisation,* 124, n. 2; Hardenberg, Stellungsnahme zum Gutachten Borgstedes, synopsis, ibid., 159–60, n.; Fritz Hartung, *Hardenberg und die preussische Verwaltung in Ansbach-Bayreuth von 1792 bis 1806* (Tübingen, 1906), 146–48; Altenstein, Entwurf einer Denkschrift (Hardenbergs) über die des Königs Majestät vorzuschlagende Veränderung in der Verfassung betreffend [Sept., Oct. 1806], Winter, *Reorganisation,* 62–67 (no. 30); Leopold von Ranke, ed., *Denkwürdigkeiten des Staatskanzlers Fürsten von Hardenberg* (Leipzig, 1877) 3: 238–46; Stein, Darstellung der fehlerhaften Organisation des Kabinetts und der Notwendigkeit der Bildung einer Ministerialkonferenz, Berlin, 26/27 Apr. 1806; Botzenhart, *Stein Briefe* 2/1, 206–14 (no. 194).

[13] Stein, Immediatbericht und Promemoria, Berlin, 27 Apr./May 1806; Winter, *Reorganisation,* 12 (no. 5); Hardenberg to Rüchel, Berlin, 5 May 1806, ibid., 4 (no. 3).

the system and its members. Frederick William, incensed, dismissed Stein in early January 1807, as the court was preparing to flee from Königsberg to Memel. Stein departed from Prussia, leaving the patriots for the time being deprived of one of their leaders and without representation in foreign policy.[14] But the patriots had chosen such a situation in preference to cooperation with the men who strove to block change and maintain the status quo.

Stein and Hardenberg enjoyed strong support among members of both the central government and the provincial bureaucracy. If we can believe the contemporary observer Zeiten, "the majority of officials" at the court belonged to the party who referred to themselves as "patriots" in the 1806 crisis. Among those were five men who in the course of the succeeding months would come to form the core of the reform government. By virtue of their personal, educational and professional backgrounds, they were men of the Enlightenment. They were officials within the Prussian government devoted to the new middle-class Weltanschauung.

Friedrich August Staegemann (1763–1840), whose enthusiastic words open this chapter, was, like most of the patriots, from a middle-class family. His father was a clergyman in a small town in the province of Brandenburg. After the age of ten Staegemann spent his youth in a Berlin orphanage. He later studied law at the University of Halle. From there he entered a government career in Königsberg and became a legal representative for the East Prussian Credit Association. Staegemann married the daughter of a Königsberg patrician family, Elisabeth Fischer. Frau Staegemann held a salon in eighteenth-century Parisian style in her Königsberg home. It was famous as a meeting place for the leading thinkers of the day. One of the most renowned of the Staegemanns' frequent guests was Immanuel Kant. As an avocation, Staegemann composed lyrics and "patriotic" verses. In a professional capacity, he represented the interests of the East Prussian nobility. At the same time he strove for better legal and political conditions for the Kölmer, the province's non-aristocratic estate owners who were overshadowed by their Junker neighbors.[15]

Just prior to the catastrophe of Jena and Auerstädt, Staegemann accepted a call as head of the Prussian Bank in Berlin to work under Stein who was then minister of finance and trade. When the military crisis of 1806 jolted Prussia, Staegemann used his literary talents to popularize the cause of

---

[14] Thielen, *Hardenberg*, 176–78; Stein, Immediatbericht, Königsberg, 3 Dec. 1806, Botzenhart, *Stein Briefe* 2/1, 306–310 (no. 292); Stein, Denkschrift, Königsberg, 20 Dec. 1806, ibid., 2/1, 324–25 (no. 307); Frederick William to Stein, Königsberg, 3 Jan. 1807 and 4 Jan. 1807, Winter, *Reorganisation*, 112–14, 116 (nos. 74, 78); Stein to Frederick William, Königsberg, 3 Jan. 1807, ibid., 114–15 (no. 75); Stein to Schulenberg, Königsberg, 18 Dec. 1806, Ranke, *Denkwürdigkeiten Hardenbergs* 3: 244–45; Ritter, *Stein*, 152–62, 165–78; [M. F. von Bassewitz], *Die Kurmark Brandenburg in Zusammenhang mit den Schicksalen des Gesammtstaats Preussen während der Zeit vom 22. Oktober 1806 bis zu Ende des Jahres 1808* (Leipzig, 1851–52) 1: 349–50.

[15] Hermann von Petersdorff, "Stägemann," *Allgemeine Deutsche Biographie* 35: 383–89; Walther Hubatsch, "Stägemann," *Altpreussische Biographie*, 688; Fritz Gause, "Stägemann, Elisabeth J., geb. Fischer," ibid.; Gause, *Geschichte der Stadt Königsberg* 2: 258, 303–304.

the patriots. In a poem spread throughout northern Germany in both printed and handwritten form, Staegemann appealed to the Russian Emperor Alexander, to "let the world confront the [French] Emperor with free sword, shining in truth. . . . Then Europe's free race will stand no more like Negroes for sale in the infamous slave market. . . . Then humanity will place [Alexander's] and Frederick William's portraits in the temple of heroes."[16]

Staegemann locked his future to those committed to renovation of state and society. He had worked previously with Beyme in an apparently harmonious relationship in the cause of agrarian reforms, and he might have been appointed to a high position, had the peace men prevailed over the patriots. "But I am completely in favor of [Stein]," he wrote his wife, "because [Beyme's] capabilities are not the type that could promote the powerful reform which we so need."[17]

Heinrich Theodor von Schön (1773–1856), ten years Staegemann's junior, was a more outspoken personality. In spite of the "von" in his name, Schön did not represent an ancient aristocratic heritage. His family had held the title for only a century. They were tenant managers of domain farms in the eastern province of Lithuania, and in this position their interests often coincided with those of prosperous non-noble members of the society. Schön studied in Königsberg under Immanuel Kant, a fact of which he was proud his whole life. Another important teacher in Schön's formative years was Theodor Anton Schmalz, author of the *Declaration of the Rights of Men and Citizens.* It was Christian Jakob Kraus who was Schön's real mentor, for the study and application of economic ideas became Schön's passion for life. Kraus considered Schön one of his most promising students and schooled him personally for a position in Prussian state service. In Kraus's lectures, Schön heard primarily discourses on Smith's *Wealth of Nations.*[18]

As a young apprentice in the Prussian government, Schön took the usual leave for "study travels" through central Germany and more importantly, for a year in England. He returned brimming with enthusiasm for everything British. His notebooks were filled with sketches of British machinery and

---

[16] Staegemann, "Der Geist Friedrichs des Grossen an den Kaiser Alexander von Russland bei Seinem Eintritt in Preussen," in Hans-Bernd Spies, ed., *Die Erhebung Gegen Napoleon 1806–1814/15,* Quellen zum politischen Denken der Deutschen im 19. und 20. Jahrhundert: Freiherr vom Stein Gedächtnisausgabe 2 (Darmstadt, 1981): 21–23 (no. 5).

[17] Rumler, "Bestrebungen zur Befreiung der Privatbauern" 37 (1925): 34–37; Staegemann to Elisabeth von Staegemann, Memel, 6 Oct. 1807, Rühl, *Aus der Franzosenzeit,* 50 (no. 44); Count Schlieben to Staegemann, Schlieben, 21 Apr. 1807, Franz Rühl, ed., *Briefe und Aktenstücke zur Geschichte Preussens unter Friedrich Wilhelm III., vorzugsweise aus dem Nachlass von F. A. von Stägemann* (Leipzig, 1899–1902) 1: 8–9 (no. 4); Nagler to Staegemann, Bartenstein, 25 Apr. 1807, ibid., 1: 10–11 (no. 7).

[18] Marion Wilson Gray, Jr., *Theodor von Schön and Prussian Reforms 1806–1808* (Diss. Univ. Wisconsin, 1971), 17–31. On the controversies in historical literature concerning Schön, see 1–16. See Schön's notebooks from Kraus's lectures: Depositum Brünneck, StA Königsberg nos. 73–79, 91; Kraus to Auerswald, Königsberg, 15 July 1799, Kraus, *Vermischte Schriften* 2: 216.

agricultural implements as well as of observations about society, government, climate and soil. The young state servant hoped to bring the ideas and the institutions of the island society to his homeland Prussia. As he wrote in his still awkward English some months subsequent to his travels:

> Since my return to my country I have attempted several things to introduce here, that are used in England. And I find that clime, constitution and therefore a different interest of individuals are great obstacles to it, to say nothing of the prejudices that every introduction of new things has to combat. I hope, however, that the great profit, necessarily arriving from the materials and plans I brought from England will convince the people of the perfection and excellency.[19]

Through his marriage with Lydia von Auerswald, Schön established close ties with a renowned liberal, noble family of East Prussia. Her father, Hans von Auerswald (1757–1833), was a friend of Professor Kraus, and the two worked closely, but in vain, to effect the abolition of serfdom in the eastern provinces in the years 1802 and 1803. Auerswald would himself become a contributor to the reform proposals of 1807–1808 and would later edit and publish thirteen volumes of Kraus's work on economics and politics.[20]

After a few years working in provincial posts, Schön came into the prestigious General Directory at the age of only twenty-seven years. He was also a member of the royally appointed Law Commission which had the responsibility for investigating the legal aspects of a proposed abolition of serfdom. In each of his offices, the young, reform-minded Schön ran into bureaucratic blockades. The Law Commission, for example, presented a forceful case for the abolition of serfdom. But the government's highest officials ignored and suppressed the recommendations.[21] Schön was a crusader. His zealousness and his self-righteous attitude offended colleagues. Smarting under the stifling atmosphere of bureaucratic conservatism, Schön bided his time, impatiently waiting for a more hopeful day.

One of Schön's closest confidants in the years before the catastrophe of Jena was Baron Karl vom Stein zum Altenstein (1770–1840). Altenstein (not to be confused with Karl vom Stein, the leader of the movement) was unusual among the young members of the patriot party in this aristocratic background. He was a member of a ten-century-old Frankish family of high nobility. His chosen career, statesmanship, led him, however, to study

[19] Wilhelm Schulze-Marmeling, *Schön und Vincke: Englische Verfassungs- Verwaltungs- und Wirtschaftseinflüsse in Preussen um 1800* (Diss. Münster, 1950), 1–80; [Theodor von Schön], *Studienreisen eines jungen Staatsmanns in England am Schlusse des vorigen Jahrhunderts: Beiträge und Nachträge zu den Papieren des Ministers und Burggrafen von Marienburg Theodor von Schön*, [ed. F. Ewald] (Berlin, 1891). This is a poorly edited version of Schön's travel journal, Dep. Brünneck, no. 57, StA Königsberg. See also his rich "Technical Journal," ibid., no. 58. Quote from draft of letter of reference written by Schön to an English acquaintance, n.d., "Reise und Aufenthalt in England/Über englisches Finanz- und Kommerzwesen/Lauderdale, Smith, 1798–1808," ibid., no. 102b.

[20] Stolze, "Auerswald," *Altpreussische Biographie*, 22; Rumler, "Bestrebungen zur Befreiung der Privatbauern," 37 (1925): 44–47.

[21] Ibid., 34 (1922): 265–96; Stadelmann, *Preussens Könige*, 36–45.

law, science and philosophy at Erlangen and at Göttingen. The latter was Germany's door to England. Göttingen was located in the Electorate of Hanover, dynastically tied to Great Britain. The university had been founded in 1737 by England's George II, and it enjoyed a reputation as one of Europe's most up-to-date institutions of higher learning. The young Theodor von Schön had stopped off in Göttingen to prepare himself for his year's stay in England. Here Altenstein absorbed the Enlightenment thought of the eighteenth century.[22]

Altenstein entered Prussian service in his home province of Ansbach-Bayreuth, one of the scattered Hohenzollern territories which lay in southern Germany. There he worked under that province's chief administrator, Hardenberg. Under the latter's leadership, Altenstein participated in an early tentative social modernization, which included a program to curtail the prerogatives of the Frankish nobility and to terminate feudal relationships. Altenstein followed his superior to Berlin when Hardenberg moved there in connection with his duties in the central administration in 1799. Throughout his early career Altenstein retained a personal loyalty to Hardenberg, even after he himself became a member of the General Directory in 1803. In Berlin Altenstein developed a close relationship with Johann Gottlieb Fichte, the famous Prussian philosopher and early German nationalist. Altenstein was never as fiery and tempestuous as Schön, with whom he corresponded regularly concerning the need for reform of the state and society. The young Frankish nobleman had a flair for expressing himself in philosophical language and a talent for making himself the spokesman for the latest ideas in political and economic thinking.

Johann August Sack (1764–1831), like Altenstein, came from one of the dispersed provinces of the Prussian monarchy. His home and first post was in Cleves, in Prussian Westphalia, bordering on the Netherlands. Sack was from a middle-class family. His father was a jurist. Typically, he studied law and cameral science, first at Halle and then at the prestigious university of Göttingen. He also made mining one of his specializations, a field of growing importance in the late eighteenth century. Like Altenstein, Sack came into a high position in Berlin by virtue of having followed his superior, in this case Stein, into the central administration. Sack had worked closely with Stein in the latter's early attempts to modernize the provincial bureaucracy and mining operations in the western parts of the monarchy. By 1798 Sack was working with the General Directory in Berlin. As a member of the Law Commission he participated in the early unsuccessful drive to abolish serfdom in Prussia. When the court hastily fled Berlin before in-

---

[22] Günther Ross, "Das Leben des Freiherrn von Altenstein bis zum Jahre 1807," ed. Hans Haussherr, *Forschungen zur brandenburgischen und preussischen Geschichte* 63 (1941): 91–128; Paul Goldschmidt, "Altenstein," *Allgemeine Deutsche Biographie* 35: 645–60; Beguelin, *Denkwürdigkeiten,* 119; On Göttingen: Götz von Selle, *Die Georg-August Universität zu Göttingen 1737-1937* (Göttingen, 1937), 35–193, passim.

vading French armies, Sack remained behind as appointed civil governor of the occupied city.[23]

The youngest member of the party surrounding Stein and Hardenberg was Barthold Georg Niebuhr (1776–1831). He was also one of the most erudite and is known primarily for his later career as a historian. He was a pioneer in the modern research of ancient history. Born in Copenhagen, Niebuhr was the son of the well-known Danish explorer and geographer, Carsten Niebuhr. His mother was German, the daughter of a medical doctor. His parents educated the precocious young man in typical Enlightenment style. He learned geography, economics, engineering, mathematics and literature in addition to languages of classical European antiquity and the Orient. Before going to the University of Kiel, Niebuhr spent a year in Hamburg with celebrated economist and social experimenter, Johann Georg Büsch (1728–1800). Büsch's Hamburg Society for Advancement of Manufacture, Arts and Practical Trades fostered free trade and manufacture, as its name implies. Among its social projects was an arrangement by which non-guild factory workers shared with managers in policy decisions. The society was well-known among the early Prussian liberals. The young Theodor von Schön made Büsch's institute a stop on his study travels.[24]

At Kiel Niebuhr studied law, science, literature and philosophy. At the age of twenty, he became private secretary to the Danish minister of finance, and by 1805 he was director of Denmark's East Indian Bureau and the Danish State Bank. In these positions Niebuhr was largely responsible for his state's commercial and financial policy. In 1805, as Prussian finance minister, Stein persuaded Niebuhr to accept the directorship of Prussia's state bank and department of overseas commerce. The learned Niebuhr came with the idea of joining Stein in a thorough reorganization of the state's financial and economic institutions. Like the men whom he joined, his model in economics and politics was Great Britain. He arrived in Berlin less than a week before the disastrous battles of Jena and Auerstädt. A sensitive person, he was overwhelmed and depressed by the chaotic state of affairs. Niebuhr was devoted to liberal values, but he was one of the most reluctant among the reform party to accept the responsibility for re-

---

[23] Hermann Petrich, "Sack," *Allgemeine Deutsche Biographie* 30: 152–53; Rumler, "Bestrebungen zur Befreiung der Privatbauern" 34 (1922); 271, 278; Wilhelm Steffens, ed. *Briefwechsel Sacks mit Stein und Gneisenau (1807/17)*, Veröffentlichungen der Historischen Kommission für Pommern, 5 (Stettin, 1931): v–xiii, 1–53.

[24] On Niebuhr: Dietrich Gerhard and William Norvin, eds., *Die Briefe Barthold Georg Niebuhrs*, Veröffentlichungen der Literatur-Archiv-Gesellschaft in Berlin, 1, 2 (Berlin, 1926–29) 1: xl–xlii; Heinrich Nissen, "Niebuhr," *Allgemeine Deutsche Biographie* 23: 646–61; Beguelin, *Denkwürdigkeiten*, 121; G. P. Gooch, *History and Historians in the Nineteenth Century* (London, 1954), 14–17; Peter Hanns Reill, "Barthold Georg Niebuhr and the Enlightenment Tradition," *German Studies Review* 3 (1980): 9–26; Seppo Rytkönnen, *Barthold Georg Niebuhr als Politiker und Historiker: Zeitgeschehen und Zeitgeist in den geschichtlichen Beurteilungen von B. G. Niebuhr* (Helsinki, 1968). On Büsch, Muther, "Büsch," *Allgemeine Deutsche Biographie* 3: 642–43; Eulen, *Vom Gewerbefleiss*, 144–45; Gustav Hasse, *Theodor von Schön und die steinsche Wirtschaftsreform, zugleich ein Beitrag zu einer Biographie Th. von Schöns* (Leipzig, diss. 1915), 36.

forming Prussian society. Perhaps this was because he was less committed to Prussia itself than his colleagues.

Staegemann, Schön, Altenstein, Sack and Niebuhr would form the nucleus of the Stein ministry of 1807–1808. As a group they were young, ranging in age from thirty-one to forty-three in 1807. Two had names which indicated aristocratic status, but only one could claim prestigious noble lineage. As a group they represented middle-class mentality and background. What they had most in common was their thorough professional education, gained in the time when Enlightenment thought and Smithian economic principles had penetrated central Europe. These young administrators were especially receptive to the new views of humanity and society which formed the basis of the liberal Weltanschauung. They idealized Great Britain and its society. They were schooled in Adam Smith's economic thought. As with Kant, the notion "freedom" was central to their values, and they used the word in its new universal sense. They proclaimed the dignity of the individual while they worked for agricultural, scientific and political "progress." Many were frustrated with the inertia and the obstructionism of the Prussian bureaucracy, though most had pursued successful bureaucratic careers prior to 1807.

The emergency of 1806 united and electrified the group. Since the crisis was external in origin, it is understandable that the would-be reformers took the name "patriots." They perceived themselves as the rescuers of Prussia. They hoped to do this by reforming institutions to bring the state in line with revolutionized France and industrial England. Patriotism, like freedom, was a new notion belonging to the middle-class ideology of the late eighteenth century. The word was frequently used at that time in the principalities of Germany to signify a progressive economic stance. For example, after 1750 a host of "economic and patriotic societies" sprang up which were generally designed to foster free trade and manufacture. As a strictly political term, patriotism jelled in Germany in response to the French invasions following the Revolution of 1789. In France itself the group which promoted the values of liberalism in the 1790s first identified itself as the patriot party. In the view of Prussian journalist Friedrich Buchholz, patriotism was by definition opposed to upholding the old regime: "The time is upon us when . . . one cannot be a patriot and a feudal aristocrat at the same time. The character of this time is not going to be . . . gentle."[25]

Stein and Hardenberg, the acknowledged leaders of the Prussian patriots, were both senior statesmen, respectively fifty and fifty-seven years old in 1807. They were ministers of the old regime who had both reached the very top of the administration by virtue of their expertise. Significantly,

[25] Eulen, *Vom Gewerbefleiss*, 180–84 and passim; G. de Bertier de Sauvigny, "Liberalism, Nationalism, Socialism," 151; Friedrich Buchholz, *Untersuchungen über den Geburtsadel und über die Möglichkeit seiner Fortdauer im neunzehnten Jahrhundert* (Leipzig, 1807), 383, quoted in Günther Schmidt, ed., *Freiherr vom und zum Stein: Schriften von und über Stein* (Berlin, 1955), 41.

neither was Prussian by origin. Stein was an imperial knight, head of the family who ruled a small principality, Nassau, where the Lahn river meets the Rhine. Hardenberg was a member of an aristocratic family of Hanover. Both men were well-educated and cosmopolitan in outlook. In preparation for careers in government, each had studied at the University of Göttingen, and Hardenberg at Leipzig as well. Neither planned to follow the traditional aristocratic model of managing a family estate or, in Stein's case, administering a family fief. Thus Stein and Hardenberg were distinguished from other members of Frederick William's old regime, many of whom were Prussian aristocrats with provincial orientations. Stein's and Hardenberg's high aristocratic status set them apart from the many capable middle-class officials of Prussian origin. They could communicate with the king of Prussia in a manner never possible with colleagues of non-noble status, no matter how talented the latter might be.[26]

Stein and Hardenberg were one to two decades older than their supporters in the patriot party. Their university education in the 1760s and 1770s, gave them outlooks different from those of the younger men, who studied when Enlightenment and Smithian thought had had a full impact upon Germany. Both older statesmen, for example, completed their work at Göttingen before Adam Smith published his *Wealth of Nations*. Stein studied political and judicial theory of mid-century thinkers under August Ludwig Schlözer (1735–1809) and Johann Stephan Pütter (1725–1807). He was also influenced by his contemporaries, Ernst Brandes (1758–1810) and August Wilhelm Rehberg (1757–1836) of the so-called "Hanoverian School." Such men were not the fiery proponents of social and economic reform with whom Stein's younger colleagues became acquainted in their university careers. Instead the Hanoverians thought of "freedom" as a privilege belonging to corporate groups. They admired the British system, and they criticized arbitrary and despotic government. Their ideal was a well-functioning government by Estates.[27]

This, it is clear, helped form Hardenberg's and Stein's mentality. Yet the ideas of one's youth need not close one's mind to new ideas. Both statesmen, well-read in their early lives, were receptive to innovative thinking. Unlike many of their contemporaries in age, they were men of the Enlightenment. Stein's personal copy of *The Wealth of Nations* is well worn and profusely marked by the minister's own hand. Hardenberg was a devotee of the rational and progressive agriculture based on Smithian principles advocated by Albrecht Thaer. Hardenberg employed the work of his fellow Hanoverian, Thaer, as a guide in effecting agrarian reform in the province of

---

[26] Ritter, *Stein*, 16–162; Thielen, *Hardenberg*, 15–161.

[27] Botzenhart, *Die Staats- und Reformideen*, 69–162. Botzenhart documents Stein's association with the Hanoverian school. He interprets Stein as an anti-Enlightenment figure. Selle, *Georg-August Universität zu Göttingen*, 189–92; Ritter, *Stein*, 28–31; James Van Horn Melton, "From Enlightenment to Revolution: Hertzberg, Schlözer, and the Problem of Despotism in the Late *Aufklärung*," *Central European History*, 12 (1979): 103–23.

Ansbach-Bayreuth. It was due in part to Hardenberg's influence that Thaer moved to Prussia in 1804.[28]

Stein and Hardenberg were hard-headed, ambitious administrators. They came to head the reform party in part as a result of their frustrations with the haphazard organization of the Prussian bureaucracy. As much through practical as through ideological considerations, they waged their fight against the cabinet government. As professionals, they believed in government run by experts as opposed to administration by the king's friends. Committed to political reform, and at ease with the ideals of early liberalism, Stein and Hardenberg were the logical leaders of the party dedicated to modernizing Prussia. Had circumstances been different, Stein and Hardenberg would not have played the roles they did. The crisis of 1806 formed the patriot party out of a disparate group of like-minded officials. It also made Stein and Hardenberg the party's leaders. In such roles they were influenced by the younger colleagues who clamored to support them.

JANUARY–OCTOBER 1807: THE PATRIOTS WAVER BETWEEN DESPAIR AND HOPE

"The year 1807 began with dashed hopes," reflected Hardenberg from his forced exile in Riga some months after the events of that January had become history.[29] He was referring specifically to the Prussian disillusionment following the unsuccessful battle of Putulsky, but the words have a much deeper significance than frustration over a single battle. The court was fleeing before France's advancing army, and the very existence of the Prussian state was in question.

In the midst of the external crisis, the patriot party suffered the severe blow of Stein's dismissal, resulting from his struggle over administrative reform. Furious over the minister's steadfast criticism of his style of government, King Frederick William fired Stein, calling him a "refractory, defiant, stubborn, and disobedient official. . . . Far from having the good of the state in mind [he is] guided by caprice, passion, personal hatred and bitterness." Niebuhr expressed the depressed sentiments of the patriots when he wrote of the "delusion, blindness and madness" of the dismissal which he saw as a manifestation of "the path of disintegration which has led this land to ruin."[30]

With Stein having left Prussian soil, the patriots pinned their hopes on Hardenberg. Frederick William, however, wavered and hesitated about forming a new government. Between January and April he reached no firm

---

[28] Dieter Schwab, *Die "Selbstverwaltungsidee" des Freiherrn vom Stein und ihre geistigen Grundlagen, zugleich ein Beitrag zur Geschichte der politischen Ethik im 18. Jahrhundert,* Giessener Beiträge zur Rechtswissenschaft 3 (Frankfurt am Main, 1971): 58; Stadelman, *Preussens Könige,* 104; Thielen, *Hardenberg,* 95.

[29] Ranke, *Denkwürdigkeiten Hardenbergs* 3: 265.

[30] Frederick William to Stein, Königsberg, 3 Jan. 1807, Botzenhart, *Stein Briefe* 2/1: 330 (no. 312); Niebuhr to Stein, Memel, 10 Jan. 1807, ibid., 2/1: 336 (no. 321).

decision. He would like to have drafted Hardenberg, but the latter, like Stein, by this time refused to participate in foreign affairs unless the cabinet government were eliminated. He hoped to exploit the desperate situation to force the hand of the king. He enjoyed unswerving support from younger colleagues of the patriot party. Schön wrote his friend Altenstein:

Hardenberg's plan for refusal is magnificent. If the great man retains the strength he has previously demonstrated, he will do great things. Wretched men (Zastrow) will have to work in his place now, and he must wait. But later he will accomplish much. . . . Auerswald, along with every other Prussian, envisions the heavens opening and all the evils of this war being abolished by a better system of government. . . . Stein said he hopes Hardenberg will remain firm.[31]

Weeks dragged by without a decision. The external situation worsened. Napoleon was advancing through East Prussia, approaching Memel. True to his style, Frederick William attempted a feeble compromise. In March he created a four-member ministerial council. Each minister was to report directly to the king. Hardenberg, softening his hard stance, accepted one of the posts, even though the cabinet government remained unchanged. But Hardenberg could not work with Zastrow who held another of the posts, and the council proved unworkable, as the patriots had predicted would be the case. By April, Frederick William, shaken by the advancing French armies and the paralyzation of his government, responded to the demands of the patriots. Appointing Hardenberg "first minister," the king took the initial step in establishing a modern ministerial system.[32] In a temporary, improvised situation, Hardenberg was Prussia's first prime minister. The long-established and once celebrated administrative organization of Hohenzollern absolutism was dead. The patriots rejoiced. They were relieved that at last Prussia had a strong figure and a workable government to deal both with the Emperor Napoleon and with Prussia's ally, Emperor Alexander.

The patriots looked forward to social, economic and political reforms. They corresponded profusely in those uncertain months about the formation of a regularly established council of ministers, about the abolition of serfdom, about the eradication of distinctions between city and countryside in economic matters, and about the establishment of a free market

---

[31] Schön to Altenstein, Königsberg, 13 Jan. 1807, Winter, *Reorganisation*, 118 (no. 82).

[32] Schön to Altenstein, Königsberg, 13 Jan. 1807, ibid., 118 (no. 82); Ranke, *Denkwürdigkeiten Hardenbergs* 3: 315–22; Anordnung des Königs Friedrich Wilhelm III für die Minister von Voss, von Hardenberg, von Schroetter und von Zastrow . . . , Memel, 11 Mar. 1807, Winter, *Reorganisation*, 141–43 (no. 102). On the impracticality of the 11 March arrangement see Niebuhr to Stein, 29 Mar. 1807, Botzenhart, *Stein Briefe* 2/1: 362 (no. 341); Hardenberg, Denkschrift to Frederick William, Memel, 3 Mar. 1807, Ranke, *Denkwürdigkeiten Hardenbergs* 5: 447–67; Hardenberg, Tagebuch, 10 Apr. 1807, Winter, *Reorganisation*, 156, n. 1. The official order granting Hardenberg the new position was not issued until 26 April, the date of the signing of the Bartenstein Convention, although it had been informally in effect since 10 April: Kabinettsordre an das Staatsministerium zu Memel, Bartenstein, 26 Apr. 1807, ibid., 173–75 (no. 123a).

system for Prussia. They allowed themselves to hope that defeat could be transformed into progress. Schön's exclamation, "We could not have achieved this at a cheaper price!" expresses his sentiment that the results, extensive reforms, would justify the high cost of military defeat, diplomatic humiliation and human suffering.[33]

Though Hardenberg's supporters talked of the dawn of a new era, they were aware that the appointment of April 1807 was a temporary measure designed to meet a crisis. But they did not know how soon uncertainty would again cloud the horizons. By 14 June, the famous battle of Friedland demonstrated that there was no hope of holding the French as they swept eastward. Twelve days later Hardenberg accompanied his king to Tilsit for the celebrated meeting among the three monarchs, Alexander, Napoleon and Frederick William, on a raft in the Niemen River. Napoleon was able to dictate the terms of the settlement. Regarding Hardenberg as his worst enemy in Prussia, the French emperor demanded the dismissal of the first minister. By mid-July Hardenberg had established an exile residence in Riga, on Russian soil.[34]

Hardenberg's brief tenure of April through July 1807 is often called the "Bartenstein ministry" because Hardenberg's staff spent most of its time at the Russian military headquarters in the East Prussian town of that name. The Bartenstein Convention of 26 April, the same date as Hardenberg's official appointment, sealed the alliance between Prussia and Russia. Hardenberg's style of administration set precedents for the reform movement. The personnel changes which the Bartenstein ministry effected established an atmosphere that prepared the way for innovation.

As his staff Hardenberg predictably drafted members of the patriot party: Niebuhr, Staegemann, Schön, Altenstein and the latter's brother-in-law, Karl Friedrich Nagler (1770–1846) who acted as the first minister's personal secretary.[35] The administrative shuffling in April 1807 involved not only new appointments, but also the replacement of several important old-regime officials. There ensued a bitter struggle, the last phase in Hardenberg's fight for power. Beyme might have been the first to receive a dismissal, for he personified the old system which Hardenberg's appointment terminated. It had long been a condition of Hardenberg's acceptance that he would not work with Beyme, and Hardenberg's supporters backed him fully on this point. But Frederick William stubbornly refused to discharge his trusted

[33] See, for example, Schön's correspondence with Altenstein: Königsberg, 25 Feb. 1807, 13 Mar. 1807, 14 Mar. 1807, ibid., 128–30, 141, 144–45 (nos. 98, 105, 107).

[34] On Hardenberg's dismissal: Hardenberg to Niebuhr, Memel, 9 July 1807, Heinrich Scheel and Doris Schmidt, eds., *Das Reformministerium Stein: Akten zur Verfassungs- und Verwaltungsgeschichte aus den Jahren 1807/08*, Deutsche Akademie der Wissenschaften zu Berlin, Schriften des Instituts für Geschichte, Series 1: Allgemeine und Deutsche Geschichte, 31a–31c (Berlin, 1966–68) 3: 898, n. 2.

[35] Kelchner, "Nagler," *Allgemeine Deutsche Biographie* 23: 233–37; *Handbuch über den königlichen preussischen Hof und Staat für das Jahr 1805* (Berlin, 1805), 8, 39, 54, 295; Ranke, *Denkwürdigkeiten Hardenbergs* 3: 240, 509; Nagler to Altenstein, Bartenstein, 29 Apr. 1807, Winter, *Reorganisation*, 176–77 (no. 124).

advisor, and Hardenberg was forced to compromise. Beyme retained the title, cabinet councilor, but was excluded from the Bartenstein staff. "Hardenberg has responsibility for reporting to the king," explained Staegemann, "even in those areas for which Beyme was formerly responsible." Beyme's repudiation of support for the Haugwitz-Lombard foreign policy made the compromise palatable for Hardenberg. The cabinet councilor expressed loyalty to the new strategy formulated at Bartenstein and voiced eagerness to work with the new government. Hardenberg's co-workers at Bartenstein, however, continued to oppose Beyme's influence and presence in the government.[36]

Hardenberg had to confront more directly three men with whom he had shared responsibility in the temporary ministerial council created the previous March. Due to the strong disagreements between Hardenberg and his colleagues, the council had never functioned satisfactorily. Especially bitter were the relations between Hardenberg and Zastrow who had been responsible for planning military strategy. Demanding Zastrow's dismissal, Hardenberg declared: "Under the present circumstances, it is absolutely essential that your majesty grant to me alone the leadership of all foreign affairs." One day later the king discharged Zastrow who left embittered, refusing an offer of a generalship as a position unworthy of his talents.[37]

The cabinet order of 26 April subordinated Otto Karl Friedrich von Voss (1755–1823), then finance minister, to the authority of Hardenberg. Voss protested bitterly to the king that Hardenberg's supervision of the finance department was an offence against his past service and "patriotism." Voss's complaining helped Hardenberg convince the king to dismiss Voss entirely, rather than retain him in the government under Hardenberg's authority. As the new first minister repeatedly emphasized, "under the present circumstances, unity is essential." Voss's former active support of the policy of the peace men discredited him. The patriots found Voss unacceptable because they considered him a representative of the old regime. Voss, who had served capably in several ministerial posts under the two previous

[36] [Bassewitz], *Kurmark Brandenburg 1806–1808* 1: 371–72, 394; Beyme to Hardenberg, Memel, 27 Jan. 1807, 3 May and 6 July 1807, Ranke, *Denkwürdigkeiten Hardenbergs* 3: 284–89, 432–38; Hüffer, *Kabinetsregierung*, 324–28. Staegemann to Elisabeth Staegemann, Bartenstein, 13 May 1807, Rühl, *Aus der Franzosenzeit*, 13 (no. 110); Beyme to Staegemann, Memel, 8 July 1807, ibid., 22–23 (no. 19). Just as there has been an attempt to rehabilitate Beyme as a reformer, historians have defended his leadership in foreign policy. It is true that he adopted the anti-French stance before Hardenberg was named first minister: Karl Disch, "Der Kabinettsrat Beyme und die auswärtige Politik Preussens in den Jahren 1805/06," *Forschungen zur brandenburgischen und preussischen Geschichte* 41 (1928): 331–66; 42 (1929): 93–134; Ritter, *Stein*, 165–66, 168–69, 203, 571, n. 6. Contemporaries viewed Beyme's espousal of the patriots' goals as mere opportunism. See Niebuhr's ironic comment: "Herr B[eyme] is a patriot and talks about his great respect [for] humanity!" Niebuhr to Stein, Memel, 29 Mar. 1807, Botzenhart, *Stein Briefe* 2/1: 326 (no. 341).

[37] Kabinettsordre an das Staatsministerium, Bartenstein, 26 Apr. 1806, Winter, *Reorganisation*, 173–75 (no. 123a); see Hardenberg's protest letter of 27 Apr. 1807, n. 3. Kabinettsordre to Zastrow, Bartenstein, 26 Apr. 1807, ibid., 176 (no. 123c). (The order is backdated; see n. 1.). Zastrow, Immediateingabe, Memel, 3 May 1807, synopsis, ibid., 178–79 (no. 127).

monarchs, was openly opposed to the fiery enthusiasm for reform professed by the young administrators in Hardenberg's ministry.[38]

The third official to be displaced by the new administrative arrangement was Baron Friedrich Leopold von Schroetter (1743–1815), provincial minister of East and West Prussia and head of the department of military provisions. Like Voss, Schroetter was a Prussian administrator of long standing. But unlike his colleague he also enjoyed a reputation as a reformer. Schroetter had long been known as a friend of Professor Kraus of Königsberg. The minister even required all candidates for employment in his department to present certification that they had studied successfully under Kraus. As provincial minister and vice president of the General Directory, he had played a significant role in the movement to free the domain peasants. He had devised several measures to abolish guilds and free the Prussian economy of its mercantilistic rigidity. Indeed there is more than one reason why Schroetter might have seemed acceptable to the new Bartenstein ministry. Schön owed much to him, for Schroetter had taken Schön into his department as a young candidate seeking an apprenticeship in government administration. The minister had made Schön's study travels financially possible by securing him an assignment from which he could absent himself for an extended time. Schroetter had recognized Schön's capabilities by bringing him into the General Directory in 1802, making him the youngest member of that austere institution. Furthermore, Schroetter had played an important part in the struggle against the cabinet government. He was one of the first to see Stein's memorandum of April 1806 criticizing the cabinet, and Stein had incorporated several of Schroetter's suggestions into the final copy intended for the king.[39]

However, Hardenberg insisted on personally assuming supervision of Schroetter's military provisions department. Like Voss, Schroetter felt himself severely wronged by his removal, and he too complained to Frederick William. He presented a long list of the services he had rendered to the state as well as a defense of his leadership in the post from which he was

[38] Kabinettsordre an das Staatsministerium, Bartenstein, 26 Apr. 1807, ibid., 175 (no. 123a). Voss to Frederick William Memel, 4 May 1807, Ranke, *Denkwürdigkeiten Hardenbergs* 3: 396–99. H. v. Petersdorff, "Voss," *Allgemeine Deutsche Biographie* 40: 352–61. On Voss's earlier work in South Prussia, see Otto Heike, *Die Provinz Südpreussen: Preussische Aufbau- und Verwaltungsarbeit im Warthe- und Weichselgebiet 1793–1806,* Wissenschaftliche Beiträge zur Geschichte und Landeskunde Mitteleuropas 12 (Marburg/Lahn, 1953), 10–11. Otto Hinze, "Preussische Reformbestrebungen vor 1806," *Regierung und Verwaltung,* Gesammelte Abhandlungen zur Staats-, Rechts- und Sozialgeschichte Preussens, 3, ed. Gerhard Oestreich (Göttingen, 1967), 523–25. See Schön's caustic comments on Voss's plan of administrative reorganization: Schön to Altenstein, Königsberg, 4 Mar. 1807, Winter, *Reorganisation,* 141, n. 1.

[39] Bruno Schumacher, "Schroetter," *Altpreussische Biographie,* 638–39; Kraus, *Staatswirthschaft,* 5, appendix, 11: 400–403. [Schön], *Studienreise eines jungen Staatswirths in Deutschland am Schlusse des vorigen Jahrhunderts: Beiträge und Nachträge zu den Papieren des Ministers und Burggrafen von Marienburg Theodor von Schön* (Leipzig, 1879), appendix, 644–77; Bruno Schumacher, "Schön," *Altpreussische Biographie,* 626–27; Hüffer, *Kabinetsregierung,* 214; Ritter, *Stein,* 156; Stein to Schulenberg, 25 Nov. [1806], Botzenhart, *Stein Briefe* 2/1, 302 (no. 287).

being removed. Schroetter expressed suspicion that he had been the victim of a cabal.[40]

Schroetter's replacement could be justified on the grounds of his disagreement with Hardenberg's foreign policy. As head of the provisions department, Schroetter concluded that the Russians were unreliable allies. He also felt that the suffering of the eastern provinces was an unjustified sacrifice for a war that was hopeless anyway. He therefore joined the peace men in their opposition to the French war and the Russian alliance.[41]

However, even if Schroetter had not been an opponent of Hardenberg's foreign policy, it would have been difficult for him to find a place in the Bartenstein ministry. His bitter accusations of a cabal working against him are exaggerated. But there was a great deal of antipathy toward him among the men who joined Hardenberg at Bartenstein. Schön was the most outspoken opponent of his former superior. He filed several reports of Schroetter's poor management of the military provisions department during the previous winter. Furthermore Schön had more than once warned colleagues: "Do not consult Schroetter [about my reform proposals]. He cannot comprehend my plans at all."[42]

The patriots regarded Schroetter as a man who, in spite of his reputation as a reformer, could never free himself from an aristocratic outlook. Schroetter was a supporter of reforms, they felt, only when they did not disturb the basic structure of the corporate society. Only on the question of free trade, a reform measure supported by the estate owners, had Schroetter taken a consistently liberal stand. In the early attempts to emancipate the serfs he could be described only as a cautious innovator. He often found that proposed reforms were good, but impractical "in the present situation." He always took care to point out when projected innovations might encroach upon the established rights of the nobility. Schroetter had never favored the cause of the Kölmer, who hoped to legally improve their position. "Hardenberg will be prime minister," Schön wrote Altenstein on 12 April, "but who will carry out his plans? Are we capable of a better constitution? I am familiar with the [administrators] of Pomerania, South Prussia, Magdeburg and Silesia . . . , and I despair. Will Voss [and] Schroetter resign? Will they somehow allow themselves to be dismissed?" Hardenberg noted with relief in his diary on 18 June that "Minister von Schroetter is considered on leave. The king will not recall the mock council any more." At about the same time Voss and Zastrow left Prussia together for Copenhagen.[43]

---

[40] Schroetter to Frederick William, Memel, 6 May 1807, Ranke, *Denkwürdigkeiten Hardenbergs,* 3: 412–19; Schroetter to Hardenberg, Memel, 7 May 1807, ibid., 3: 419–25.

[41] Krause, *Der Provinzialminister Schroetter,* 52–67; B. Schumacher, "Schroetter," *Altpreussische Biographie,* 638–39.

[42] Schön to Altenstein, Königsberg, 25 Feb. 1807, Winter, *Reorganisation,* 128 (no. 98); see also 174, n. 5.

[43] On Schroetter's earlier participation in reform work, see the following: Rumler, "Die

Hardenberg and his staff members at Bartenstein were bent on pushing aside the ministers of the old regime in order to start over with a clean slate. They sought to work free of the bureaucratic and conservative hindrances they had encountered in the past. In spite of Hardenberg's seniority, the patriots' struggle to eliminate Beyme, Schroetter, Voss, Zastrow and others was a generational conflict. It is obvious that the latter two, conservative aristocrats, could not work in a reform government, for its goals were threatening to their values and life-styles. Beyme and Schroetter, however, considered themselves fair-minded and modern. They bitterly resented what they saw as a personal plot against themselves. But the civil servants of the younger generation were adamant: these elder bureaucrats were incapable of understanding the reform plans. The patriots, it would turn out, were only partly successful. The presence of Beyme and Schroetter in the government would affect the nature of the reform work in 1808. Voss and Zastrow would work behind the scenes as outright opponents of change.

If the patriots had expected to begin the work of drafting reform legislation under Hardenberg's leadership, they were disappointed. They spent their time instead trying to hold together a government in desperate condition. "The minister is setting to work without fanfare . . . ," reported Nagler in April. "For the present I can see no [overall] plan of operations. In the matter of military provisions, the minister has good designs." Indeed, providing supplies to soldiers and trying to bring together scraps of a shredded government exhausted the energies of the Bartenstein group until the Peace of Tilsit.[44]

The three-month administration was a personal ministry in a literal sense. Hardenberg kept his helpers close by his side. He employed their specialized skills, and they carried out his orders. His staff spoke of him as "prime minister," though the term was not used in official documents. Everyone agreed that the most pressing task at hand was that of terminating the war and rescuing as much as possible for Prussia. Nevertheless, the patriots who eagerly joined Hardenberg's staff sensed that their long-term plans were being sidetracked or ignored. Schön, for example, was vexed over

---

Bestrebungen zur Befreiung der Privatbauern" 34 (1922): 1–24, 265–96; 37 (1925): 31–76, passim; Eicke, *Der ostpreussische Landtag von 1798*, 57–59; Ritter, *Stein*, 67; Hans Lippold, *Die Kriegs- und Domänenkammer zu Bialystock in ihrer Arbeit und Bedeutung für die preussische Geschichte* (Königsberg, diss., 1914), 37–39; Schön to Altenstein, Königsberg, 12 Apr. 1807, Winter, *Reorganisation*, 157 (no. 119); Altenstein to Schön, Nimmersatt, 12 July 1807, Theodor von Schön, *Aus den Papieren des Ministers und Burggrafen von Marienburg Theodor von Schön* (Leipzig, Halle and Berlin, 1875–1883) 2: 33; Niebuhr to Stein, Memel, 10 Jan. and 29 Mar. 1807, Botzenhart, *Stein Briefe* 2/1: 337, 362 (nos. 321, 341); Krause, *Der Provinzialminister Schroetter*, 51; Staegemann to Elisabeth Staegemann, Memel, 7 Sept. 1807, Rühl, *Aus der Franzosenzeit*, 34–35 (no. 29); Hardenberg, Tagebuch, 18 June 1807, Winter, *Reorganisation*, 182, n. 1.

[44] Thielen, *Hardenberg*, 190–91; Nagler to Altenstein, Bartenstein, 29 Apr. 1807, Winter, *Reorganisation*, 176 (no. 124); Staegemann, Promemoria über den Geschäftskreis des unter Leitung Hardenbergs gestandenen kombinierten Departments, ibid., 212–13 (no. 149). The latter document provides a good survey of the tasks which occupied the Bartenstein ministry.

having to function as a mere secretary whose work amounted to taking care of "meal and oats." "It is a great handicap," he complained to Hardenberg during the Tilsit negotiations, "that I always have to stand behind the curtains." He resented not having full "representation" in the decision-making of the administration. Hardenberg's staff was also disappointed that the first minister remained aloof toward Stein. They had hoped that once Hardenberg had won the first battle over administrative reform, he would set about reinvolving Stein in the ministry. "Schön is taking it hard," remarked Nagler, "that Hardenberg does not breathe a word about Stein."[45]

It cannot be known whether or not a reform program such as the patriots envisioned would have taken place under Hardenberg had Napoleon not forced him from office at the conclusion of peace. The Bartenstein staff's hints of frustration are tied up with the government's conception of the primacy of its diplomatic endeavors. The patriots believed that nothing could be accomplished toward reforming society until the war was terminated. The crisis allowed them little perspective on their work and plans.

There is in the Bartenstein experience something characteristic of the whole Prussian reform movement. Hardenberg's ministry represents the reform movement's first accomplishment in bureaucratic reorganization: creation of a modern ministerial government in rudimentary form. It was not a new administrative system built according to blueprint. Rather, similar to the one that would follow it, it was a hastily contrived expedient designed to meet a crisis which was almost beyond control. The patriots, of course, thought of the Bartenstein ministry as a temporary measure, precedent to more adequately planned measures. But they sometimes failed to distinguish clearly between stop-gap efforts and well-executed reforms. Perhaps Hardenberg would have enjoyed the authority of the post of first minister on a permanent basis if that had been an option to him. Some of his subsequent experiences suggest this.

Members of the Bartenstein ministry had two distinct goals: saving the state and reforming the society. The way in which they perceived these as part of the same large task is emblematic of their thinking. The patriots were, after all, bureaucrats who had a stake in the Prussian monarchy. They could not afford to let things get too far out of hand. Either an obliteration of the state or a complete social disintegration would have been anathema to them. Their visions of a new society were limited by their commitment to orderly progress within an existing social and political framework. At Bartenstein little social reform was accomplished because preservation of the monarchy took precedence.

In office Hardenberg had ignored the perhaps unrealistic desires of his subordinates to reinvolve Stein in the Prussian government. There is evi-

[45] Schön to Altenstein, Memel, 30 June 1807, ibid., 209–10 (no. 144 and n.); Schön to Altenstein, Königsberg, 12 Apr. 1807, ibid., 157 (no. 119); Sack to Stein, Berlin, 26 May and 4 June 1807, Botzenhart, *Stein Briefe* 2/1: 372–73, 375–76 (nos. 348, 350); Nagler to Altenstein, Bartenstein, 29 Apr. 1807, Winter, *Reorganisation*, 176 (no. 124).

dence to suggest that the two were in some ways personally incompatible. But, forced from office by Napoleon's dictates, Hardenberg prevailed upon King Frederick William to swallow his pride and recall the minister whom he had recently dismissed with anger and disdain. Hardenberg drafted the summons, appealing to Stein both in the name of the monarch and on a personal basis. On Hardenberg's counsel, Frederick William offered Stein the ministerial posts of finance and interior. It was understood that he should follow the precedent of the Bartenstein ministry in assuming informally the role of prime minister until a permanent administrative structure could be established.[46]

At Nassau Stein was completing a project which revealed his continued interest in Prussia and the shape of his vision of reforms. His friend, Prince Anton Radziwill, had requested that he compose a plan for restoration of Prussian administration in the estranged Polish provinces. Stein did not believe that this was feasible without a thorough restructuring of the Prussian government. Like other patriots Stein was convinced that Prussia's only hope of recovery from military and economic prostration lay in an all-embracing reform program. His response to Radziwill's request was the celebrated Nassau Reform Memorandum of June 1807.[47]

Above all, Stein called for a complete reorganization of the governmental edifice of the monarchy. In agreement with several of the reform proposals coming out of the fight against cabinet government, Stein advocated a single, unified administrative organ to replace the unwieldy General Directory and the myriad of other organizations with interlocking responsibilities answerable to the monarch. But the Nassau document was more extensive than those of the previous winter. Certainly recalling the bitter frustrations of his previous career, Stein argued that the effects of bureaucracy in Prussia were more detrimental than positive. Officialism led to a "hireling mentality . . . a fear of change and innovation."

In place of the system of rule by career bureaucrats, Prussia should establish an administration based upon representation. Stein believed that a reformed government should rest upon the participation of "property owners, and indeed of all classes." He argued that self-government would enliven the "dormant or misled forces and the widely scattered talents" of society. It would reconcile "the needs . . . of the nation with those of the government, rekindling a feeling for the Fatherland, for independence and for national honor."

The Nassau plan gave a significant preview to the work of a Stein ministry. For the time being, uncertainty ruled in Prussia. At Hardenberg's

---

[46] Hardenberg, Tagebuch, Piktupöhnen, 6 July 1807, ibid., 211–12 (no. 148); Hardenberg to Stein, Memel, 10 July 1807, Botzenhart, *Stein Briefe* 2/1: 408–12 (no. 357); Ranke, *Denkwürdigkeiten Hardenbergs* 3: 501.

[47] For this and the following paragraphs: Stein, Über die zweckmässige Bildung der obersten und der Provinzial-, Finanz- und Polizei-Behörden in der preussischen Monarchie, Nassau, June 1807, Botzenhart, *Stein Briefe* 2/1: 380–98 (no. 354).

emphatic recommendation, his Bartenstein staff formed a temporary council designed to provide transition between the ministry of Hardenberg and a new one, hopefully led by Stein. Called the Immediate Commission because it was to have direct or "immediate" access to the king, the provisional body faced obstacles from the outset. One of the major problems was Beyme, who, as Hardenberg departed, slid back into his position as "invisible prime minister." Upon assuming responsibility, the Immediate Commission confronted Beyme in a bitter three-day controversy over who was to chair the body. Beyme attempted to install three different handpicked candidates as chairman of the temporary government. The members of the Immediate Commission absolutely refused to work with "outsiders," men of the old regime or others who were not a part of their group of patriots. Beyme's three candidates, all of whom held the title finance councilor, were Otto Christoph von Quast-Ganz, August Heinrich Borgstede, and Georg Wilhelm von Schlabrendorff. The debate reached the pitch of a shouting match, and Schön threatened to resign before working under one of Beyme's men.[48]

Finally a fourth candidate emerged as an acceptable compromise to both parties, Theodor Anton von Klewitz (1760–1838). Like most of the patriots, Klewitz was of middle-class background. Like several members of the Immediate Commission, he had studied at Halle and Göttingen. His fields were law, mathematics, technology and chemistry. Klewitz had followed the career of a typical successful bureaucrat. So thriving was his professional life that he had been granted a title of nobility in 1803. Members of the Immediate Commission knew Klewitz as a bright person and an able worker sympathetic to their plans for modernization, though he was not outspoken. Perhaps most important to them was their belief that he would be no pawn of Beyme.[49]

It is significant that this compromise candidate was acceptable to Beyme and King Frederick William as a spokesman for the temporary government, whereas none of the original members of the Immediate Commission were. While Klewitz did not enjoy the status of men like Hardenberg or Stein, he surpassed all members of the temporary government in age and years of service, and most in social rank. This underlines the fact that the reform party was built of men whom the court and the old bureaucracy regarded

[48] Hardenberg, Immediatbericht, Memel, 10 July 1807, Winter, *Reorganisation*, 216–17 (no. 152); Kabinettsordre to Altenstein, Schön, Staegemann and Niebuhr, 14 July 1807, ibid., 220–22 (no. 158); Schön to Altenstein, Memel, 12–14 July 1807, ibid., 222–27 (no. 159); Ranke, *Denkwürdigkeiten Hardenbergs* 3: 379. On Quast, Borgstede and Schlabrendorff, see the following: *Handbuch über den preussischen Hof 1805*, 48, 220; Kabinettsordre to Hardenberg, 30 May 1807, Winter, *Reorganisation*, 181 (no. 131); ibid., 117, n. 1; Schlabrendorff to Beyme, Riga, 7 July 1807, ibid., 567–68 (no. 148a); Hardenberg to Schlabrendorff, Königsberg, 1 June 1807, ibid., 184 (no. 135); Schlabrendorff, Promemoria, Memel, 4 June 1807, ibid., 184–86 (no. 136); ibid., 158–160, n.; [Bassewitz], *Kurmark Brandenburg* 1: 399–402; Hintze, "Reformbestrebungen," 521 and n.; Beguelin, *Denkwürdigkeiten*, 121.

[49] Bailleu, "Klewitz," *Allgemeine Deutsche Biographie* 16: 180–81; Hans Herzfeld, "Klewitz," *Mitteldeutsche Lebensbilder*, (Magdeburg, 1926) 1: 12–30.

as on the fringes of acceptability. Age, status and schooling in traditional patterns were thought necessary to hold these wild young administrators in check.

With Klewitz as their spokesman, the Immediate Commission experienced a three-month administration characterized by conflicts with Beyme over prerogative and authority. Schön referred to Beyme contemptuously in correspondence as "Herr stumbler," calling him "in essence a weak person who allows others to sway him." But King Frederick William, withdrawn to his "cabinet" more than ever, gave few audiences and little respect to the Commission. He acted on the principle, Schön related, "that men like ourselves are fit only to stand behind the curtains, although [Klewitz] is his own secretary. . . . The situation seems unbearable. . . . We are secretaries' secretaries and nothing more."[50]

For six weeks the Immediate Commission worked in complete uncertainty about the question they considered most vital to their purposes: Would Stein accept the summons to return to Prussia and head a reform ministry? The members knew that Stein's recent, ignominious dismissal would make it easy for him to decline. They feared that Hardenberg's failure to reinvolve Stein in the government might have increased his alienation. The patriots knew that Stein, after all no Prussian himself, had seriously considered a position in the administration of Tsar Alexander. They were aware, moreover, that Frederick William had no contingency plan, should Stein decline. They saw their own designs for Prussia hanging precariously in the balance. "It causes me great pain to hear of the miserable conditions" at the court, wrote Altenstein on 12 August from Riga, whence he had accompanied Hardenberg. "Certainly only the cornerstone and foundation stone can save us," he said, playing upon the literal meaning ("stone") of Stein's name. "An answer must come soon!" Niebuhr was most depressed over the situation. He made it clear that he would continue to work in Prussia only under Stein's leadership, and he threatened to resign in any case. He advised Schön too to resign, "before it becomes too insulting." "If Stein does not come, everything will go with the current trend into dissolution and decay."[51]

---

[50] On Frederick William's bewilderment and withdrawal, see Altenstein to Schön, Piktupöhnen, 1 July 1807, Dep. Brünneck, no. 5, St. A. Göttingen. An important part of a sentence, "but the king grows daily weaker," as well as other unflattering remarks about Frederick William have been omitted from the printed version, Schön, *Aus den Papieren* 2: 16–17. Almost every letter of Schön to Altenstein contains the complaint about having to "stand behind the curtains." Schön to Altenstein, Memel, 14 July, 6 Aug. and 14 Aug. 1807, Winter, *Reorganisation,* 227, 257, 264 (nos. 159, 195, 207). See also Hans Haussherr, *Erfüllung und Befreiung: Der Kampf um die Durchführung des Tilsiter Friedens 1807/1808* (Hamburg, 1935), 28, 31.

[51] Altenstein to Schön, Riga, 12 Aug. 1807, Schön, *Aus den Papieren* 2: 40. The play upon the literal meaning of the word "stein" was common among the patriots. See Altenstein's reference to Stein as a "powerful column" who alone could support a "mighty building" in a "sea of muck." Altenstein to Schön, Riga, 19 July 1807, ibid., 2: 35–36; Hardenberg to Schön, Riga, 20 July 1807, ibid., 1: appendix, 56; Niebuhr to Schön, Riga, 11 July 1807 and 17/29 July 1807, ibid., 2: 95–100; Niebuhr to Stein, Riga, 16/28 July 1807, Botzenhart, *Stein Briefe* 2/1: 420–23 (no. 366).

The patriots discussed among themselves the possibility of carrying on without Stein. "Friend," wrote Schön to Altenstein in July,

> you write me about my substituting for Stein. Your friendship deceives you. It will not work. . . . I would like to manage the affairs. . . . However I lack an essential requisite, . . . representation at the court. My principles are heretical to the people there, and I would not be able to overcome the mountain of intrigue which would arise against me. . . . For me there is no possibility if Stein does not come.[52]

It took until late August for the summons to reach Stein in far-off Nassau and for his reply to return to Memel. His answer was positive: he would come. The patriots rejoiced. This is the occasion of Staegemann's ecstatic words to his wife: "Herr vom Stein is returning. Serfdom will be abolished, . . . compulsory guilds will be destroyed."[53] At last they could develop a reform program. Until October they worked at a feverish pace, preparing reform memoranda and putting them aside for their future prime minister to present to the king. Stein was prevented by illness and by distance from arriving before that date.

Hardenberg, meanwhile exiled at Riga, undertook the task of mapping a comprehensive plan for the reform of the Prussian state and society. Altenstein left the day-to-day tasks of running the government to his colleagues and joined the former first minister to assist him in composing the reform program. Two extensive documents emerged from their efforts, one written by each. They consulted all the works they could obtain on political and economic thought, but in the small Russian seaport libraries were not extensive. Both Niebuhr and Schön corresponded regularly with them, contributing suggestions and ideas in their own specialized areas.[54] Beside Stein's Nassau plan, the two Riga memoranda are the most systematic statements behind the reform movement. The fact that they were written in an atmosphere of crisis contributes to this quality. Neither before 1807 nor after he rejoined the government in 1810, did Hardenberg pen any proposal so comprehensive. Instead, when in office, he tackled problems individually, creating a more patchwork effect.

In Riga Altenstein composed drafts, and Hardenberg refined them to fit his own style and taste. Apparently the original plan was to produce one rather than two documents. But Altenstein's, completed first, is an independent proposal, three times the length of Hardenberg's. Altenstein's memorandum is expressed in flowery, philosophical language. Hardenberg, more concise, limited himself to practical solutions, of concrete problems. For those subjects on which Altenstein was most eloquent and complete,

---

[52] Schön to Altenstein, Memel, 23 (July) 1807, Winter, *Reorganisation*, 236 (no. 171).

[53] Staegemann to Elisabeth Staegemann, 26 Aug. 1807, Rühl, *Aus der Franzosenzeit*, 30 (no. 25).

[54] Hardenberg, Tagebuch, Tauerlauken, 11 July 1807, Winter, *Reorganisation*, 220 (no. 155); Ranke, *Denkwürdigkeiten Hardenbergs* 3: 514–16; Altenstein to Schön, Riga, 17/29 [July] 1807, Dep. Brünneck, no. 5, StA Königsberg, edited with changes in Schön, *Aus den Papieren* 2: 45; Hardenberg, Tagebuch, Riga, 15 Aug. and 2 Sept. 1807, Winter, *Reorganisation*, 265, 283 (nos. 210, 245); Schön to Altenstein, Memel, 12 July and 14 July 1807, ibid., 223–27, 264 (nos. 159 and 207).

such as religious and educational questions, Hardenberg simply referred readers to his helper's plan. In the sections on foreign policy and military affairs, Hardenberg worked independently of Altenstein's preliminary drafts.[55]

Hardenberg and Altenstein approached their work with the view that the Prussian state had perished and a new one would be forged in its place. They hoped to bring to a reformed Prussia the same advantages France had gained through revolution, but to avoid the bloodshed and violence the French had experienced. They advocated an orderly "revolution from above." "The time could never be more favorable. . . . There is no room for prejudice which clings to old ways. . . . If one wants to rescue the state and to see it prosper again, let there be no delay. . . . A phoenix will arise out of the ashes."

The new society which Hardenberg and Altenstein projected was to be based on the concept of greatest possible freedom for all. They urged abolition of the rigid, feudal class structure. They called for removal of mercantilistic restrictions on the economy. They were especially critical of the old-regime economic limitations resulting from the strict separation of city and countryside which, they complained, excluded holders of capital from agricultural enterprise. The two reformers in Riga were advocates of freedom in its new and universal sense. In application, they thought primarily of economic freedom which would benefit entrepreneurs. While calling for "abolition of serfdom," Hardenberg did not think it necessary to destroy the institution of compulsory labor owed by peasants to landlords.

In the area of political reform, the two planners advocated supplanting Prussia's traditional network of overlapping and entangled administrative bodies with a simple, central bureaucracy. They wanted to effect a "practical remaking of the domestic government" in order to bring it into "harmony with the spirit of the times and the providential world plan." They called for creation of representative institutions. However, they drafted concrete plans for representative bodies only on a community level. More extensive were their outlines of bureaucratic organs, building a pyramidal structure of local, county, provincial and national administration. Hardenberg and Altenstein provided for an authoritative prime ministerial post, the occupant of which would hold the title "first minister" or "state chancellor." Others in the reform party were beginning to discuss a more thorough type of participatory government. And the discussion would widen as the Stein ministry took form. But in the late summer of 1807, when Hardenberg thought of political reform, he was primarily concerned with establishing a system of bureaucratic efficiency.

---

[55] Altenstein, Über die Leitung des preussischen Staats, Riga, 11 Sept. 1807, ibid., 364–566 (no. 262); Hardenberg, Über die Reorganisation des preussischen Staats, ibid., 302–63 (no. 261). See Eduard Spranger, "Altensteins Denkschrift von 1807 und ihre Beziehung zur Philosophie," *Forschungen zur brandenburgischen und preussischen Geschichte* 18 (1905): 471–517; Hans Haussherr, "Hardenbergs Reformdenkschrift Riga, 1807," *Historische Zeitschrift* 157 (1938): 267–308.

While Altenstein assisted Hardenberg at Riga, the other members of the Immediate Commission worked at an almost frantic pace to develop a reform program which they could finish after Stein arrived to carry their plans to the king. In correspondence during these weeks, the patriots used phrases such as "the good cause" and "the great plan" in reference to their designs. "Why are we being destroyed?" questioned Theodor von Schön, perhaps the most passionate devotee of the great plan. "The evil is more fundamental than the bureaucracy. It lies in the very structure of the state." Schön diagnosed Prussia's condition in terms of four main ills. The first was hereditary serfdom: "The slave [*sic*] has no interest in preserving the state; it is rather to his advantage to destroy his master and the government which protects the master." The second malady was restriction in property ownership and the aristocracy's exclusive hold on agriculture: those who have capital are denied the right to possess property, and the noble estate owners lack money. "Few men are interested in land under these conditions." Thirdly, Schön attacked the social privilege of the aristocracy. "This deadens all self-respect of commoners and gives a servile mentality to 23/24 of the nation." And finally he assaulted the rigidity of the mercantilist economic system, a "forceful suppression of the national well-being." These four problems the patriots set out to correct with an intensity of purpose and a mood of optimism. They hoped with their plans to make an antiquated society into a modern one.[56]

The urgency and devotion with which the Immediate Commission toiled is illustrated by a tragic circumstance in the life of Theodor von Schön. Working tirelessly to complete a proposal for reforming the agrarian economy, Schön learned in early August that his wife Lydia, living in Königsberg, was critically ill. She wrote repeatedly during the late summer urging him to visit, but his work prevented his leaving Memel, he felt. After 10 August, she was too weak to write and dictated her letters. Anxious to hurry to her side, but feeling he could not leave without someone replacing him, Schön sent urgent messages to Altenstein in Riga requesting him to hurry to Memel. On 14 August he wrote:

> I do not want to take you away from the minister. I cannot leave here. Staegemann has too much to do, and Klewitz is afraid. Therefore I must carry the heaviest load and live through the hard times here. Until [next week when I will leave in any case] I will work as hard as I can. . . . I have composed a long report for the king on the reestablishment of Prussia. It contains some important ideas and is one of the best of my latest pieces of work. I wish Hardenberg could read it.

The Immediate Commission report was complete on 17 August, but Schön did not sign it. He was hurrying to his wife, having received an urgent message from his father-in-law, Auerswald. He did not arrive in time to

---

[56] References to "the great plan" and "the good cause" in Altenstein to Schön, Riga, 19 July 1807, Dep. Brünneck, no. 5, StA Königsberg, altered in Schön, *Aus den Papieren* 2: 36; Schön to Altenstein, Memel, 12 July 1807, Winter, *Reorganisation*, 223–24 (no. 159).

see her again. She died while he was en route. The reform proposal, meanwhile, was ready for presentation to Stein.[57]

The energy from years of pent-up frustration went into the frantic, high-pitched work of the Immediate Commission. This energy would sustain the reform party throughout the thirteen-month Stein ministry. A group of young idealistic officials, nurtured on the values of early liberalism, had been disappointed by the slow, grinding machinery of the bureaucracy, and by its conservative leaders. Finally they saw their opportunity when the French Revolution struck Prussia in the twisted form of Napoleon's methodic military advances. The disasters united the scattered liberal bureaucrats into the party of the patriots. For a year, from the Battle of Jena in October 1806 to Stein's arrival in October 1807, the patriots were alternately overcome with depression and bolstered by optimism. By the fall of 1807 they saw sun on the horizon. They believed they could remake Prussia. One of their chosen leaders, Hardenberg, was for the time being out of the picture. But Stein, like his younger colleagues, was sustained by the faith that a new society could be forged. He was anxious to preside over the remaking of Prussia.

---

[57] See Dep. Brünneck, No. 47, StA Königsberg, passim, which contains letters of Lydia von Schön to her husband from 5 June to 10 Aug. 1807. Altenstein to Schön, Riga, 12 Aug. and 19 Aug. 1807, Schön, *Aus den Papieren* 2: 40 and 1: appendix, 57; Schön to Altenstein, 14 Aug. 1807, Winter, *Reorganisation*, 263–64 (no. 207).

IV. BUREAUCRATIC CHANGE AND ACCOMMODATION OF THE ARISTOCRACY

BUREAUCRATIC SUPREMACY AND AD HOC ADMINISTRATIVE STRUCTURE

The establishment of Stein's ministry was a triumph of bureaucracy over personal absolutism. The conflict over the cabinet government—royal rule versus ministerial rule—had been bitter and drawn out, but Frederick William capitulated when he recalled the previously dismissed Baron vom Stein to lead Prussia out of its crisis. Never before had a Prussian king turned over the affairs of the state to his ministers so completely as Frederick William did in 1807. Never again would the Hohenzollerns claim the right to rule "from the king's cabinet." For at least a century, they would continue to name and dismiss ministers as servants of the crown, but it was the matter of initiative which shifted in 1809. Unlike Frederick the Great, who recruited state servants to carry out his personal will and whim, Frederick William III and his successors would appoint professionals to formulate and execute policy for Prussia. After 1807 ministers and bureaucratic officials, rather than kings and their appointees, ran the monarchy.

Hardenberg's brief Bartenstein ministry of April-July 1807 had already established a precedent. Hardenberg's appointment as "first minister" destroyed once and for all the old structure of government at the top administrative level, the famous General Directory. Had the military-diplomatic situation not curtailed it, this experiment might have come to be considered Prussia's historic turning point. But Hardenberg and his staff were so overwhelmed with keeping Prussia alive, and their tenure was so brief, that they had no chance to start intentionally laying the foundations for a new government. By October, when Stein resumed office, the diplomatic crisis had intensified, rather than abated, yet Stein and his staff had had time to develop a longer-range perspective on their roles. They were able to think of themselves as the builders of a new Prussia. Hardenberg had the job of holding the state together. Stein, in contrast, had a specific mandate to reform, as well as to administer the civil affairs of government.

Setting his staff to work on the blueprints for a revised administrative structure of the state, Stein nevertheless accepted the ad hoc organizational arrangement which he found when he arrived in Memel. This consisted of bare remnants and shattered pieces of the former system as well as some hastily devised temporary offices. The crisis of 1806–1807 had swept away not only the structure, but also much of the personnel, of the old-regime leadership. Through his ministerial rank with the portfolios of Finance and Interior, Stein enjoyed the privilege of "immediacy," that is, he had the right of direct access to the king. This in addition to his understood, but unofficial, role as prime minister, made him the most powerful official in the land.[1] Only two other persons enjoyed the right of access to the king by virtue of ministerial titles. One was Leopold von Schroetter, ousted from the central administration under the shakeup of the Bartenstein ministry. Schroetter still held his position as provincial minister of East Prussia, through which he had the right of immediacy. This time the reform party did not object to Schroetter's presence, perhaps realizing that they could do worse, and perhaps seeing his participation as beneficial to their cause. Though Schroetter was an old-regime administrator, he enjoyed a reputation as an advocate of change. He had long supported Stein in the latter's attack upon the cabinet government. The king was pleased to have in Schroetter a trusted advisor with years of experience in the Prussian system, who could work well with the reform government. Frederick William possibly regarded Schroetter as a potential check on the younger, more impetuous members of the reform movement. The other remaining minister, whose tenure reached back to the days before the French Revolution directly confronted Prussia, was August Friedrich von der Goltz (1765–1832), head of the Office of Foreign Affairs. Goltz was not a reformer, but he posed little threat to the Stein party, in part because he possessed no strong commitments and no great leadership potential. One member of Stein's staff characterized Goltz as a "good man," who has "not the faintest idea about government administration." In effect, Stein directed foreign as well as domestic policy during his year's tenure, in spite of Goltz's formal position.[2]

The king's favorite, Beyme, was the single remaining old-regime figure, and his presence provoked controversy. Neither the Bartenstein government nor the Immediate Commission had been successful in effecting the dismissal of this state servant, dear to the king, rhetorically committed to reform, yet distasteful to the reform party. Before his arrival in Memel, Stein sent messages through Altenstein, Staegemann and others that he would not assume office if he had to work with Beyme. Frederick William's response was to appoint Beyme as the supreme judicial administrator. Grosskanzler, which would remove him from any direct relationship with the ministerial administration, yet still give him the privilege of immediacy. Beyme was bitter at being pushed aside from the mainstream of activities, but at the urging of the queen, he accepted his new office with good grace.[3]

---

[1] Hardenberg, Tagebuch, Piktupöhnen, 6 July 1807, Winter, *Reorganisation,* 211–12 (no. 148); Hardenberg to Stein, Memel, 10 July 1807, Botzenhart, *Stein Briefe* 2/1: 408–12 (no. 357); Ranke, *Denkwürdigkeiten Hardenbergs* 3: 501.

[2] Schön to Altenstein, 20 [July], and 6 Aug. 1807, Winter, *Reorganisation,* 235, 257 (nos. 171, 195); Raack, *Fall of Stein,* 55, 66; Schramm-Macdonald, "v. Goltz," *Allgemeine Deutsche Biographie* 9: 351–53.

[3] Beguelin, *Denkwürdigkeiten,* 123–25; Kieswetter to Staegemann, Berlin, 26 Oct. 1806, Rühl, *Briefe und Aktenstücke* 1: 20–21 (no. 15); Ritter, *Stein,* 207–208; Beyme to Stein, Memel, 6 Oct. 1807, Scheel, *Reformministerium* 1: 8 (no. 4); Raack, *Fall of Stein,* 35–36.

Beyme's shifting roles illustrate how personalities, individual whims, and remnants of absolute royal power helped shape the activity of reform.

Under the temporary but precedent-setting arrangement of 1807–1808, the ministry functioned as a series of committees commissioned by Stein. (See schematic illustration). The most important of these with regard to the drafting of reform measures was the Immediate Commission which had functioned as a government without a head in the interlude between the Bartenstein ministry and Stein's arrival. It consisted of the most dedicated core of the reform party: Altenstein, Schön, Staegemann, Klewitz, and Niebuhr. (Niebuhr was soon to be reassigned to diplomatic responsibilities.) This group bitterly resented their lack of access to the king, perhaps doubly so because the Commission's title implied the right of immediacy. Their inability to communicate directly with the monarch meant lack of any real power to realize their reform goals. Hence they welcomed Stein's leadership enthusiastically. While some members of the Immediate Commission had privately hoped for ministerial positions, they saw that this was not feasible, and did not press the issue once Stein's acceptance was received. Instead they prepared a lengthy document for the new prime minister outlining their previous work and suggesting new roles for themselves pending a final administrative reform. They petitioned to be relieved of all responsibility for overseeing day-to-day administrative affairs, which would free them to devote their entire energy to developing reform proposals. In fact they sought to secure the exclusive right to draft the reform legislation of the Stein government.[4] Stein did not act upon the Immediate Commission proposal, indicating instead that he would draw upon a wider group of advisors and specialists than the five-member group. In July 1808 the Commission was officially abolished when it was made a part of the "General Conference" under a temporary reorganization plan. Its members remained the most active originators and discussants of reform legislation.[5]

The second most important committee in the ad hoc arrangement of Stein's ministry was the East Prussian ministerial office under Schroetter's direction. Stein's method of developing new legislation was to request proposals from one or more individuals or groups on specific topics such as agrarian, administrative, and financial reform. The drafts then circulated in multiple copies to others for criticism, counterproposal, and revision, with the hope that consensus would be reached. This not often being the case, Stein would, himself, weigh the various proposals and responses,

---

[4] Immediate Commission to Stein, Memel, 12 Oct. 1807, Scheel, *Reformministerium* 1: 19–23 (no. 9). On Niebuhr's new responsibilities see: Ministerialreskript an die Immediat-Friedensvollziehungskommission, Memel, 17 Nov. 1807, ibid., 1: 81 (no. 37). On Schön's and Altenstein's discussion of ministerial posts for themselves, see Altenstein to Schön, Riga, 19 July 1807, Dep. Brünneck, no. 5, StA Königsberg (edited, so as to alter meaning in Schön, *Aus den Papieren* 2: 37–38); Altenstein to Schön, Riga, 17/29 July 1807, ibid., 2: 42–43; Schön to Altenstein. Memel, 23 [July] 1807, Winter, *Reorganisation,* 236 (no. 171).

[5] Immediatkommission to Stein, Memel, 12 Oct. 1807, Scheel, *Reformministerium* 1: 23, n. 6 (no. 9); Plan zu einer interimistischen verbesserten Einrichtung des Geschäftsganges, [25 July 1808], ibid., 2: 675–82; Sitzungsbericht des Generaldepartements der Polizei und der Finanzen, Königsberg, 4 Aug. 1808, ibid., 3: 724–26 (no. 227).

TEMPORARY STRUCTURE OF THE HIGHEST PRUSSIAN BUREAUCRACY DURING THE REFORM YEAR 1807–1808

KING

Administrators with direct access to the king

Schroetter, Minister of East Prussia. Schroetter's staff functioned as drafters and revisers of reform measures.

Stein, Minister of finance and interior (informal prime minister).

Goltz, Foreign minister

Beyme, Grosskanzler

Individuals and committees with no access to the monarch except through Stein

Commission for Completion of the Peace. Headed by *Sack* in Berlin, the Commission had the responsibility of communicating with French authorities concerning a final peace treaty.

Immediate Commission (after 25 July 1808 reorganized as the *General Conference*). This was the major body mandated to draft the reform measures. Members included: *Altenstein, Schön, Klewitz, Staegemann*.

Miliary Reorganization Commission. Membership included *Scharnhorst* and *Gneisenau*. Drafted military reforms.

Other reformers who contributed to reform work on *ad hoc* basis as solicited by Stein. Among others: *Vincke, Rehdiger, Auerswald, K. v. Schroetter, Frey*.

finally directing one of the participants to prepare a final draft to be laid before the king. The East Prussian ministerial office was especially significant in the origination of agrarian reforms, but there is hardly an aspect of the reform activity in which it did not participate. Schroetter's staff included the fiery civil servant, Ernst Gottlieb Morgenbesser, author of the *Commentaries on the Republican Lawbook* which seven years previously had provoked heated controversy between himself and the conservative bureaucracy. The Königsberg office also included Privy Councilors Karl Ferdinand Friese and Gustav Ferdinand Wilckens, two administrative professionals known for their devotion to the cause of social change.[6]

Reform memoranda flowed from the pens of many others who were otherwise occupied in administration, statesmanship, or private affairs, from whom Stein nevertheless requested proposals, because of their special expertise or experience. These included men like Ludwig von Vincke, Hans von Auerswald, Johann Gottfried Frey, Karl Nikolaus von Rehdiger, Prince Friedrich Wilhelm von Reden, and Karl Wilhelm von Schroetter, brother of the East Prussian minister. Academics like Professors Hoffmann and Süvern took part in the discussions as well. There were others within the government whose presence was felt during the reform debates, although administrative or diplomatic responsibilities prohibited a very active role. Sack, head of the Commission for Completion of the Peace in Berlin, is an example. Generals Scharnhorst and Gneisenau headed the Military Reorganization Commission which played a role similar to that of the Immediate Commission, but in the sphere of military reforms. The whole arrangement was tied together by the person of Stein. It functioned as a "ministry" only in a loose understanding of the term. But it is typical of the reform government that it worked with such temporary arrangements awaiting the enactment of more formal and final measures.

GOALS AND IDEALS OF BUREAUCRATIC REFORM

Empowered to steer the state into the modern world, the reformers were resolved to make permanent their victory over absolutism. One of their top priorities was the formation of a rationally organized bureaucracy from the level of the king's top minister down to the local village. Their reforms would replace the cumbersome and arbitrary arrangement of intertwined boards, commissions, committees, and independent offices which had developed under absolutist rulers. The existing system was highly inefficient, argued the reformers. More importantly, it had assumed a life of its own, creating a barrier between the populace and the government. Altenstein complained that the royal bureacracy had "taken over everything and placed it in the hands of paid servants. . . . Out of this situation has grown a comlete indifference toward government." Stein deplored the "hireling

[6] Schroetter, Immediatbericht, Königsberg, 16 Oct. 1807, ibid., 1: 28–31 (no. 13). On Friese, see Hoffmann, "Nekrolog des Staats-Sekretärs Friese," 688–708.

mentality" of the state's officials which he believed produced a "life of forms and machine-like service, . . . a fear of change and innovation." He promised to terminate "all unnecessary and harmful interference of the goverment" in private affairs of Prussians. A simpler, more streamlined administration would bring new vitality to Prussia. It would replace the stifling top-heavy officialism with civil servants who were not only in touch with the people but also well trained in their professions.[7]

While, by the beginning of the nineteenth century, a strong sense of professional identity had developed in Prussia's bureaucracy, the particular historical circumstances under which this happened made the civil service an especially powerful agent of the crown, pitting it against other elements of society. This situation stood in contrast to that of France, for example. In that state there was a pronounced amalgamation of feudal and professional elements in the officialdom, keeping it in touch with at least the elite of society, rather than totally at odds with the kingdom's subjects.[8] While the Prussian reform party sought further to emancipate the state's officials from royal control, their ideological context was that of reestablishing ties between the people and the government. Paradoxically they saw the processes of establishing bureaucratic independence and popular government as one and the same. Stein believed, for example, that a more rational administration could eliminate unhealthy competition between provincial Estates and the central bureaucracy. Despite centuries of absolutist erosion of aristocratic privilege, numerous noble political institutions remained, including standing committees, fire insurance associations, credit associations, and provincial assemblies. All of these saw their function as that of guarding provincial interests against the powers of the central government. In a modern state, Stein reasoned, local leadership and bureaucratic institutions should not be in opposition to one another. They should be mutually supportive. Administrative reform would replace wasteful conflict with harmonious cooperation, thus restoring "unity and strength" to Prussia. State servants would represent the interests of "the nation" rather than of a particular class or of the crown.[9]

As Stein emphasized in a memorandum to the king early in the reform year, a future governmental administration in Prussia must strictly avoid the disadvantage of being run by people whose sole motivation was their

---

[7] Altenstein, Über die Leitung des preussischen Staats, Riga, 11 Sept. 1807, Winter, *Reorganisation,* 393–94 (no. 262); Stein, Über die zweckmässige Bildung der Behörden, Nassau, June, 1807, Botzenhart, *Stein Briefe* 2/1: 389–91 (no. 354); Stein to Schroetter, Königsberg, 27 June 1808, ibid., 2/2: 764 (no. 729); Wilhelm Isenberg, *Das Staatsdenken des Freiherrn vom Stein,* Schriften zur Rechtslehre und Politik, 58 (Bonn, 1968): 159.

[8] Peter Lundgreen, "Gegensatz und Verschmelzung von 'alter' und 'neuer' Bürokratie im Ancien Régime: Ein Vergleich von Frankreich und Preussen," in Wehler, ed., *Sozialgeschichte heute,* 104–18.

[9] Stein, Über die zweckmässige Bildung der Behörden, Nassau, June, 1807, Botzenhart, *Stein Briefe* 2/1: 389–91; Isenberg, *Das Staatsdenken,* 162. Growth of modern civil service to represent the interests of the state rather than a single class: Wunder, *Privilegierung und Disziplinierung,* 13.

pay. To prevent this, the Prussian government must integrate scientifically, academically and technically trained persons from private life into its departments and boards. Men active in the commercial world as well as scholars and artists must contribute to administrative decisions. It is imperative to grant "the nation . . . the Estates . . . and their representatives an appropriate participation in and influence upon administration."[10]

The goal, then, was the establishment of a truly professional bureaucracy, but one whose work and spirit was shaped by the people whom it served. How was this to become a reality? The answer to this question lies in the actual reform plans of the 1808 ministry. A striking aspect of the envisioned bureaucracy, as one views it from the top down, is that "private" influence would be incorporated in accord with a hierarchical conception of society.

Six weeks after assuming office, Stein endorsed an extensive proposal (150 pages in print plus appendices and accompanying letters) drafted by Altenstein and entitled "Plan for a New Organization of Administration in the Prussian State." It outlined a future shape for the top bureaucracy consisting of four ministers: Finance and Interior, Foreign Affairs, War and Justice. As their titles implied, each was responsible for a particular administrative specialization, replacing the overlapping provincial and technical responsibilities of Prussia's old General Directory. The Stein ministry, as well as outside critics, debated, criticized, revised and battled over the various parts of this plan for the following year. The memoranda and correspondence concerning it alone would fill volumes. Besides the arguments over organizational matters, such as the division of responsibilities between ministries and the subdepartments of each ministry, there were disagreements of deeper significance. Klewitz and Schön were concerned that the plan did not insure a proper degree of popular contribution to the administration.[11] Hardenberg and Beyme feared the top decision-making group was too large; it should be narrowed to only a few ministers.[12] Stein and others disagreed.[13] Beyme criticized the proposal for not taking into consideration the views of the dismissed minister Voss, "one of the first statesmen with a practical education in the old regime who declared the old structure untenable and proposed a total restructuring."[14] Commentators from the military complained about the plan's subordination of the minister of war to a predominantly civilian cabinet.[15] As the debate widened,

---

[10] Stein, Immediatbericht, Memel, 23 Nov. 1807, Scheel, *Reformministerium* 1: 94–99 (no. 44). See also Ernst Walter Zeeden, *Hardenberg und der Gedanke einer Volksvertretung in Preussen 1807–1812*, Historische Studien, 365 (Berlin, 1940; Vaduz, 1965): 23–27.

[11] Klewitz, Gutachten über Steins Organisationsplan, Memel, 14 Dec. 1807, Scheel, *Reformministerium* 1: 222–31 (no. 68); Schön, Schluss eines Gutachtens über die Zentralverwaltung, ibid., 1: 342–45 (no. 104).

[12] Beyme, Gutachten zum Organisationsplan, ibid., 1: 194–99 (no. 59); Hardenberg, Gutachten zum Organisationsplan, ibid., 1: 213–21 (no. 66).

[13] Stein, Immediatbericht, Memel, 9 Jan. 1808, ibid., 1: 290–92 (no. 88); Zusammenstellung der Bemerkungen über den Organisationsplan, ibid., 1: 292–304 (no. 89).

[14] Beyme, Gutachten zum Organisationsplan, ibid., 1: 194–99 (no. 59).

[15] Lottum, Gutachten zum Organisationsplan, ibid., 1: 238–42 (no. 72).

several participants developed and refined the idea of separating legislative from administrative functions in government.[16]

On the very day of Stein's enforced abdication of office, 24 November 1808, he was able to lay before the king a revision of the administrative reorganization plan.[17] It represents the final consensus of those closest to the reform leader in the 1808 ministry. Its basic feature was a Council of State (Staatsrat) which would include not only ministers, but also royal princes, as well as the privy councilors and other high officials who served as heads of the several sections of each ministry. The king would be presiding officer "when he could be present." The Council was to have been organized according to a collegiate principle. This meant that while each member functioned within a prescribed area of expertise, the council would arrive at uniform decisions, resolving differences by debate and vote. The entire Council would accept responsibility as a body for its decisions and policies. The collegiate form of organization had long been the key to the reform party's plans for reform of Prussia's top administration. Unity was essential: "If administrators work independently," Schön had written several months before the formation of the Stein ministry, "they work according to their own views." If they do not function as an integral part of a council, they lack insight into overall policy, resulting in one-sided decisions. "We should surround his highness with . . . a [council of ministers] . . . which acts in the place of the ruler in small matters and is his closest advisor in important ones."[18] Besides unity in decisions, the other critical feature of the plan was the rational distribution of responsibility. The new cabinet would consist of five ministries: Domestic Affairs, Finance, Foreign Affairs, War, and Justice. Each would be divided into sections, divisions and subdivisions, every subunit handling minutely prescribed responsibilities and prerogatives.

Because the plan was not enacted in its originally intended form, its significance lies not in what it did for Prussia as much as in its revelation of the reformers' objectives. The Staatsrat embodies important principles upon which the Stein government insisted. The most important of these was government by professionals. In this regard it is significant that the section chiefs and privy councilors in the Council outnumbered the ministers themselves. The former were civil servants protected by the status of permanent tenure, the core of a professional bureaucracy, and they could theoretically outweigh the politically appointed administrators of ministerial rank. The king's presiding role in the Council brought him into the bureaucratic decision-making process rather than pitting him against it. It is

---

[16] Vincke, Denkschrift, mit Marginalien Steins und Redens, Berlin, 24 March 1808, ibid., 2: 430–52 (no. 136).

[17] Verordnung, die veränderte Verfassung der obersten Verwaltungsbehörden in der preussischen Monarchie betreffend, Königsberg, 24 Nov. 1808, ibid., 3: 1088–134 (no. 328).

[18] Schön to Altenstein, Königsberg, 14 March 1807, Winter, *Reorganisation*, 144–45 (no. 107).

to be assumed that he would not have been present at most of the meetings, held as often as three times a week, and his "representative," predictably the minister of interior, would have presided in his place.[19]

Development of reform plans for administration on the provincial level followed a similar pattern to that of the national: proposal after proposal, critique after critique, and revision after revision. The document which can be regarded as the Stein ministry's final conceptualization (though typically, it was altered after Stein's fall) is a draft prepared by Schroetter's East Prussian ministry with significant input from Friese and Wilckens. The "Regulations Concerning Improved Organization of the Provinicial Administrative and Financial Offices in East Prussia, Lithuania, and West Prussia" was intended as a model for other provinces as soon as they were freed from French occupation.[20] The reform aimed at streamlining provincial government. It would replace the old-regime "War and Domain Chambers" with bodies of simpler names and less complicated functions: "governments" (*Regierungen*). The executive professional personnel of each provincial office would consist of one director (*Präsident*) and several government councilors (*Regierungsräte,* in place of the old *Kriegs- und Domänenräte*), each to work in one of several outlined departments: General Welfare and Administration (*Polizei*), Finance, Education and Cultural Affairs, and Military Affairs. This all amounted to a rationalization of administrative function and establishment of professional civil service categories at the provincial level.

More noteworthy about the "Regulation" is its provision for eight "Estates representatives" (*ständische Repräsentanten*) in each provincial government. If not at the very top level of state administration, then at least at the provincial level, the reformers were serious about amalgamation of "nation and administration." Provincial assemblies[21] would name two candidates for each post, one of whom would be selected by the king. These representatives, the reformers reasoned, would "bring more life to the affairs of the provinces and . . . , by virtue of their expertise and knowledge of local people and conditions, rectify the defects which they find in public administration." They were to have full voting rights in the plenary meetings, were to sit at the president's left across from the government councilors, and were from time to time to take on certain tasks and "be re-

---

[19] Verordnung, Königsberg, 24 Nov. 1808, Scheel, *Reformministerium* 3: 1088–134 (no. 328); Otto Hintze, "Das preussische Staatsministerium im 19. Jahrhundert," in *Gesammelte Abhandlungen zur Staats-, Rechts- und Sozialgeschichte Preussens* 3: Regierung und Verwaltung, ed. Gerhard Oestreich (Göttingen, 1967): 544–51; Willerd R. Fann, "The Rise of the Prussian Ministry, 1806–1827," in Wehler, *Sozialgeschichte heute,* 119–22.

[20] Herbert Obenaus, "Verwaltung und ständische Repräsentation in den Reformen des Freiherrn vom Stein," *Jahrbuch für die Geschichte Mittel- und Ostdeutschlands* 18 (1969): 146; Reglement wegen verbesserter Organisation der Provinzial-, Polizei- und Finanzbehörden in Ostpreussen, Litauen, und Westpreussen, [Königsberg, 27 Sept. 1808], Scheel, *Reformministerium* 3: 873–81 (no. 265).

[21] Still in the planning stage. See Chapter 5.

sponsible for carrying them out properly just like every other servant of the state."[22]

A strongly debated issue in the conceptualization of the Estates representatives was that of compensation. Early in the discussion Auerswald argued that it was inappropriate to ask Prussia's property owners and businessmen to donate their services without pay. Schroetter agreed. Others in the discussion doubted whether enough men willing to make the necessary sacrifice could be found. Stein and Altenstein emphasized that good government was built upon willingness to share one's expertise and feared that the representatives would seek office for the sake of pay rather than for the contribution they could make, if the positions were salaried. Altenstein proposed granting the representative "honors" rather than money. Stein put forward a compromise: the Estates themselves could compensate their representatives rather than letting them be paid out of the treasury of the central government.[23]

The issue remained unresolved, for the "Regulations" do not mention compensation. The discussion, however, illustrates a dilemma the Prussian reformers created for themselves with their goal of amalgamating illustrious nonprofessionals into the administration. It is comparable to the nearly contemporary debates in France, England and North America: Should the people's representatives in parliaments and other assemblies donate their time or be remunerated for it? But there is a unique feature to the Prussian situation, for here the representatives under discussion were to become, in effect, part of the bureaucracy, rather than members of a separate legislative branch of government.

With regard to administration in Prussia's counties and villages, the reformers agreed that local inhabitants should be granted "greater participation in public affairs."[24] All reform proposals assumed the continued or revived existence of popular county assemblies[25] which would work side-by-side with—and in some cases intertwined with—royal administrators. The reformers were also unified in the conviction that the power of "police" (Polizei) in the local communities belonged to the central administration. The Stein government worked with an eighteenth-century conception of the police. The notion embraced almost any governmental function pertaining not only to security and safety, but also to the public welfare of inhabitants. Functions of the police included supervision of commerce, markets, education, religious institutions, charity systems, public health, road and bridge maintenance and transfer of public property.[26] It was under

---

[22] Reglement, see note 20.

[23] Obenaus, "Verwaltung und ständische Repräsentation," 147–48; Auerswald, Bemerkungen . . . zu dem Aufsatz über die zweckmässige Bildung der . . . Behörden, [28 Jan. 1808], Scheel, *Reformministerium* 1: 347–56 (no. 107); Vincke, Denkschrift mit Marginalien Steins und Redens, Berlin, 24 March 1808, ibid., 2: 449–50 (no. 136); Altenstein, Bemerkungen zu dem Gutachten Vinckes, [Königsberg, after 24 March 1808], ibid., 2: 467 (no. 137).

[24] Schroetter to Stein, Königsberg, 13 Oct. 1808, ibid., 3: 906–14 (no. 278).

[25] See Chapter 5.

[26] Franz-Ludwig Knemeyer, "Polizei," in Brunner, *Geschichtliche Grundbegriffe* 4: 875–97; Ritter, *Stein*, 259, 261, n. 30.

the concept of police authority that the reformers developed their plans for what they hoped would become a new, effective bureaucracy in the rural landscape.

Members of the Stein government disagreed about the specific form the new local bureaucratic institutions should take. The three primary discussants of this issue were Schön, Schroetter, and Ludwig von Vincke (1774–1844). The latter was one of those who contributed to the reforms in response to specific requests from Stein rather than because he was a member of one of the committees responsible for developing reform measures. A former administrator from Prussia's western province of Westphalia (which by April 1807 was no longer a Hohenzollern jurisdiction due to Napoleon's rearrangement of Central Europe), Vincke was an outspoken admirer of British institutions. He had close ties with Schön, with whom he had frequently corresponded since their student days. He had worked closely with Stein in Westphalia and was known for his social and economic reform initiatives on the provincial level. He had succeeded Stein as chief administrator of the Rhine province when the latter had moved into the central administration. In 1807 Stein brought Vincke into his government for a series of ad hoc responsibilities, but primarily to carry out diplomatic assignments. Constantly traveling, he did not work on a day-to-day basis with the reformers in Memel and Königsberg. However, between trips and during his travels, he composed at least four major documents contributing to the discussion of governmental reform. Vincke envisioned that the reforms he and his colleagues were undertaking would have the effect of "awakening and stimulating the most intelligent inhabitants to [assume] management of their own local affairs."[27]

Central to Vincke's scheme of county administration was the office of county councilor (*Landrat*) which would be responsible for exercising police power in rural localities. Vincke thought it appropriate to use the "old, respected and familiar title, [Landrat]" but to transform the office, eliminating its character as a stronghold of the nobility. His model for reform was the justice of peace, local officer of the crown in the British administrative system. In reformed Prussia, Vincke planned, county councilors would be responsible for peace and order, including protection of life and property. As well, they would supervise guild activities, the practice of medicine, public ceremonies, and charitable institutions. They would maintain public facilities like roads, bridges, street lamps, wells, springs, rivers and ditches. The Landräte were to work as members of commissions in each *Kreis* (county), not as individuals bound to specific villages. They would meet every three months like the quarter sessions in England. A county of 40,000 inhabitants would have 15 county councilors, appointed

[27] W. Schulze-Marmeling, *Schön und Vincke,* 22 and passim; [Heinrich] Kochendörffer, *Vincke* (Soest in Westfalen, 1932–33) 1: 70; Dieter Menne, *Die Mitarbeit des Freiherrn von Vincke an den preussischen Reformbestrebungen 1806 bis 1809* (Staatsexamenarbeit, Bochum, 1967) passim; Vincke, Über die Organisation der Unterbehörden, 4: Für die Kommunalverwaltung, Berlin, 13 July 1808, Nachlass Vincke, A V, 29, Staatsarchiv Münster.

by the crown. Unlike their old-regime predecessors, Landräte would not come exclusively from the aristocracy. Criteria for office would be property ownership:

In the selection, neither the caste of birth, nor social status, nor religion, but rather a certain degree of wealth, would be taken into consideration. Real estate above all else would receive emphasis. For example, whoever has a yearly income after liabilities and debts of 400 thaler from real estate, of 800 thaler from capital investment, personal income or mercantile trade, or a fourteen-year tenancy worth between 3[000] and 4,000 thaler [would be eligible]. Practicing lawyers as well as judicial and financial administrators would be ineligible.[28]

Village administrators, *Shulzen,* patterned after the constables in England, were to support the work of the Landräte in the communities. These, too, were to be drawn from the propertied inhabitants: "No one should be appointed who does not possess property of at least sixty *Morgen* [sixteen ha. or forty acres] or a private house in the cities."[29]

Schroetter's office presented an alternative plan five weeks before Stein was to leave office. Drafted by Wilckens, this proposal advocated the division of the three provinces of East Prussia, Lithuania, and West Prussia into thirty-nine counties (Kreise) and each county into an average of five administrative districts. Each county would be administered by a board consisting of one Landrat, a deputy from each district, and several minor officials. "The new county administrative boards are at the same time officers of the central government and heads of local communal affairs." Authority of the county boards would apply equally to "all properties and persons of every Kreis, regardless of whether they belonged to royal farms, aristocratic estates, or lands under the jurisdiction of the cities or counties. Key to Schroetter's proposal was the fact that the Landräte and deputies were subject to control by county assemblies (*Kreistage*). They would be elected or named by the assemblies, subject to ratification by the king and the top administration. Eligibility for office was property, with standards similar to those Vincke outlined. "The Kreistag is the controlling body of the county board, the county councilor, and the individual county deputies in all affairs affecting the county."[30]

---

[28] For this and the following paragraph: Vincke, Über die Organisation der Unterbehörden zunächst für die Polizeiverwaltung, Berlin, 4 June 1808, Scheel, *Reformministerium* 2: 588–97 (no. 179). On justices of the peace in England, see Sidney and Beatrice Webb, *English Local Government* (Hamden, Conn., 1963, reprint of 1906 ed.) 1: 319–87 and George Burton Adams, *Constitutional History of England* (London, 1965, first ed., 1921), 260–61. See Vincke's manuscript describing the British governmental system, written during the reform year for the purpose of depicting models for the Prussian reformers, later published by Niebuhr; L. von Vincke, *Darstellung der inneren Verwaltung Grossbritanniens,* ed. B. G. Niebuhr (Berlin, 1815).

[29] Vincke, Polizeiverwaltung, 4 June 1808, Scheel, *Reformministerium* 2: 594 (no. 179). In calculating the size of these plots I assume Vincke refers to Magdeburg Morgen, as in his memorandum of 14 June 1808, ibid., 2: 612. See Friedrich-Wilhelm Henning, *Bauernwirtschaft und Bauerneinkommen in Ostpreussen im 18. Jahrhundert,* Beihefte zum Jahrbuch der Albertus-Universität Königsberg/Pr. 30 (Würzburg, 1969): appendix, 236.

[30] Schroetter, Plan zur Einrichtung der Kreisverwaltungsbehörden in Preussen, [13 Oct. 1808], Scheel, *Reformministerium* 3: 914–33 (no. 279).

Within a month, just days before Stein's departure, Schön countered Schroetter's proposal with an alternative of his own. His planned county administrative office (Kreispolizeibehörde) was complex in its composition. It was to consist of one Landrat, appointed by the king, a justice of the peace and a police inspector, each appointed by the provincial executive, and several other members named by the Landrat and the justice of the peace. The justice's appointees were to be recommended by the county inhabitants. This complicated arrangement was Schön's attempt to integrate all levels of administration from the monarch to the local inhabitant. It can be compared with the British petty, special and quarter sessions court which displayed an independent community spirit in spite of its several royal appointees. However, affairs which were strictly local in nature belonged to the local county inhabitants and were to be taken care of by the county assemblies.[31]

These three proposals, all of which were still under consideration for revision when the Stein government fell, are similar in several important respects. But their authors saw in them crucial differences. The major disagreement was over the ultimate location of authority in local government. While all three reformers envisioned a sharing of responsibilities between administrators and popular assemblies, Schroetter's conceptualization represented those who would like to have subordinated royal bureaucrats to local control. Schön, on the other hand, sought to distinguish clearly between community matters, belonging to jurisdiction of the deputies, and the Polizei which, he argued, should be independent of local supervision. He made a clearer distinction than Schroetter did between administrators and deputies. Schroetter's plan, in fact, was in many ways inconsistent with the trend of developing a professional bureaucracy. Schroetter still thought in terms of Estates, and his emphasis on community control would have perpetuated predominance of noble landowners in local government.

Vincke's plan stands between those of the two East Prussian reformers. He separated the spheres of community and central government responsibility more clearly than Schroetter. But whereas Schön's county councilor was strictly an official of the king, Vincke saw this officer as a paternalistic figure in the local community. Vincke himself had been a Landrat in Minden between 1799 and 1803. Possibly out of this experience grew his idealized notion of the county councilor, a spokesperson for local inhabitants who at the same time mediated between community needs and those of the crown.[32]

Whereas all three reformers were concerned that the county councilor position not be a sinecure of the local aristocracy, Schroetter and Vincke

[31] Schön, Votum zum Schreiben Schroetters vom 13. Okt. 1808, Königsberg, 14 Nov. 1808, ibid., 3: 1016–21 (no. 309). See S. and B. Webb, *English Local Government* 1: 279–313.

[32] Georg Christoph von Unruh, *Der Landrat: Mittler zwischen Staatsverwaltung und kommunaler Selbstverwaltung* (Köln and Berlin, 1966), 34–37.

tied the office to local property ownership, while Schön did not. Schön was thinking more in terms of professional bureaucracy.[33]

The proposals of Schroetter, Vincke and Schön, perhaps more than any others of 1808, illustrate the reformers' confusion over the two goals of placing governmental administration in the hands of a professional bureaucracy and simultaneously involving local citizenry in public affairs. The one feature they all had in common was their expressed commitment to terminating the direct political function of land proprietorship, Gutsherrschaft. No longer would local rural Prussians, because of their place of birth and residence, regard their landlords as their "government."[34] Varying in degree, the three plans aimed at eliminating Junkers' control of community affairs. Ironically, however, they all would have given the old aristocratic families a means of perpetuating their supremacy in local politics. This reform of the Stein government, if it had reached the status of promulgation, would have altered the manner in which estate owners dominated the countryside, but it would not have effected an eclipse of their authority.

A modern form of municipal government was of highest priority to the reformers. From the outset, Stein argued that the office of tax councilor (Steuerrat) had robbed the merchants and artisans of the right to control their own affairs. The reform administration worked with incredible energy to effect a reorganization of the city and town government. They produced the famous Cities Ordinance (*Städteordnung*)[35] of 19 November 1808, which became the basis of city government in Prussia throughout the nineteenth century. The measure represents an effort to place municipal affairs in the hands of indigenous leaders. In terms of the state bureaucracy, however, the reformers operated from their conviction that police authority belonged to the central administration alone. Johann Gottfried Frey, the principal author of the municipal ordinance, argued the point unequivocally: "The exercise of police authority cannot be . . . a special power of the communes, but rather can only be administered in the name of the ruler . . . because it is a facet of the supreme governmental dominion and cannot be alienated." Schroetter, who more than other reformers thought in terms of traditional corporate society, opposed this position, arguing for the cities' autonomy. Schön and Stein advocated a compromise, maintaining that municipalities should have the integrity of independence but should be under supervision of a police director who assures "that nothing be undertaken which opposes the purposes of the central government." So the bureau of police director, later renamed police president, an organ of the crown, became a part of every city's power structure.[36]

---

[33] Schön, Votum zum Schreiben Schroetters, Königsberg, 14 Nov. 1808, Scheel, *Reformministerium* 3: 1018 (no. 309).

[34] Stein to Sulzowsky (drafted by Schön), Memel, 29 Dec. 1807, ibid., 1: 276 (no. 80).

[35] See Chapter 5.

[36] Schroetter to Frey, 3 Aug. 1808, Scheel, *Reformministerium,* 3: 703–704 (no. 224); Frey [to Schroetter], Königsberg, 29 Aug. 1808, ibid., 3: 801 (no. 248); Protokoll der Generalkon-

What this reform accomplished was a separation of local initiative in cities from that of the central government. While the municipal ordinance abolished the old-regime office of tax councilor, it did not diminish the power of the crown within the city walls. The central government was now represented by the director of police. The new system was more streamlined than the old. The pre-reform police directors in cities had been frequently the same person as the mayors-in-chief, theoretically representing the crown and the local inhabitants at the same time.[37] Subsequent to the reform, the royal administrators were strictly professionals, owing no allegiance to the towns or their power groups.

Under the reformers' plans, the new bureaucracy would be a major factor in overcoming the ill effects of absolutism and the oppressive dominance of semi-feudal aristocracy. As for the civil servants themselves, Stein and his colleagues pictured predominantly educated professionals. Where the reform goal of amalgamating the administration with representatives of popular goverment found its way into concrete proposals, property and wealth were the criteria, not hereditary status. The 1808 reform blueprints are the best possible indication of what Stein's government would have effected, had it had the time to carry out its plans. They clearly point to the conclusion that Prussia would have gained on every level, from the ministry to the local village, a more professional bureaucracy than it had had under absolutism. Its form and the social origins of its members would have differed somewhat from that of the old regime. Whether it would have been less oppressive or more in touch with the interests of the populace can only remain a matter of conjecture.

THE PRECEDENTS OF 1808: POWERFUL BUREAUCRACY IN ALLIANCE WITH ARISTOCRACY

Everything about the way in which the Stein ministry functioned was temporary in the minds of its members. It was a hastily thrown-together system. Its organization and way of conducting business were perceived to be mere expedients, pending the finalization of the real reforms. But how much were the ad hoc arrangements of 1808 on the way to becoming permanent patterns in Prussia? Were the practices of Stein and his coworkers setting precedents that were liable to become the real reforms themselves, in spite of the reformers' commitments to long-range visions?

The Stein government placed a high priority on the establishment of a rationally organized ministry based on the collegiate principle. But anxious

---

ferenz, Königsberg, 19 Oct. 1808, ibid., 3: 934–39 (no. 281); Ordnung für sämtliche Städte der preussischen Monarchie, Königsberg, 19 Nov. 1808, Botzenhart, *Stein Briefe* 2/2: 986 (no. 902); Ritter, *Stein,* 259–62, 591, n. 30; Gause, *Geschichte der Stadt Königsberg* 2: 339; Harald Schinkel, "Polizei und Stadtverfassung im frühen 19. Jahrhundert: Eine historisch-kritische Interpretation der preussischen Städteordnung von 1808," *Der Staat: Zeitschrift für Staatslehre, öffentliches Recht und Verfassungsgeschichte* 3 (1964): 316–34.

[37] Gause, *Geschichte der Stadt Königsberg* 2: 76.

to undertake their work, and needing to debate and refine their ideas on the shape of the state's future ministerial bureaucracy, the members of the Stein party accepted roles in bits and pieces of hastily devised committees. In effect, between October 1807 and November 1808, the Prussian government had the shape of a prime ministerial system with a loosely organized staff of assistants, though there is no document naming Stein as the executive minister. The final ministerial reorganization program of the Stein government, dated 24 November 1808, similarly did not emphasize the role of a prime minister. The position which existed in practice was nowhere explicitly spelled out in the documents, for the reformers were not sure that what they insisted upon for the sake of smooth political administration corresponded with thier ideal objectives. The Prussian experience of the following four decades was a perpetuation of the pattern of wavering between a collegiate system and one dominated by a single, powerful executive minister. Neither tradition became firmly established, for solutions varied according to circumstances and personalities.[38] Stein's reform government laid the foundation for a powerful ministry which would dominate the affairs of state. It also established a pattern of ad hoc arrangements, arrived at through compromise and political struggle, which would be a lasting characteristic of Prussian government.

Another, perhaps more significant precedent established by the high bureaucracy of 1808 was the role it assumed as the initiator of legislation. This, too, was perceived as a temporary strategy. Having wrested the prerogative from the king, the bureaucrats would write new laws and edicts until they could turn the power of legislation over to the people in popular assemblies.[39] The Immediate Commission expressly petitioned that it be allowed to assume this legislative function as Stein assumed office. Stein preferred to spread the authority out, but he kept it within the confines of a small group of hand-picked professional bureaucrats.[40] As we have already seen, the Stein ministry devoted the bulk of its considerable energy to writing, debating, revising, and promulgating new laws and edicts. This pattern is important because, for much of the nineteenth century, the ministerial bureaucracy retained this function. In some other states developing along similar lines, bureaucrats shared this prerogative more fully with the rising commercial middle class, usually expressing itself through parliamentary assemblies.[41] The growing strength of bureaucracy itself was not unique in Prussia, but its role in initiating legislation was characteristic.

---

[38] Fann, "Rise of the Prussian Ministry," 119–22.

[39] Actual reform proposals for popular assemblies are discussed in Chapter 5.

[40] Immediate Commission to Stein, Memel, 12 Oct. 1807, Scheel, *Reformministerium* 1: 19–23 (no. 9).

[41] Barbara Vogel, "Die 'allgemeine Gewerbefreiheit' als bürokratische Modernisierungsstrategie in Preussen: Eine Problemskizze zur Reformpolitik Hardenbergs," in Dirk Stegmann et al., eds., *Industrielle Gesellschaft und politisches System: Beiträge zur politischen Sozialgeschichte. Festschrift für Fritz Fisher*, Schriftenreihe des Forschungsinstituts der Friedrich-Ebert-Stiftung 137 (Bonn, 1978): 70.

This can be attributed to the historical circumstances in which the reformers functioned. As professionals, they received their mandate to write a new constitution, in the broad sense of the word, when the old one crumbled. There were neither mobs in the streets nor revolutionary assemblies to give the bureaucrats authority or to check their powers. When Stein and his associates were forced out of office in an untimely manner, they passed on the prerogative of legislative initiative to their successors. Whether the leaders of 1808 would have given up this right as they planned to do can never be known. What is documented is that they were the first in a long line of top-level administrators to exercise the privilege of functioning as the promulgators of legislation in Prussia.

Having wrested the power of initiative from the monarch in governmental affairs, how would the new bureaucracy relate to the other powerful element in society, the semi-feudal aristocracy? If one can believe their rhetoric, the reformers were intent on creating a new society in which heredity was not the basis of status. As Stein declared to an inquiring estate owner in the early months of the ministry:

> [In our] age the [dominance] of a few [aristocrats] is no longer appropriate. The people who comprise the state have progressed to the point where they can represent themselves individually. . . . They neither need nor desire paternalistic leadership. . . . The position of the aristocracy must be fixed so that . . . all classes can contribute harmoniously [to the state and society].[42]

Theodor von Schön was even more explicit. He hoped to see the aristocratic class ultimately fade away as a social and political entity. "The nobility as it exists must decline. . . . If it is tied to other classes, it will unconsciously, gradually dissolve and disappear."[43]

Would the bureaucrats then ignore the provincial nobility? Would they take measures to destroy it? Or would they regard it as a political force to be reckoned with? Might they even look to noble Estates as political allies? Answers to these questions can be sought in the events growing out of the financial crisis of the Napoleonic war. Exiled and bankrupt after the disasters of 1806–1807, the Prussian government faced demands for enormous reparations in addition to the cost of restoring the devastated cities and countryside. Final reparations figures were not established until late in the year 1808, but the Prussian leaders knew from the beginning that the sum would be crippling. The final figure of 120 million francs equalled approximately the entire 1806 annual budget of Prussia. The Stein government was certain that if massive sources of new revenue were not found, the very existence of the state was in jeopardy. The need for unprecedented taxation is a classic test of the relationship between kings of the early modern era and their noble Estates. The central function of the Estates

[42] Stein to Sulzowsky, Memel, 29 Dec. 1807, Scheel, *Reformministerium* 1: 278 (no. 80).

[43] Schön, Gutachten, [1808], in G. H. Pertz, *Das Leben des Feldmarschalls Grafen Neithart von Gneisenau* (Berlin, 1864–1880) 1: 412–15.

after the Middle Ages had been that of granting taxes and enabling monarchs to survive crises.[44] Prussia was no exception. Like governments before them, Stein and his colleagues, in need of revenue, turned to the proud, independent noblemen of East Prussia, the only province with whose institutions they could work, following the Peace of Tilsit.

However, the traditional Estates assembly was a dormant institution in East Prussia. Since 1740 only two *Landtage* had convened, and they were called for the limited purpose of expressing homage to the newly crowned kings in 1786 and 1798. Prior to each, it had been necessary to determine anew the composition and means of convening the assembly.[45]

Instead of repeating this practice in 1808, or of attempting to establish a new assembly based on their conception of modern representation, the reformers chose to adapt an existing institution, the East Prussian Aristocractic Credit Association, the Landschaft, to meet the demands of the moment. In the provincial economic crisis, the credit association appealed to the king on 29 August 1807, for permission to hold a general assembly of its organization to consider an emergency source of revenue for meeting their own obligations. To the surprise of the credit association, the government in granting the request stipulated that the organization was to constitute itself as an East Prussian Estates assembly. The delegates were to include on their agenda "not only matters concerning the credit system, but also those of the province in general."[46]

Since its founding, the Landschaft had not only fulfilled its function of channeling investment into aristocratic agriculture, it had also served as the political voice of the provincial aristocracy. Contemporaries employed the two terms, "Landschaft" and "Estates" interchangeably.[47] So when the Immediate Commission, pending Stein's arrival, recognized the credit

---

[44] On the amount of the reparations: Koselleck, *Preussen*, 167. On the role of Estates: A. R. Myers, *Parliaments and Estates in Europe to 1789* (London, 1975), 29–33 and passim. Estates elsewhere in Germany: Benecke, *Society and Politics*, 181–225.

[45] Johannes Voigt, *Darstellung der ständischen Verhältnisse Ost-Preussens vorzüglich der neuesten Zeit* (Königsberg, 1822), 26–31, 65–71; [Georg] Bujack, *Das erste Triennium des Comités der ostpreussischen und littauischen Stände* (Königsberg, 1887), 7–8; Manfred Botzenhart, "Verfassungsproblematik und in Peter Baumgart, ed., *Ständepolitik in der preussischen Reformzeit," Ständetum und Staatsbildung in Brandenburg-Preussen: Ergebnisse einer internationalen Fachtagung*, Veröffentlichungen der Historischen Kommission zu Berlin 55: Forschungen zur preussischen Geschichte (Berlin and New York, 1983), 435–36.

[46] Ostpreussische Generallandschaftsdirektion, Immediatbericht, Königsberg, 29 Aug. 1807 (copy), Rep. 2, Tit. 23, no. 1, Vol. 1, fols. 7–8, StA Königsberg; Kabinettsordre to Generallandschaftsdirektion, Memel, 10 Sept. 1807 (copy), ibid., fol. 3.

[47] Mauer, *Das Landschaftliche Kreditwesen Preussens*, 9–11; Brünneck, *Die Pfandbriefsysteme*, 37; Rosenberg, *Bureaucracy, Aristocracy, and Autocracy*, 169–70; Büsch, *Militärsystem und Sozialleben*, 107–108, 141–42, 147–48; Botzenhart, "Verfassungsproblematik," 436–37. A contemporary source indicates that other provinces had "Estate constitutions," through which institutions practically identical with the credit associations were empowered to speak for the Estates on matters other than credit and mortgages. There is no mention of such an institution in East Prussia. Leonhardi, *Erdbeschreibung* 1: 349, 360–62. In other parts of Germany the term "Landschaft" was used to mean "Estates": Benecke, *Society and Politics*, 110–15.

organization as the political organ of East Prussian noblemen, they were confirming an eighteenth-century practice. The plans for an assembly were underway when Stein arrived, and he furthered them.

Yet the reformers did not plan to allow the provincial leaders to hold their assembly without some significant alterations in its composition and purpose. First, they insisted that representatives of the Kölmer, East Prussia's prosperous, non-aristocratic estate owners, be seated as members of the organization. Secondly, Stein informed the Credit Association directors that "His Majesty the king has decided to enter the Aristocratic Credit System [as a proprietor of] the royal farms (domains) of East Prussia and Lithuania." And finally, the government appointed a member of its own party, Hans von Auerswald, as presiding officer of the forthcoming assembly. The first two measures, both expressly forbidden by the Landschaft charter, were prompted in part by economic reasons. The Kölmer would play a vital role in the provincial agricultural economy and would add to the tax base. As for the domains, the government planned to issue semi-negotiable mortgage bonds on the extensive crown lands. Membership in the credit association was designed to guarantee a firm security for the mortgages. But the political implications were ominous. By making the king a member, by dictating membership criteria, and by handpicking the presiding officer, the government would undermine the independence of the assembly. The Landschaft would become a tool of central governmental power.[48]

The Credit Organization Directory protested vigorously. They objected specifically to the appointment of Auerswald, proposing instead Karl von Schroetter, brother of the minister and a person they considered more friendly to their own perspectives. They opposed the inclusion of the Kölmer, regarding it as an insult to noble tradition. They rejected the plan of including royal domains in their organization, suggesting as an alternative, a separate association for crown lands. Finally, the estates owners' organization contested the government's proposal of convening the credit association as a provincial assembly. The association's officers argued that

[48] Kabinettsordre to Generallandschaftsdirektion, Memel, 10 Sept. 1807 (copy), Rep. 2, Tit. 23, no. 1, Vol. 1, fol. 3, StA Königsberg; Kabinettsordre to Auerswald, Memel, 10 Sept. 1807, ibid., fol. 1; Stein to Generallandschaftsdirektion, Memel, 21 Dec. 1807; Botzenhart, *Stein Briefe* 2/2. 581 (no. 506). Similar letters were sent to other provinces: Stein to Massow, Memel, 21 Dec. 1807, Scheel *Reformministerium* 1: 242 (no. 73); Ritter, *Stein*, 276. See also: Auerswald to the Immediate Commission, Königsberg, 29 Sept. 1807, "Preussische Finanzpolitik von 1806–1815," Nachlass Eckart Kehr, Bundesarchiv, Koblenz, Kl. Erw. 508, fols. 39–40 (no. 21); Ost-Preussisches confirmirtes Landschafts-Reglement, Berlin, 16 Feb. 1788, Part 1, chapt. 2., § 1, 9, *Novum corpus constitutionum prussico-brandenburgensium praecipue marchicarum* (Berlin, 1791) 8: 1791–94. On the privileged position Stein envisioned for the king in the association: [Staegemann], Plan zur Credit-Assoziation der königlichen Domainen mit dem ritterschaftlichen Credit-System [n.d.], Rep. 2, Tit. 23, no. 1, Vol. 1, fols. 65–66, StA Königsberg. See Marion W. Gray, "Der ostpreussische Landtag des Jahres 1808 und das Reformministerium Stein: Eine Fallstudie politischer Modernisation," *Jahrbuch für die Geschichte Mittel- und Ostdeutschlands* 26 (1977): 129–45.

the forthcoming meeting should be limited to "deliberation and decision of matters which relate to land evaluations and [matters authorized by] our charter."[49]

One might expect that the credit organization, which had in the past spoken for the Estates on a variety of issues, would have welcomed an official recognition of its expanded role. By insisting on remaining narrowly within the limits of its charter in 1807, the officers were resisting what the members must have viewed as unwarranted meddling in provincial affairs on the part of the central government. It is also possible that they hoped to bring about the convocation of an authentic Estates assembly, and thus to reestablish more thoroughly the traditional political role of the Estates. In previous centuries the provincial nobility had often seized upon crises to reassert their eroded political influence.

Stein's government treated the protests lightly. In the name of King Frederick William, the government assured the credit system members that they need not worry about the crown's mixing into their affairs. However, no alteration in the previous orders would be considered. Auerswald would preside at the meeting; non-credit matters would be on the agenda; and Kölmer deputies would be invited. Auerswald dismissed the proposal for a separate royal credit association as "entirely superfluous" It was appropriate for the domain farms to be in the credit association and thus for the king to belong.[50]

The central government's bureaucratic singlemindedness is mirrored in its instructions to Auerswald on procedures for the meeting. Contrary to traditional practice in the credit association, delegates were not to vote according to mandates from their constituents. Nor were they to cast collective ballots from their respective districts. The assembly's decisions were to be based upon the votes of individual delegates who would decide their stance during the assembly's debates. The reformers insisted that this method would inspire "more versatile and freer opinions . . . and greater contemplation."[51] Stein must have known when he drafted the directive that the elective Kreis assemblies had ordered their delegates to oppose admission of the royal domains into the credit system. If the delegates were to reach their decisions on the basis of instructions given prior to the session, the government would have no leverage to influence the meeting's actions,

---

[49] Generallandschaftsdirektion, Immediatbericht, Königsberg, 14 Sept. 1807 (copy), Rep. 2, Tit. 23, no. 1, Vol. 1, fol. 4, StA Königsberg; Generallandschaftsdirektion, Einige Bemerkungen zu dem Plan zur Credit Association der Domainen, [n.d.] (copy accompanying a letter from L. v. Schroetter to Auerswald, Königsberg, 26 Dec. 1807, fol. 73), ibid., fols. 78–79.

[50] Kabinettsordre to Generallandschaftsdirektion, Memel, 17 Sept. 1807, ibid., fol. 13; Scheel, *Reformministerium* 1: 238, n. 4; Auerswald to Schroetter, Königsberg, 29 Dec. 1807 (draft), Rep. 2, Tit. 23, no. 1, Vol. 1, fol. 80, StA Königsberg Auerswald to Stein, Königsberg, 26 Dec. 1807 (draft), ibid., fols. 71–72; Immediatkommission to Auerswald, Memel, 25 Dec. 1807, ibid., fols. 81–82.

[51] Kabinettsordre to Auerswald, Königsberg, 31 Jan. 1808, Scheel, *Reformministerium* 1: 361–64 (no. 110). Compare: Botzenhart, *Stein Briefe* 2/2: 639, in which the document is abbreviated, but its origin is more explicitly described.

a situation which, from the government's point of view, could have thwarted the whole purpose of the Landtag. In the same vein, Stein issued unequivocal directions regarding Kölmer lands which the government wished to see permanently admitted to the credit association. Auerswald was to allow the noble delegates to debate this issue, but if they should prove recalcitrant, the presiding officer was to *suspend the meeting* until he received further directions.[52] The reform bureaucrats were willing to put up with the inefficiency of long-winded debates. But they were inflexible in their demands regarding the final outcome of the meeting.

Between 2 and 17 February 1808, the Landtag convened in Königsberg with a membership of twenty-four aristocratic delegates, twelve Kölmer, and the five noble directors of the credit association. Whatever original objections the Landschaft may have had to debating issues outside the competence of the credit association, the delegates of 1808 arrived well-disposed to make their business the affairs of the province in general. In addition to the agenda items of the central government, the East Prussian delegates drew up petitions on such diverse topics as a new road building ordinance, clarification of noble rights in use of forests, the rights of water mill owners to alter the flow of streams, the need for unified weights and measures, and the right to wear uniforms. Most of the topics initiated by the delegates were related to the wartime destruction of the province.[53]

From the ministry's viewpoint, Auerswald conducted the meeting skillfully. Through a combination of pressure, flattery and threats, he was able to extract the results desired by Stein. The delegates admitted the crown lands into the credit system. They seated the Kölmer deputies, and they endorsed the new tax ordinance[54] which would help solve the financial crisis. Staegemann and Stein drafted a response to Auerswald on behalf of the king, expressing his "special satisfaction [and] applause" for the conduct of the meeting.[55]

Regarding the petitions which the delegates themselves initiated, the Stein government took whatever action it deemed appropriate, usually

---

[52] Kabinettsordre to Auerswald, Königsberg, 31 Jan. 1808, Scheel, *Reformministerium* 1: 363 (no. 110). Italics added.

[53] Auerswald, Immediatbericht, Königsberg, 18 Feb. 1808, ibid., 1: 382–96 (no. 120), and in more detail: Rep. 2, Tit. 23, no. 1, Vol. 2, passim., StA Königsberg.

[54] Tax ordinance discussed in Chapter 6.

[55] Protokoll des Generallandtages, Königsberg, 4 Feb. 1808 (draft), Rep. 2, Tit. 23, no. 1, Vol. 2, fols. 51–60; Auerswald, Immediatbericht, Königsberg, 8 Feb. 1808 (draft), Rep. 2, Tit. 23, no. 1, Vol. 2, fols. 110–13; Reglement, das Kriegs-Schulden-Wesen der Provinz Ostpreussen . . . betreffend, 23 Feb. 1808, *Sammlung der für die königlichen preussischen Staaten erschienenen Gesetze und Verordnungen von 1806 bis zum 27sten Oktober 1810, als Anhang zu der seit den Jahre 1810 edierten Gesetz-Sammlung für die königlichen preussischen Staaten* (Berlin, 1822), 193–213 (no. 27). Kabinettsordre to Auerswald, Königsberg, 16 Feb. 1808, ibid., fol. 133. On the origin of this document see Botzenhart, *Stein Briefe* 2/2: 655 (no. 592); Lehmann, *Stein* 2: 209–13. The aristocratic membership of the Landschaft attempted, both during the meeting and again later in the year, to reject the Kölmer by insisting that membership required a title of nobility. They attempted also to regain the right to determine their presiding officer. See the Stein ministry's reply: Protokoll der Generalkonferenz, Königsberg, 21 Sept. 1808, "Preussische Finanzpolitik von 1806–1815," Nachlass Kehr, Bundesarchiv, Koblenz, fol. 186 (no. 113).

following the recommendations of Auerswald, but maintaining the prerogative to make final decisions in every case. For example, the Landtag appealed for the enactment of a new *Gesindeordnung*, an ordinance regulating the relationships between servile classes and their masters. Auerswald presented the assembly's draft of a new regulation, remarking, however, that the plan was "so illiberal" that it should be rejected.[56] In this manner, the presiding officer sought to "reconcile" the wishes of the assembly and those of the reform bureaucrats.

The outcome of one issue of the agenda is especially telling for the relationship of the Prussian ministerial bureaucracy and the provincial Estates. Seeking to establish a relatively permanent voice for East Prussia's aristocracy, the delegates petitioned for official recognition of an "Estates committee," which had been established at the homage Landtag of 1798. A primary function of the four-member body had been to communicate the views of the provincial nobility to the central government. Like the Landschaft, it had served to preserve the political role of the hereditary upper class in a time when traditional aristocratic institutions had deteriorated. Its membership had often overlapped with that of the credit association directory.[57]

Acting in accord with Auerswald's advice, Stein sanctioned the committee, emphasizing, however, that this narrowly constituted body should not become the sole political voice of the province. Instead, a Landtag, based upon a revised organizational plan, was to convene annually in order to "maintain public spirit, to encourage participation in the general welfare [and] to . . . present the wishes and the needs of the subjects to the monarch."[58]

It is unclear whether or not Stein envisioned that the Estates committee would continue functioning after the revised Landtag was inaugurated. Yet his recognition of the committee represents endorsement of an antiquated aristocratic institution whose very existence stood in conflict with the expressed intent of the reforms. As early as June 1807, Stein had laid plans to eliminate narrow provincial organizations like the one in question. Yet not only in East Prussia, but also in Silesia, Stein encouraged the nobility to retain its Estates committee.[59] The provincial organ was useful in the

---

[56] Auerswald, Immediatbericht, Königsberg, 18 Feb. 1808, Scheel, *Reformministerium* 1: 382–96 (no. 120).

[57] Protokoll des Generallandtages, Königsberg, 11 Feb. 1808, Rep. 2, Tit. 23, no. 1, Vol. 2, fols, 81–82, St. A. Göttingen. J. Voigt, *Darstellung der ständischen Verhältnisse*, 99. For a comparison of the roles of the Estates committee in another province, see Otto Schönbeck, "Der kurmärkische Landtag vom Frühjahr 1809," *Forschungen zur brandenburgischen und preussischen Geschichte* 20 (1907), 2–3.

[58] Auerswald, Immediatbericht, Königsberg, 18 Feb. 1808, Scheel, *Reformministerium* 1: 383–84, n. 3 (no. 120); Kabinettsordre to Auerswald, Königsberg, 27 Feb. 1808, Botzenhart, *Stein Briefe*, 2/2: 672–73 (no. 619). The complete document is located in Rep. 2, Tit. 23, no. 1, Vol. 2, fols. 140–41, StA Königsberg; Botzenhart, "Verfassungsproblematik," 438–40.

[59] Stein to Bismarck, Berlin, 19 April 1808, Scheel, *Reformministerium* 2: 510–12 (no. 154); Stein to General-Komitee der schlesischen Stände, Berlin, 23 April 1808, Botzenhart, *Stein Briefe* 2/2: 708–709 (no. 674).

negotiations concerning reparations with the French. But the government's short-term answer to an immediate problem, recognition of the Estates committees, set patterns which endured well into the *Vormärz* era. Long after Stein's departure, the government continued to communicate with provinces through the Estates committees.[60]

The Stein ministry employed the East Prussian Assembly of 1808 as a device to achieve its own ends. It used an organization designed for another purpose, the Aristocratic Credit Association, violated its traditional rights, and exacted concessions as well as financial support. This fits firmly within the tradition of bureaucratic absolutism characteristic of nineteenth-century Prussia. At the same time, however, the bureaucracy made the aristocracy its ally. Perhaps the reformers sensed the need of political support in the uncertain conditions of 1808. Or possibly they grasped at the only solution to the financial problem which they could imagine. Whatever its motivation, the Stein government effected a working relationship—albeit a sometimes tense one—with the Prussian noble leaders. The situation can be compared in some respects to that of the French monarchy in 1787, also in a state of financial crisis. The king's minister, Calonne, had the opportunity at that time of pushing the aristocracy aside, drawing on new sources of support in the Third Estate. He chose, instead, to consult with the Estates, in their traditional form, making the dominant noble class allies in the solution of the kingdom's problems, and bringing about the aristocratic phase of the French Revolution.[61] Prussian leaders of 1808, like the French of 1787, called upon the old provincial leadership for support, thus legitimizing its authority.

The uneasy bureaucratic-aristocratic alliance worked itself out in many ways. One example is to be found in the Stein ministry's approach to the problem of abolishing patrimonial courts. Under the system of "patrimonial jurisdiction" estate owners were responsible for legal matters involving inhabitants of their lands. Since the enactment of a judicial reform in 1781, they had been required to employ judges who were supervised by county judicial officers and who were theoretically guaranteed some professional immunity from arbitrary or self-serving actions of their employers. In effect, the patrimonial courts comprised the old manorial justice system in slightly revised form: landlords were the judges of their villagers. Since the eighteenth century there had been repeated attempts to revise this situation so obviously open to abuse, but to little avail. Economic reforms, such as emancipation of peasants from ties to the land, had proceeded at an uneven pace, for landlords often saw the advantage to themselves in this type of

---

[60] The archival sources show that the *ständische Comité* continued to speak for the Estates long after Stein's departure. See the numerous volumes of correspondence between the committee and the central government: Rep. 2, Tit. 23, passim, StA Königsberg. See Koselleck, *Preussen,* 183–85; Botzenhart, "Verfassungsproblematik," 440–44.

[61] Georges Lefebvre, *The Coming of the French Revolution: 1789,* tr. R. R. Palmer (Princeton, 1947), 25–27.

changed relationship. But they hung on to patrimonial jurisdiction tenaciously as a symbol of their authority in society.[62]

The reform party considered the abolition of patrimonial courts basic to their destruction of the evils of the old aristocratic institutions. In his Nassau memorandum, Stein put it simply: "In the place of patrimonial courts, which are flawed in principle and in practice, county courts will be established." It would have been logical to abolish the institution of patrimonial jurisdiction along with other feudal obligations in the Edict of 9 October 1807, but Stein saw this as a more logical part of his overall projected reform of the judiciary. So he let the peasant village courts temporarily stand. In January 1808 he directed Karl von Schroetter, a judicial expert, to devise a plan combining the numerous branches and departments of the Prussian judiciary into one single, efficient system which would include new lower courts with state, rather than aristocratic, jurisdiction. Schroetter was to work with his brother, Leopold.[63]

In August 1808, a full nine months after the peasant edict had been enacted, Stein was obliged to remind the Schroetters that nothing had been accomplished regarding reform of the rural courts. The situation was producing confusion: peasants were being released from feudal ties on estates but were still subject to landlords' courts. A few months later Schön drafted a more insistent letter. Writing for Stein, Schön expressed dissatisfaction that the brothers Schroetter had concentrated their efforts on the municipal judiciary and had ignored the patrimonial courts. "This does not correspond to my plans. Have [your associates] prepare a proposal for abolition of patrimonial jurisdiction," he ordered.[64]

By now it was appropriate to question whether the Schroetters were purposefully delaying action on this reform. Karl von Schroetter informed Stein that he deemed it advisable to have the landowners themselves determine the means for revising the judicial system, rather "than to arouse dissatisfaction" by simply decreeing reforms. "I recognize the value of the proposed [changes]. . . . But patrimonial judges will protest vigorously if we take from them a prerogative which has been previously recognized."

---

[62] Eicke, *Der ostpreussische Landtag*, 23–26; Voigt, *Darstellung der ständischen Verhältnisse*, 70.

[63] Stein, Über die zweckmässige Bildung der obersten Behörden, June, 1807, Botzenhart, *Stein Briefe* 2/1: 397 (no. 354); Schön, Gutachten, Memel, 30 Nov. 1807, Scheel, *Reformministerium*, 1: 183-84 (no. 52). On the larger question of judicial reform see Koselleck, *Preussen*, 155–58; Kabinettsordre to K. v. Schroetter, Königsberg, 21 Jan. 1808, Scheel, *Reformministerium* 1: 334–35 (no. 100). On the system of patrimonial jurisdiction see Epstein, *Genesis of German Conservatism*, 372–73; Schrimpf, *Herrschaft, Individualinteresse und Richtermacht*, 55–58, 61–62, 69–70; Koselleck, *Preussen*, 544. On the move to abolish patrimonial jurisdiction in other parts of Germany: Elisabeth Fehrenbach, *Traditionale Gesellschaft und revolutionäres Recht: Die Einführung des Code Napoléon in den Rheinbundstaaten*, Kritische Studien zur Geschichtswissenschaft 13 (Göttingen, 1978), 60–65, 135–37.

[64] Stein to K. and L. von Schroetter (based on a note from Schön to Auerswald), Königsberg, 12 Aug. 1808, Scheel, *Reformministerium* 3: 744–45 (no. 235); Stein to K. and L. von Schroetter (drafted by Schön), Königsberg, 25 Sept. 1808, ibid., 3: 864–65 (no. 262). On Schroetter's inclination to protect noble prerogatives, see Marion W. Gray, "Schroetter, Schön and Society: Aristocratic Liberalism versus Middle-Class Liberalism in Prussia, 1808," *Central European History*, 6 (1973), 77–80. See also B. Schumacher, "Karl von Schroetter," *Altpreussische Biographie*, 639.

And indeed they did protest. A committee of East Prussian noblemen formally presented their argument to the government. While they had consented to abolition of serfdom, they said, patrimonial jurisdiction was a separate issue. It was not selfish interests which induced them to oppose reform of the rural court system, for "to the estate owner, patrimonial jurisdiction is far more costly than profitable." They were concerned, rather for the welfare of their peasants who "had learned for centuries to turn to their lords in judicial affairs as well as in domestic and economic matters." They feared that if patrimonial jurisdiction were abolished, the necessity of traveling to distant courts, the cost involved, and the impersonality of state courts would prevent the rendering of true justice. "The estate owner therefore would prefer to see patrimonial jurisdiction remain, costly as it is for him, . . . rather than see his people wander about."[65]

Stein and Schön sent firm rebuttals both to the Schroetters and to the committee of estate owners.[66] Their letters had no effect. The resistance of aristocratic landowners who had the sympathetic ear of the men responsible for drawing up reforms, prevented Stein's and Schön's plans from even coming to the drawing board. Frustrated, Stein took an unprecedented step, publishing his plans for abolition of manorial courts in the newspapers. He must have hoped to create a climate of opinion favorable to the reform among the middle class. In effect he was appealing to the public over the heads of his own staff. Even more drastic was the action taken in November after Stein's dismissal had become certain. Schön, at the behest of his superior, directed officials in all chambers to distribute a pamphlet attacking patrimonial jurisdiction to both the administrators and the inhabitants of their provinces. The publication entitled "Can the Nobility Desire Abolition of Patrimonial Jurisdication?" was written by Professor J. G. Hoffmann, an active supporter of reform who assumed Kraus's chair of cameral science at Königsberg after the latter's death in 1807. These final desperate attempts to appeal for support outside the bureaucracy and aristocracy only strengthened opposition to the Stein ministry. Stein's enemies were able to use the issue in appealing for his dismissal. The manorial courts remained in operation until the revolutions of 1848.[67]

---

[65] K. von Schroetter to Stein, Königsberg, 28 Sept. 1808, Scheel, *Reformministerium* 3: 881–83 (no. 266); Promemoria des ostpreussischen ständischen Komitees, Königsberg, 25 Oct. 1808, ibid., 3: 954–56 (no. 286). See Franz Mehring, "Das Oktoberedikt von 1807," *Gesammefte Schriften und Aufsätze*, vol. 4, *Zur preussischen Geschichte*, 136–37.

[66] Stein to Schroetter, Königsberg, 6 Oct. 1808, Scheel, *Reformministerium* 3: 895–96 (no. 272); Stein to the deputies of the nobility of East Prussia (drafted by Schön), Königsberg, 27 Oct. 1808, ibid., 3: 962–63 (no. 290).

[67] Semi-official article in the *Königsberger Zeitung* and the *Hamburger Korrespondent*, Königsberg, 26 Sept. 1808, Botzenhart, *Stein Briefe* 2/2: 876–78 (no. 833). Stein to Bismarck (drafted by Schön), Königsberg, 16 Nov. 1808 (corresponding letters to each chamber office, all drafted by Schön), Scheel, *Reformministerium* 3: 1024 (no. 312). See ibid., 3: 1025, n. 2. On Hoffmann, see Treue, "Adam Smith in Deutschland," in W. Conze, ed., *Deutschland und Europa* (Düsseldorf, 1951), 121, 128–30; Raack, *Fall of Stein*, 120–22; Samuel Sugenheim, *Geschichte der Aufhebung der Leibeigenschaft und Hörigkeit in Europa um die Mitte des neunzehnten Jahrhunderts* (St. Petersberg, 1861), 470–71; Schrimpf, *Herrschaft, Individualinteresse und Richtermacht*, 324–32.

The ministerial bureaucracy of Stein's government was a powerful political machine. But by allying itself with the old aristocracy, and by including among its own members people who feared to offend the estate owners, the reform party set limits on what it could accomplish. Not all members of the Stein government were sympathetic to the aristocratic perspective on reforms. But they chose to work with those who were, giving a tone to the reform discussions which ultimately shaped the potential of their work.

In many ways there is a clear clash between the day-to-day political behavior and the long-range objectives of the Stein ministry. The short-term measures, such as ad hoc use of ministerial power and consultation with the aristocracy, were of greater importance than the reformers themselves realized. This is not to suggest that the outcome of the reform movement would not have been different if Stein's ministry had not been forced from office prematurely. It is an argument, however, that the innovators of 1808 held values which are not expressed literally in their reform memoranda. These values had an effect upon post-reform society, and this would have been the case, even if Stein had remained in office longer. First among these unexpressed values was the bureaucracy's belief in itself as the savior of state and society. Second was the emphasis placed on orderly, gradual reform which resulted in an accommodation with the aristocracy, allowing, or even assisting, the semi-feudal elite's transition through the crisis of 1806–1808. Is it surprising that the hereditary class gained a new footing in the nineteenth century rather than "gradually dissolving and disappearing" as Schön predicted would happen?

V. GOVERNMENT BY PROPERTY OWNERS

Modern representative government is an idea born in eighteenth-century western Europe. French philosophes, rejecting the theoretical foundations of absolutism, articulated the concept of government by consent of the governed. French revolutionaries attempted to put this ideal into practice in their national assemblies. British colonials in North America waged their victorious war of independence under the then radical slogan, "no taxation without representation." The British parliament had been evolving for some time into an institution which claimed the right of governing in the name of the nation, rather than the aristocracy.

The theme that tied together these and many other eighteenth-century experiments in government was "property." Those who spoke of the "nation" or the "people" always meant the property-owning elite. Ownership of land, capital and resources was replacing hereditary status in Europe's thinking about who should have voice in government.

Prussian thinkers who considered the new ideas of voting, constitutions, and assemblies were no exception. As Immanuel Kant wrote in 1793:

> The person who has the right to vote under [a representative system] is called a citizen . . . as distinguished from a resident. . . . The qualification for this (besides the natural ones of not being a child or a woman) is solely that the person be his own master. . . . [He must] possess property which supports him, under which may be reckoned any art, craft, fine art or science.[1]

In his famous essay, "Metaphysics of Morals," Kant described his ideal of a "civic union" comprised of citizens who governed their own affairs. He distinguished between economically independent citizens, to be regarded as "active members" of the state and others, the "passive" members of the civic body.[2]

Governmental leaders, as well as philosophers, advocated republican institutions in Prussia before the turn of the century. The jurist Ernst Ferdinand Klein, one of the major collaborators on Prussia's General Lawcode, expressed a typical Enlightenment attitude when he wrote:

---

[1] Immanuel Kant, "Über den Gemeinspruch: Das mag in der Theorie richtig sein, taugt aber nicht für die Praxis" (1793), *Gesammelte Schriften* 8 (Berlin and Leipzig, 1923), 295. This chapter is a revision of the article: Marion W. Gray, "Government by Property Owners: Prussian Plans for Constitutional Reform on the County, Provincial and National Levels in 1808," *Journal of Modern History* 48 (1976): on-demand reprint, 1–51.

[2] Kant, "Die Metaphysik der Sitten" (1797), ibid., 6 (Berlin, 1914), 311–18 (§43–49).

The state is not a marionette show in which the puppets are manipulated according to the will of a single individual. A state is successful when it consists of people who act unhindered according to their convictions. . . . However uneducated the nation might be, it must eventually become accustomed to ruling itself if it is not to remain perpetually in a condition of childhood.[3]

Judicial Counselor Ernst Gottlieb Morgenbesser, who ran into conflict with his superiors on account of his radical ideas, published his *Commentaries on the Republican Lawbook* in the year 1800. The only political arrangement consistent with the laws of nature, reasoned Morgenbesser, was one in which "every community elects its legislative representatives [who will] make laws according to majority will."[4]

The journalist Theodor Gottlieb von Hippel (1775–1843), nephew and namesake of the famous mayor of Königsberg who crusaded for improvement of women's status, presented Stein with a packet of suggestions upon the latter's assumption of office. He outlined what he called a "new, better organization of the state which should be founded on a representative system." The chief body of this new system was to be a national legislative assembly.[5]

Advocates of republicanism established themselves as opponents of the status quo, and they succeeded in making their ideas widely known throughout Prussia before the crisis of 1806–1807. Liberals worked both silently and publically to prepare for the time when "the people" would become Prussia's lawmakers. Many were not sure Prussians were ready for the responsibility, but they looked forward to the day when the nation would rule itself.

As soon as the crisis struck and reform-minded officials began considering how to rebuild the devastated society, the notion "representation" gained a sudden currency in government circles. The province of South Prussia, lost to the Hohenzollern crown when local insurrectionaries joined the French armies, became an early object of discussion. In recommending a path for reintegrating the territory into Prussia, should it be rewon, officials advocated an administration based on "representatives of the nation" to replace the royal-aristocratic alliance which had characterized the government of the province before 1806. This and several other early attempts to formulate plans for representative institutions sprang directly from the military-political crisis. They are almost uniformly vague and naive.[6] In

---

[3] Ernst Ferdinand Klein, ed., *Annalen der Gesetzgebung und Rechtsgelehrsamkeit in den preussischen Staaten,* 4 (1796), 334, quoted in Hermann Conrad, *Staatsgedanke und Staatspraxis des aufgeklärten Absolutismus,* Rheinisch-Westfälische Akademie der Wissenschaften, Geisteswissenschaften, Vorträge G 173 (Opladen, 1971), 61.

[4] E. G. Morgenbesser, *Beyträge zum republikanischen Gesetzbuch,* vii, 12–13.

[5] Theodor Bach, *Theodor Gottlieb von Hippel, der Verfasser des Ausrufs: "An mein Volk". Ein Gedenkenblatt zur fünfzigjährigen Feier der Erhebung Preussens* (Breslau, 1863), 116–21; Brenning, "Hippel," *Allgemeine Deutsche Biographie* 12: 466.

[6] Hardenberg and Altenstein, Denkschrift betreffend die Vorschläge von Radziwill und Gruner für Südpreussen, March 1807, Kurt Schottmüller, ed., *Der Polenaufstand 1806/07:*

the wake of military defeat the notion of representation was becoming fashionable, but its proponents were novices at drafting workable plans.

Stein himself gave a focus to the reform party's considerations of representative government. In his famous Nassau Memorandum, composed before he knew he would be summoned to lead a reform government, Stein advocated granting "property owners, and indeed all classes, participation in provincial and municipal government." Writing in forced retirement from Prussian service, Stein argued in the summer of 1807 that self-government would enliven the "sleeping or misled forces and the widely scattered talents" of society. He conceptualized municipal self-rule, county assemblies and provincial representative institutions.[7] He drew up no plans for a national legislature, perhaps because his memorandum focused upon provincial and local affairs, but possibly also because he did not favor such a far-reaching idea at the time. The Nassau Memorandum became the foundation for the reformers' discussion of representation, especially after Stein's return to Prussia in October 1807 to lead the government.

As the new ministry commenced its work in October 1807, plans for representative institutions rapidly took on concrete form. Stein's staff had in their hands two versions of the massive program of reform composed by the exiled minister Hardenberg and Karl zum Altenstein in the Baltic coastal town of Riga. The two proposals, totalling hundreds of pages, outlined a "constitution" for Prussia. The drafters hoped their design would establish "the greatest possible freedom and equality" for all citizens. The Riga Memoranda, as the two documents came to be known, called for a government of "national deputies," of "elected officials," and of a "national representation." Elections were not to be based on social classes. They were to be open to all citizens. The system which "seems to conform most perfectly to the spirit of the age," wrote the planners, was one of "democratic principles under a monarchical regime."[8]

In spite of their rhetorical devotion to popular government on all levels, Hardenberg and Altenstein were more than cautious about representation above the local community. At each step in a pyramidal system from the community to the national government, popular will was increasingly checked by bureaucratic institutions and royal appointees. Like Stein, they envisioned no national parliament. Rather "national representation" was to consist of three delegates elected from provincial assemblies, akin to the Stein government's plans for "Estates representatives" to help the bureaucracy function smoothly. Stein's staff used the Riga Memoranda as spring-

---

Urkunden und Aktenstücke aus der Zeit zwischen Jena und Tilsit, Sonder-Veröffentlichungen der Historischen Gesellschaft für die Provinz Posen 4 (Lisa, 1907), 158–80 (no. 63).

[7] Stein, Über die zweckmässige Bildung der Behörden, Nassau, June 1807, Botzenhart, *Stein Briefe* 2/1: 380–98, esp. 390 and 394 (no. 354).

[8] Hardenberg, Denkschrift über die Reorganisation des preussischen Staates, Riga, 12 Sept. 1807, Winter, *Reorganisation,* 302–63. Altenstein, Über die Leitung des preussischen Staates, Riga, 11 Sept. 1807, ibid., 364–566. See Haussherr, "Hardenbergs Reformdenkschrift," 267–308 and Spranger, "Altensteins Denkschrift," 471–517.

boards, and it is remarkable how far they developed plans for representation within a year.

By December Stein had set his colleagues to work on patterns for self-governing bodies on all levels, including a national parliament.[9] By the spring of 1808 the reformers were already drawing up a final draft of their proposal for a provincial representative assembly. During the summer and fall of that year, they were refining their scheme for a Prussian national assembly. On 19 November King Frederick William signed the ordinance establishing city government (Städteordnung), the one facet of the plans for representative institutions which was effected as law. The other plans did not get beyond the drafting stage before Stein was forced out of office at the end of the year. As he left, he pled with his successors to continue the work: "The life of our state depends upon the enactment of a plan [of national representation]."[10]

One cannot know with certainty where the reformers might have led Prussia if they indeed had forged their drafts into the state's first written constitution. Nevertheless the reformers' proposals, debates and revisions of 1808 are good indications of the nature of the change Stein and his colleagues might have effected. They sought to streamline government and make it capable of responding to the challenges of the post-French Revolution world. Like other innovators of their times, they strove to broaden the basis of government while tapping the energy and resources of society's most prosperous members, primarily the educated and propertied middle classes.

GOVERNMENT ON THE LOCAL LEVEL: RURAL COMMUNITIES

The October Edict, the Stein ministry's first major reform, was designed to terminate the feudal relationships between landlords and peasants.[11] From this starting point the Prussian leaders of 1808 worked to rebuild village government. Corollary to the abolition of class relationships was the termination of the century-old tradition of noble administrative, judicial, and police prerogative in the countryside: Gutsherrschaft. While this seems merely a logical conclusion to modern analysts, the reformers saw themselves compelled to spell out again and again the political implications of their social reform. "No one should be vassal of a fellow subject," insisted Schön in a letter drafted for Stein to an aristocratic provincial leader. "No one should be obligated to a fellow subject for any reason just because he was born on this or that plot of soil, or because his father owns or owned [a certain] piece of land."[12] Since landlords would no longer rule, a new structure for village government would have to be devised.

---

[9] Winkler, *Johann Gottfried Frey,* 122.

[10] Stein to the General Department, Königsberg, 24 Nov. 1808, Scheel, *Reformministerium* 3: 1138 (no. 330).

[11] This important agrarian reform measure is discussed in Chapter 6.

[12] Edikt, den erleichterten Besitz und den freien Gebrauch des Grundeigentums sowie die

The entire staff of Stein's ministry took part in drafting, debating and revising this reform measure. Their plans for communal self-government were intertwined with their attempts to streamline the administrative structure of rural areas. Police authority, exercised by the Landrat in local communities, was to be a function of the central government. However, the reformers were also dedicated to the establishment of representative assemblies which would determine matters of local concern, those that did not touch national interests. "The county (Kreis) administers its community affairs for itself alone," stipulated Schön in his brief but significant proposal for a local assembly.[13]

Ludwig von Vincke worked out a more extensive plan which was designed to make finances and taxation the responsibility of taxpayers themselves. Believing that people would pay taxes readily if they had a voice in the fiscal administration of their area, Vincke drafted plans for an annual meeting patterned after the Assembly of Heirs (*Erbentag*) of the counties of Cleves and Mark in his home, Westphalia.[14]

The Westphalian provinces from which Vincke took his conception had retained a stronger tradition of local self-rule in the centuries of absolutism than Prussia's eastern territories had. There was also a more prosperous class of non-serf farmers in the West. In Cleves and Mark, the Erbentage convened yearly under the supervision of the Landräte to establish community budgets. Participation was tied to property. Five categories of people had voting rights in the Erbentage, explained Vincke: First, all personally present landowners; second, hereditary tenants with thirteen Morgen [three ha. or seven-and-a-half acres] of taxable land on the estates of noble or middle-class landlords; third, where no land measure existed, those who had paid ten thaler in taxes during the previous year; fourth, guardians of minor heirs who met the qualifications; and finally, religious authorities. The last group, a small minority, was the only one whose participation was not tied to proprietorship.[15]

Vincke proposed to "transfer this institution, which has been tested by long use, to other [Prussian] provinces after the abolition of the most constraining aspects of serfdom." Because many rural inhabitants of the eastern Hohenzollern territories owned no land and held no hereditary tenancy,

---

persönlichen Verhältnisse der Landbewohner betreffend, Memel, 9 Oct. 1807, Scheel, *Reformministerium* 1: 11–16 (no. 7); Stein to Sulzowsky, Memel, 29 Dec. 1807 (drafted by Schön), ibid., 1: 276–77 (no. 80). Similar expression in Altenstein's Riga memorandum: Über die Leitung des preussischen Staates, 11 Sept. 1807, Winter, *Reorganisation,* 391.

[13] Stein, Votum zum Schreiben Schroetters vom 13. Okt. 1808, Königsberg, 14 Nov. 1808, Scheel, *Reformministerium* 3: 1020 (no. 309).

[14] Vincke, Über die Organisation der Unterbehörden, 2, Für die Finanzverwaltung, [Berlin], 14 June 1808, ibid., 2: 612–15.

[15] Ibid. On the Westphalian *Erbentag* see Richard Capelle, "Beiträge zur Geschichte der Erbentage, namentlich derjenigen in der Grafschaft Mark," *Beiträge zur Geschichte Dortmunds und der Grafschaft Mark* 23 (1914): 75–169, and Alfred Hartlieb von Wallthor, *Die landschaftliche Selbstverwaltung Westfalens in ihrer Entwicklung seit dem 18. Jahrhundert,* Veröffentlichungen des Provinzialinstituts für westfälische Landes- und Volkskunde, Series 1, Book 14 (Münster/ Westfalen, 1965) 1: 52–55.

the requirements should be lowered to include twelve-year lease holders, or those who paid ten thaler in taxes, "until the October Edict has created a middle class of property owners." Stein, who had spent his early career as a Westphalian administrator, knew the Erbentage by personal experience and regarded them highly. He regretted that in several areas of Westphalia they had been suppressed by the "fatal spirit of the bureaucracy," and he instructed both Altenstein and Schroetter to use them as models for planning representative rural assemblies.[16]

Believing that their social reforms would eliminate the rigid class structure of semi-feudal society, the Prussian leaders foresaw the development of a prosperous, independent class of yeoman farmers. This remarkable optimism, despite the fact that historically rural freedom in Prussia had not led to ownership but rather to propertyless conditions, was basic to the reformers' belief that they were creating a new kind of society composed of people who could rule themselves. Since the independent agricultural class was a goal and not yet a reality, the planners were willing to make concessions, enfranchising relatively small farmers who enjoyed only a degree of independence and paid a minimum tax. The tax liability was key. Those on the other hand, without a "stake in society,"[17] to borrow a phrase from the American Founding Fathers, would be excluded from the county assemblies. This broad category would encompass agricultural wage earners, subsistence farmers, small tenants, household servants, artisans, and many others, certainly most of the rural populace. Vincke, Schön and Stein planned to institutionalize a new concept of political rights and privileges. Their objectives were based on the belief that success, measured in terms of property rather than in terms of hereditary class, made people articulate in political matters and hence entitled them to a voice in their own government.

SELF-GOVERNMENT IN THE CITIES

As early as his Nassau Memorandum of June 1807, Stein argued imperatively for returning the government of municipalities to local leadership. He viewed the office of tax councilor (Steurerrat) as an absolutist creation which denied Prussia's townspeople the right to oversee their own affairs. He also was convinced that Prussia's middle Estate, lacking self-government, was estranged from the monarchy and less responsive to national needs than it could be.[18] The Stein administration worked with zeal to restructure city and town administration, and this became the one facet of

---

[16] Stein to Altenstein, Berlin, 10 Apr. 1808, Botzenhart, *Stein Briefe* 2/2: 700 (no. 662); Stein to Schroetter, Königsberg, 25 July 1808, ibid., 2/2: 793 (no. 754).

[17] J. R. Poole, *Political Representation in England and the Origins of the American Republic* (New York, 1966), 26, 138–48.

[18] Stein, Über die zweckmässige Bildung der Behörden, Nassau, June 1807, Botzenhart, *Stein Briefe* 2/1: 390–92 (no. 354); Stein, Anweisung zur Kabinettsordre an Schroetter, [Königsberg, 25 July 1808], ibid., 2/2: 794 (no. 755).

their governmental reform program which was actually put into effect before Stein was forced from office. The scheme which the reformers devised in their thirteen-month tenure became the model for all Prussian cities, and its basic provisions shaped municipal political life until the early twentieth century.

Königsberg, capital of East Prussia and the temporary residence of the court during the reform year, was the laboratory for experimenting with new forms of municipal structure. Typically, a complex system of privileged corporations dominated the affairs of this busy port of 50,000 people. Guild representatives performed intertwined duties of business and governmental nature. Like other Prussian cities, Königsberg's internal authority was superseded by the royal tax councilor, appointed specifically to see that the city functioned smoothly in the larger absolutist-mercantilist system.[19]

Königsberg suffered terribly in the war of 1806–1807, enduring economic chaos, French occupation, and a special "War Contribution" of twelve million francs levied by Napoleon on the city and surrounding province. This paralyzing state of affairs induced local leaders themselves to seek a streamlining of their municipal administration. This they did through a series of proposals drafted by the lawyer, Criminal Councilor Friedrich Brand, legal consultant to the Königsberg merchant guilds. In addition, Königsberg's elders themselves petitioned for a simplified administrative structure which would strengthen the hand of the city fathers to meet their extraordinary challenges. Brand and the merchants intended not only to retain, but even to reinforce the corporate nature of the city's society and government. Their plans would have solidified the traditional privileges of the patrician families.[20]

The reform party headed by Stein had their own ideas, however. Their debates over urban reform were among the most widespread of the ministry. The planner who emerged as most prominent in this particular endeavor was Johann Gottfried Frey (1762–1831), police director (i.e., chief administrator) of the city. A native Königsberger of a modest family, Frey had climbed to his important post after a university education and through positions in the municipal court and the city council. He was respected among the merchant families, and he was a familiar figure in the liberal academic circles and literary salons of the city. Already political friends, Stein and Frey strengthened their personal ties when the minister lodged in the police director's house while the Prussian government was in Königsberg during the reform debates.[21]

---

[19] Winkler, *Johann Gottfried Frey*, 31–35.

[20] Ibid., 85–111; Gause, *Geschichte der Stadt Königsberg* 2: 306–19, 334–35; Immediatvorstellung der ältesten der königsberger Bürgergesellschaft, Königsberg, 15 July 1808, Scheel, *Reformministerium* 2: 648–53 (no. 204), Entwurf zu einer neuen Verfassung der königsberger Bürgergesellschaft, Königsberg, 15 July 1808, ibid., 2: 653–56 (no. 205).

[21] Winkler, *Johann Gottfried Frey*, 35–85; von Poschman, "Frey," *Altpreussische Biographie*, 195; Gause, *Geschichte der Stadt Königsberg* 2: 300–301.

At Stein's request, and probably with his informal collaboration, Frey drafted a municipal reform proposal which he submitted to his associates for discussion in July 1808, along with commentaries by Ernst Gottlieb Morgenbesser and two city council members, Horn and Buck. The General Conference, taking the place of the Immediate Commission in August, debated the proposal and presented alternative recommendations. Schroetter's staff also discussed the plan in detail, suggesting several significant modifications. It was the latter group, the East Prussian Ministerial Office, which produced the version of the document signed by the king as the City Government Act of 19 November 1808, which has come to be known simply as the Prussian Städteordnung.[22]

The ordinance established a government with an assembly of elected deputies (*Stadtverordnetenversammlung*). This body in turn elected the magistrates which included a mayor and other administrative executives. The assembly approved the municipal budget and was empowered to supervise all executive actions of the city. Enfranchised citizens elected the assembly, voting in buroughs which, significantly, were geographical districts, having nothing to do with guilds or corporations.

As one could expect, there were two official classes of people in cities, citizens (Bürger) and residents (*Schutzverwandte*). The qualifications for citizenry were low. "Citizenship may not be denied anyone of reputable character who has taken up residence in the city [and who] wishes this privilege. . . . Also unmarried persons of the female gender may, when they possess these qualifications, receive citizenship." This does not mean, as one might at first conclude, that all residents of a city enjoyed citizenship rights. It did not need to be written into the law, for everyone understood, that wives, children, servants and apprentices were not reckoned as citizens, but rather as members of citizens' households. Those without permanent residence—vagabonds, the unemployed, and paupers—were excluded. Soldiers stationed in a town were ineligible for citizenship. Furthermore, those entitled to become citizens did not receive the status automatically. They had to apply for it. And for decades after the reform, great numbers did not petition for citizenship, apparently not understanding the process, not seeing an advantage to themselves, or not being able or willing to pay the twenty-five thaler application fee. Jews, for example, were granted the right to petition for citizenship, but for years few chose to exercise this right.[23]

---

[22] Frey, Vorschläge zur Organisation der Munizipalverfassungen, [before 17 July 1808], Scheel, *Reformministerium* 2: 657–70 (no. 206); Stein to Schroetter, Königsberg, 17 July 1808, ibid., 2: 671–73 (no. 207); Morgenbesser, Bemerkungen zum Entwurf Freys, [Königsberg, 23 July 1808], ibid., 699–70 (no. 221); on the dating of this see Rep. 2, Tit. 35, no. 38, fols. 32–34, StA Königsberg where the document accompanies a letter of 23 July. [Buck and Horn], Bemerkungen zu Freys Vorschlag, ibid., fols. 35–49; Protokoll der Generalkonferenz, Königsberg, 19 Oct. 1808, Scheel, *Reformministerium* 3: 934 (no. 281); Schroetter and Stein, Immediatbericht, Königsberg, 9 Nov. 1808, ibid., 3: 987–91 (no. 302); Ordnung für sämtliche Städte der preussischen Monarchie, Königsberg, 19 Nov. 1808, Botzenhart, *Stein Briefe* 2/2: 947–79 (no. 902).

[23] Gause, *Geschichte der Stadt Königsberg* 2: 336.

One group of residents was required to become citizens, those who conducted a business. Put another way, non-citizens were prohibited from engaging in commercial practices, so the first step in establishing one's self in the business community was the process of applying for citizenship.

Finally, and perhaps most importantly, citizenship was not equivalent to the right to vote in the elections of representatives to the city assembly. Owners of property and owners of businesses were automatically enfranchised. All others had to demonstrate that they received a yearly income of 200 thaler (150 thaler in small towns) in order to participate in the privilege of suffrage. One can get a sense of the significance of this figure by considering that Frey recommended a "modest" salary of 150 to 300 thaler as appropriate for the mayors of small towns. Female citizens were automatically excluded from the electorate. So were members of the magistracy. All collaborators on the reform agreed upon the property-income standard as appropriate measures for citizens' political maturity and hence their right to vote. Even Morgenbesser, often regarded as the most extreme reform advocate, thought that not only suffrage, but also citizenship should be denied anyone with less than 200 thaler income in order to prevent a "great mass of . . . unreliable people" from flooding the political life of the city. Stein himself emphatically favored the commercial interests: "An intelligent, world-experienced businessman judges better about city affairs than the scholar, and it is highly desirable that among the representatives there be many individuals from the merchant class."[24]

The new constitution broke down the old notion of privilege or freedom connected with membership in a corporation. It was an experiment with the new definition of freedom which, in the view of its advocates, was a universal claim. Because business experience and property were written into the system, the ruling members of the old society would easily continue to maintain dominant positions in city affairs for years to come. City politics was still a club whose first members were the male business leaders. In Königsberg's first election of 1809 only 3,426 of the 50,000 inhabitants qualified as voters, less than 7 percent. By 1817 there were still only 4,110 citizens in the city.[25]

The composition of the magistracy provided a further guarantee that the propertied elite would find permanent voice in urban government. The reformers debated strongly whether the magistrates should be unsalaried elected officials, and hence very responsive to the citizenry, or whether they should be permanently employed civil servants who would possess a high degree of expertise and training. Stein, Schön and Morgenbesser argued that the latter option would result in a bureaucratically run gov-

---

[24] Morgenbesser, Bemerkungen zum Entwurf Freys, Scheel, *Reformministerium* 2: 699–700 (no. 221); Stein to Schroetter, Königsberg, 17 July 1808, ibid., 2: 671 (no. 207).

[25] Gause, *Geschichte der Stadt Königsberg* 2: 336; Werner Conze, ed., *Die preussische Reform unter Stein und Hardenberg: Bauernbefreiung und Städteordnung,* Quellen- und Arbeitshefte zur Geschichte und Politik, 4128 (Stuttgart, 1973), 60. Similar percentages of enfranchised citizens in the Silesian cities: J. Ziekursch, *Das Ergebnis der friderizianischen Städteverwaltung,* 151.

ernment, distant from the wishes of the burghers. Hence these reformers favored unpaid officials who would serve out of selfless dedication to municipal affairs. This, of course, would guarantee predominance of wealthy families, for only they could afford to devote years of service to civic administration without remuneration. Frey, on the other hand, believed the *Magistrat* should be composed of professionals. The final compromise reflected the reformers' bias for property. It provided for a mayoral staff of salaried officials elected for six- to twelve-year terms working in conjunction with a group of unpaid city fathers, with members varying according to the size of the municipality. Salaries were set low. "Although the mayor cannot carry on a business in addition to his governmental post," explained Frey, "it is nevertheless desirable that he be a well-to-do resident." The elected representatives themselves should come explicitly from "the wealthiest resident citizens."[26]

Nevertheless, the old middle class of the patrician families saw the Städteordnung as an attack on their status. They wanted corporate membership, not residence or wealth, to determine people's political position. Right up until the edict was signed by the king, they waged their campaign for a more traditional and more restrictive definition of citizenship. Frey, aware of the opposition of the city elders, warned Stein not to present the new law to them for discussion. Like all the reform measures of 1807–1808, it was enacted by royal fiat, without consultation with those it affected. The reform gave Königsberg and other Prussian cities self-rule whether they wanted it or not. Many showed their opposition at the polls by electing representatives hostile to the reforms. Frey endured a resounding defeat in his bid to become the town's first mayor under the new regime, receiving only thirteen votes in the city assembly while the top candidates, including the pre-reform mayor, Gervais, the lawyer Brand and wealthy merchants polled over four times as many. Similarly Berlin elected as its first mayor Karl Friedrich Leopold von Gerlach, an outspoken critic of the Stein ministry and member of a notoriously conservative Prussian family whose members resisted political change at least until Bismarck's time.[27]

A potential, powerful check on the proud municipal patricians was, of course, the police authority (Polizei), placed not under control of citizens, but of the national government. In Königsberg this office of the central bureaucracy was housed in the city hall until 1831 when it was moved to

---

[26] Stein, Über die zweckmässige Bildung der Behörden, Nassau, June 1807, Botzenhart, *Stein Briefe* 2/1: 390–92 (no. 354); Winkler, *Johann Gottfried Frey*, 140; Protokoll der Generalkonferenz, Königsberg, 19 Oct. 1808, Scheel, *Reformministerium* 3: 934–39 (no. 281); Frey, Vorschläge zur Organisierung der Munizipalverfassungen, [before 17 July 1808], ibid., 2: 669 (no. 206).

[27] Brand, Plan über die künftige nähere Verbindung der königsberger Bürgerschaft mit dem Magistrat, Königsberg, 24 Aug. 1808, ibid., 3: 786–96; Winkler, *Johann Gottfried Frey*, 143–45; Gause, *Geschichte der Stadt Königsberg* 2: 337–38; Hans Joachim Schoeps, ed., *Aus den Jahren preussischer Not und Erneuerung: Tagebücher und Briefe der Gebrüder Gerlach und ihres Kreises 1805–1820* (Berlin, 1963), 344, 384. Ziekursch, *Das Ergebnis der friderizianischen Städteverwaltung*, 149–51.

separate quarters, signifying its external source of authority. Ironically Frey became Königsberg's police director, guarding the interests of the state in his hometown for which he had designed self-rule.[28] The reformers' solution to the question of central versus local authority is typical. They wished to establish self-government, but they feared it as well, reasoning that a national government representing all, rather than special groups, would supersede local citizens' authority. The ideal of the reformers, put into practice in Prussia's cities, was government by property owners, checked by a central bureaucracy.

"Trust ennobles a person, and eternal tutelage hinders one's maturity," wrote Frey in his first formal draft for the municipal reform. "Participation in public affairs fosters political [growth], and the more this increases [the more] the interest grows in the common good."[29] If Prussian cities retained a corporate character after the reforms, they were no longer the closed guilds of pre-modern times, but rather open corporations to which all could aspire regardless of birth. This opened the way for the new middle class who would become society's economic leaders, anticipating the growth of an industrial age. The electorates were small, consistent with the early liberals' notion that the undisciplined propertyless classes were not yet mature enough to accept political responsibilities. They had not yet earned enfranchisement, but they had the right to strive for it. Even citizenship itself had to be actively sought through an application process. Those who were successful were the appropriate leaders of the new society. Under these rules, the nineteenth century would witness the growth of an unenfranchised urban proletariat headed by a prosperous, powerful middle class.

Perhaps it was mere chance that the reorganization of municipal government was the single component of the reformers' constitutional program which became a working reality, while other proposals never got beyond the planning stage. But it is also possible that the cities received foremost attention because they and their commercial interests were high among the priorities of the Stein government. It is consistent with the reformers' goals that the Prussian middle class, the business community, should gain a high proportion of their attention.

PROVINCIAL ASSEMBLIES

When the haphazardly composed East Prussian provincial assembly of February 1808 petitioned for a permanent "Estates Committee" to oversee provincial affairs, Stein consented, but only temporarily until genuine re-

---

[28] Schroetter to Frey, 3 Aug. 1808, Scheel, *Reformministerium* 3: 703–704 (no. 224); Frey [to Schroetter], Königsberg, 29 Aug. 1808, ibid., 3: 801 (no. 248); Protokoll der Generalkonferenz, Königsberg, 19 Oct. 1808, ibid., 3: 934–39 (no. 281); Ritter, *Stein*, 259–62, 591, n. 30; Gause, *Geschichte der Stadt Königsberg* 2: 339; Ordnung für sämtliche Städte der preussischen Monarchie, Königsberg, 19 Nov. 1808, Botzenhart, *Stein Briefe* 2/2: 968 (no. 902).

[29] Frey, Vorschläge zur Organisierung der Munizipalverfassungen, [before 17 July 1808], Scheel, *Reformministerium* 2: 657 (no. 206).

forms could be enacted. He emphasized that in the future an annual elective assembly would replace the makeshift institutions dominated by the semi-feudal aristocracy. This assembly was to have the purpose of "maintaining public spirit and encouraging participation in the general welfare [as well as] presenting the wishes and needs of the subjects to the monarch." Stein commissioned the reform-minded provincial administrator, Hans von Auerswald, to draft the plans for such an institution. Auerswald's role in the discussion of provincial government is analogous to that of Frey's in the city.[30]

By May, within three months of his charge, Auerswald completed his plan for a provincial legislature. It was to be a unicameral body which would share with the crown the prerogative to initiate and veto legislation. This would bring about "no limitation in the legislative power of the regent," Auerswald assured critics, "but rather a strengthening of it" by linking it with popular will.[31]

Inspired by the Hanoverian statesman and political theorist, August Wilhelm Rehberg, Auerswald sought to establish an assembly which represented the "whole land," as opposed to specific classes. Quoting Rehberg, Auerswald argued: "It is . . . very detrimental when the deputies . . . assemble as members of individual Estates."[32] Nor should they convene with mandates from constituents, but rather as representatives, free to debate and decide issues in their meetings.

The legislative body should consist of a single house. If there were an upper and a lower chamber, the former would come under the influence of the old aristocracy, and this would lead to "an oligarchy." The majority of the "high nobility and large estate owners," Auerswald contended, "have been conditioned to an unproductive and idle life, and their intelligence is considerably lower than that of the educated and prosperous middle class." They have never enjoyed the "trust of the nation, and the atmosphere of the times gives no cause to expect that they can earn it now." In revolutionary America, colonial leaders had taken pains to establish senates or upper houses in order to institutionalize an elite leadership in a society which lacked a formal aristocracy.[33] In contrast, Auerswald hoped to elim-

---

[30] Protokoll des Generallandtages, Königsberg, 11 Feb. 1808, Rep. 2, Tit. 23, no. 1, vol. 2, fols. 81–82, StA Königsberg; Kabinettsordre to Auerswald, Königsberg, 27 Feb. 1808, Botzenhart, *Stein Briefe* 2/2: 672–73 (no. 619).

[31] Auerswald, Plan zur Organisierung eines jährlichen Generallandtages für Ostpreussen und Litauen, [Königsberg, 20 May 1808], Scheel, *Reformministerium* 2: 572–80 (no. 174).

[32] The direct references to Rehberg were eliminated apparently before the final drafting of Auerswald's plan. See his quotes from Rehberg in an earlier draft: Rep. 2^2, no. 2604, fols. 8–9, StA Königsberg. August Wilhelm Rehberg, *Ueber die Staatsverwaltung deutscher Länder und die Dienerschaft des Regenten* (Hanover, 1807). See Ursula Vogel, *Konservative Kritik an der bürgerlichen Revolution: August Wilhelm Rehberg*, Politica, 35 (Darmstadt-Neuwied, 1972).

[33] Gordon S. Wood, *The Creation of the American Republic 1776–1787* (Chapel Hill, N.C., 1969), 206–22, 483–99; Jesse Lemisch, "The American Revolution Seen from the Bottom Up," in Barton J. Bernstein, ed., *Towards a New Past: Dissenting Essays in American History* (New York, 1968), 10–11.

inate domination of the entrenched Prussian nobility by assuring that there would be no upper chamber in the provincial Landtage.

Who was entitled to vote for representatives? Auerswald established separate qualifications for the urban and the rural electorates. For the countryside, he proposed that "estate owners" be enfranchised, but not only those of aristocratic lineage. Like Vincke, Auerswald expected that, as a consequence of the October Edict, the nonaristocratic segment of society would gradually assume a dominant position in rural landholding. Hence he favored a corresponding shift in political enfranchisement.

> Everyone eligible to vote is also eligible for election; the competition here cannot be broadened enough, for sometimes the owners of small estates have excellent ability, education, reputation and trust, and this will be daily more and more the case if capitalists move into rural areas.[34]

In rural Prussia, then, landed proprietors should elect representatives to provincial assemblies. But the cities were a different matter, and for one so concerned with property, Auerswald drew up a surprising proposal of political enfranchisement:

> I believe we should extend suffrage in the cities (a) to all citizens, (b) to all who independently practice middle-class professions, even if they are non-citizens, and (c) to all who reside in the administrative jurisdiction of the city, even if they are not citizens and do not belong to middle-class professions.

In other words, mere residence was the requirement. "If voting rights were limited to citizenship, or simply to ownership of property, persons who might . . . exert a significant influence could be excluded. . . . No class and no talent should be barred from municipal government." Auerswald classified town dwellers as a special category among the population. One might expect this from an eighteenth-century administrator who viewed society as composed of Estates, for the city populace had traditionally enjoyed the status of a separate corporation. Yet the striking aspect of Auerswald's plan is the wide base of suffrage. He had a deep and unusual faith in the urban electorate, to whom he granted a disproportionate thirty-nine percent of the seats in the planned assembly.[35]

The most substantial criticism of Auerswald's plan came from Staegemann and Schön. In disagreement with the provincial leader, both of these planners considered an upper house essential. However, they reached this conclusion for quite different reasons. Schön agreed with his father-in-law that a chamber dominated by the nobility would produce only negative results. But like Vincke, Schön was an admirer of British institutions, and he maintained that two houses were necessary in order to balance each other's weaknesses. Prussians, he argued, were unaccustomed to self-government. Representatives were bound to make mistakes. "If the delegates

---

[34] Auerswald, Generallandtag, [20 May 1808], Scheel, *Reformministerium* 2: 576 (no. 174).
[35] Ibid., 576–77.

of the people completely understood their responsibilities and acted totally free of prejudice and influence, then a single chamber would suffice. But even the most sophisticated people are still far from these perhaps unreachable goals." In order to construct an upper house which would not merely promote the interests of the hereditary upper class, Schön proposed a random selection process. Every third person on the list of elected delegates, ordered by age, should be made members of the higher chamber, while the other two-thirds would comprise the lower house.[36]

Staegemann generally favored deferring establishment of provincial representation until a complete constitution had been devised for Prussia. However, if a Landtag were to be established, he argued, it should not deprive the aristocracy of its political role within a constitutional system:

> I consider a middle factor between the sovereign and the people [popular house] . . . necessary and essential [because] in an immoral and lethargic age the impulses of the people lead to the destruction of the constitution and the ruin of the common welfare. This middle power must be an Estate. . . . I believe . . . that only a purified, higher nobility can constitute the upper house.[37]

As for the Landtag constituency, Schön objected to Auerswald's proposal of dividing the electorate into an urban sector with fourteen delegates and a rural one with twenty-two. With the implied argument that society consists of individuals rather than corporate groups, Schön advocated the more modern idea of directly proportional representation. "The most suitable method would be to ascertain the number of enfranchised citizens in the state and provide that a certain number elect one deputy." This would have made place of residence, profession and social class immaterial. Nevertheless, since he lacked the statistics to devise a concrete proposal according to this principle, Schön fell back on a modified conception of corporate society. Reckoning in economic rather than statistical terms, he advocated allotting one-fourth of the Landtag seats to urban delegates and three-fourths to rural representatives. This would have reflected, in Schön's estimation, the contribution of each segment to the economic welfare of the province.[38] Schön disagreed with Auerswald's heavy emphasis upon the urban factor in the electorate.

On the question of suffrage as well, Schön differed with Auerswald. For rural areas he proposed that large tenants be counted equally with owners,

---

[36] Schön, Zum Immediatbericht Auerswalds vom 20. Mai, 1808, Königsberg, 20 June 1808, ibid., 2: 616 (no. 190).

[37] Staegemann, Über den Plan zur Organisierung eines General Landtages für Ostpreussen, 19 Aug. 1808, Max Lehmann, *Knesebeck und Schön: Beiträge zur Geschichte der Freiheitskriege* (Leipzig, 1875), 304–306. The idea that a constitution must precede other social and political reforms was also common to many non-Prussian reformers in Central Europe. See, for example, Elisabeth Fehrenbach, *Der Kampf um die Einführung des Code Napoléon in den Rheinbundstaaten,* Institut für europäische Geschichte, Mainz, Vorträge, 56 (Wiesbaden, 1973), 27.

[38] For this and the following paragraphs: Schön, zum Immediatbericht Auerswalds, Königsberg, 20 June 1808, Scheel, *Reformministerium* 2: 616–19 (no. 190).

so that voting would not be strictly tied to possessions. This measure would have enfranchised the important, innovative class of tenant managers (to which Schön's father had belonged). In any case, Schön was considering political rights for the well-off. Tenants should manage plots of at least four hufen (68 ha. or 170 acres), large enterprises in Prussia's agrarian economy. None of the reformers considered the peasantry or free villagers qualified to participate in provincial politics.

Not surprisingly, for the cities as well Schön stipulated higher qualifications than Auerswald:

> It seems advisable . . . to enfranchise only the person who has [either] real estate valued at four thousand thaler (approximately the value of 4 kulmische hufen) or who has a yearly trade of eight thousand thaler. Otherwise it is to be feared that deputies without interest [in the state] will be sent from the cities.

One can be certain that if the Stein government had realized its goal of establishing a Landtag, the urban electorate would have been significantly narrower than that of Auerswald's far-reaching proposal.

While Auerswald, Schön and Staegemann disagreed on several noteworthy issues, they held one very important common conviction: The haphazard, informal political domination of the aristocracy should be terminated. New criteria would grant a voice to nonnoble classes. Schön and Auerswald hoped to place political leadership in the hands of the middle class. If the old aristocracy should continue to play a role, it would be because they met new qualifications. Auerswald stressed the importance of a "national representation . . . consisting of men from the most varied businesses and interests." All three reformers agreed upon one measure of political capability, property ownership. Even Staegemann, who still looked to the nobility for political authority, consented to the decisive role of property advocated by his co-workers: "Since it is difficult to apply a measurement (and to determine which one), it is fair that ownership of landed property should determine [qualifications] for voters and for representatives."[39]

A PRUSSIAN NATIONAL ASSEMBLY

Relatively late in the reform year, Stein's staff undertook their discussion of national representation, *Reichsstände.* For the purpose of drafting such plans, Stein recruited the Silesian nobleman, Karl Nikolaus von Rehdiger (1765–1826), who enjoyed a reputation as an authority on constitutions. An observer in revolutionary Paris, he had seen French assemblies first hand. More consciously than Stein's other co-workers, Rehdiger borrowed ideas from French models. He produced a surprising proposal for a national assembly, rejecting traditional social classes, provincial Estates, and prop-

[39] Auerswald, Generallandtag, [20 May 1808], ibid., 2: 573 (no. 174). Staegemann, General Landtag, 19 Aug. 1808, Lehmann, *Knesebeck und Schön,* 306.

erty as bases for representation. Rehdiger advocated simply that every five thousand Prussian inhabitants should send one delegate to the assembly. Yet tempering this plan, which had a radical tone by Prussian standards, was an indirect electoral process, a complicated pyramid of three electoral colleges. This system would remove the assembled delegates several steps from popular influence. Rehdiger argued that it would result in "ennoblement and intellectualization of the general popular will."[40]

Moreover, those who would enjoy the right to serve as delegates, far from representing a cross section of society, were to epitomize a new elite, "an aristocracy of reason and integrity." They would be men who had proven themselves leaders in civic life and had won the respect of their fellow citizens. The following were to be eligible for election: active civil servants, military officers, city and village magistrates, noblemen, members of royal orders, church officials, academicians, teachers, artists, the bearers of medals, and savers of lives! Also included were senior members of merchant, professional and artisan associations, large factory owners, masters of at least three dependent servants, and contributors to charitable institutions.

Rehdiger, clearly more able than his colleagues to distance himself from Prussian tradition, invented a system of representation which he felt would mirror a new society. According to his conception, society was composed of individuals, in contrast to the corporate system of the eighteenth century, but its leadership would come from a select class in which there was room for every kind of distinction, service or achievement. Unlike others associated with the Stein government, Rehdiger, in this first draft of his plan, repudiated property as a measure of political talent. "Nothing is more false," he argued, "than the conception that the state consists of shares of property and wealth." He made room for the old aristocracy, by virtue of birth, to exert roles of authority alongside other talented and endowed groups. He believed peasants and propertyless agricultural workers would be adequately represented by landlords and pastors. Middle-class leaders would enjoy an influential role. And Rehdiger planned a dominant place for professional civil servants in the elective branch of government.[41]

Stein, with his own critique of Rehdiger's proposal, brought the discussion much closer to the mainstream of thought among the reformers. Stein found Rehdiger's outline lacking because it provided no place for provincial assemblies. He also criticized what he perceived as an overbalance of administrators in the Rehdiger scheme. Representative institutions were to

---

[40] This plan by Rehdiger is lost or unaccessible. I have relied upon the description of Ritter, *Stein*, 279–82. The major features of the plan can be gleaned from Stein's critique of it: Beurteilung des Rehdiger'schen Entwurfs über Reichsstände, Königsberg, 8 Sept. 1808, Botzenhart, *Stein Briefe* 2/2: 852–56 (no. 813). Alfred Stern, ed., "Beiträge zur Biographie des preussischen Staatsrats von Rehdiger. Aus dem Nachlass von Paul Lenel," *Historische Zeitschrift* 124 (1921): 220–49.

[41] Ritter, *Stein*, 279–82, 597.

counteract an overbearing bureaucracy, Stein argued, and they should not risk domination by professionals. Most important, Stein could not accept Rehdiger's rejection of Estates as the basis for national representation, asserting: "We find all known . . . nations with any degree of cultivation divided into Estates. . . . Can we expect that such a universal institution could be abolished . . . without damage?"[42] What were Stein's plans for the aristocracy in a modern Estate system?

> The dominance of one Estate over its fellow citizens is [a] harmful disruption of social order, and it should be curtailed. The nobility of Prussia is burdensome because it is numerous [and] largely poor. It demands salaries, offices, privileges and advantages of every sort. A result of its poverty is lack of education. . . . The number of aristocrats should be reduced; the poor nobility should be eliminated; and the remaining, decreased number of wealthy families should be given a political and governmental function. Wealth [gives] the property owner [interest in] the general welfare. . . . Thus from the prosperous aristocracy there should be built an upper house, and its brilliance should be maintained through inclusion of men of great prestige, whether it result from wealth or services to the state.[43]

Stein hoped a reformed nobility could adequately bear the responsibilities of the upper Estate. Rather than Rehdiger's nobility of intelligence, Stein foresaw an aristocracy of wealth. He equated prosperity, especially in the form of landed property, with ability. Property owners, he said, "predominate in the whole store of ideas which belong to a nation. . . . Determination of the means for maintaining order, clearheadedness and freedom of expression should be left to [them]."

Joining with Stein, Vincke also emphasized the importance of Estates: "In all localities and in all time periods, well-organized Estates have proven beneficial." But the existing social system had little to do with "well-organized" Estates. Vincke counted upon the social reforms of the Stein government to nullify hereditary class distinctions in Prussia. Nobility would become an anachronistic concept "which cannot serve as the basis for representation." Instead, he advocated a return to what he termed "the original Germanic practice of basing representation on property ownership." While he acknowledged that "real estate alone is no longer a fitting criterion for the present times which know other sources of income and wealth," he believed nevertheless that "stable, permanent landed property always deserved a priority." Ownership qualified men for political responsibilities not only for historical reasons, but also for practical ones, Vincke argued. "He who is most established, he who has the most to lose, he who must pay the greatest taxes . . . can be assumed [to have] the greatest interest in public affairs." Like his co-workers, Vincke had no reservations about a social hierarchy, but he saw the existing class distinctions as no longer

---

[42] Stein, Beurteilung des Rehdiger'schen Entwurfs, Königsberg, 8 Sept. 1808, Botzenhart, *Stein Briefe* 2/2: 852–56 (no. 813).

[43] Ibid., 854–56, for this and the following paragraph.

tenable. He argued strongly for property as the means of determining who would belong to the new elite.[44]

In response to the objections of his colleagues, Rehdiger revised his plan to include the concept of Estates, proposing a tricameral assembly. The first house, the College of Estates, would represent Prussia's highest nobility and religious dignitaries. The second chamber, the National College, would be divided into eight separate sections to represent the following "professions": merchants; manufacturers and members of guilds; urban property owners; proprietors of rural estates; landowning peasants; academicians, clerics and artists; civil servants; and military officials. Representatives of the royal bureaucracy were to comprise the third house, the College of the State. Here administrators from six categories (justice, economics, general administration, foreign affairs, defense and public education) would presumably give a professional balance to the popular side of government.[45]

Except that it was divided into three chambers, the legislature which Rehdiger's revised plan would have produced might have differed little in composition from the one envisioned in his earlier draft. However, the electorate was significantly altered. Instead of the proportional representation of the earlier plan—one delegate for five thousand inhabitants—the revision would institutionalize three classes of citizens within the state: nobility, professions, and civil servants. These three "Estates" would form the basis of representative government. Property would play a role as one of the several qualifications for the "professions."

Rehdiger charted a complicated path for legislation before it came to the king for his approval. Drafts of bills were to be debated in committees of each house, then in the three chambers, and finally in a plenary session. Rehdiger envisioned the divisions and subdivisions as checks upon one another. He was anxious to avoid in this way "conflict of the classes . . . which in these times of agitation can be highly detrimental." With regard to the College of Estates, he was careful to stipulate that this was not an "upper house" with veto power, but rather an integral part of the legislature, equal with the others. The voice of the second and the third chambers could outweigh that of the first. To grant an aristocratic upper house a veto privilege would be to provide "a number of magnates with the means of destroying everything liberal." For Rehdiger knew that "the mentality of our magnates will, at least in the beginning, [produce] a decided antagonism toward . . . reorganization of the state."[46]

---

[44] Vincke, Organisation der ständischen Representation, 20 Sept. 1808, G. H. Pertz, ed., *Denkschriften des Ministers Freiherrn vom Stein über deutsche Verfassungen* (Berlin, 1848), 2–13.

[45] [Rehdiger], Entwurf einer Representation [n.d.], Rep. 92 Gneisenau, 17 A 11, Geheimes Staatsarchiv Preussischer Kulturbesitz, Berlin-Dahlem, fols. 77–85. The document is described, but not printed, in Pertz, *Das Leben des Feldmarschalls Grafen Neithardt von Gneisenau* 1: 406–11. It had long been considered lost by historians. See Ritter, *Stein* (1st ed., Berlin, 1931) 1: 538, n. 47. It is incorrectly identified in the contents of the Gneisenau papers.

[46] [Rehdiger], Entwurf einer Representation, Rep. 92 Gneisenau, 17 A 11, Geheimes Staatsarchiv, fols. 77–89; Bemerkungen zu dem Entwurf nebst Anhang I und II, ibid., fols. 90–94.

Stein was pleased. Although still critical of Rehdiger's proposed heavy representation of military and civil bureaucrats, Stein concluded:

> The present proposal for national representation is based upon intellectual ability and property of every type. . . . The representation is complete. . . . It gives [property] the necessary preponderance through which the government receives stability. . . . At the same time the nobility will be granted certain prerogatives.[47]

Stein proposed a simplification of Rehdiger's complicated election procedures and advocated linking eligibility for election more closely to standards of property ownership.

Schön also found the basic concepts of Rehdiger's revised plan acceptable. He agreed that the reformers' task was that of "assembling the smartest, most educated, and best citizens of the state, and of finding a means for selecting them." Yet he too considered it important to emphasize the vital character of property. While rhetorically maintaining that property was not the best means of selection, he conceded that it was indeed "essential" as a "security measure—but only as this." Furthermore, "the more immobile [the property is] the more certain it is as a test."[48]

With several practical suggestions concerning the electorate, Schön underlined the role he believed property should play in the representative system. For example, he would grant a vote to every "large estate" in the elections for provincial representatives. As for "small estates," the village magistrate, *Schulze,* should cast a vote for the community, so long as he was a property holder. If the Schulze were only a tenant, "then twenty small property owners should form a voting body and choose their electors. The Schulzen and electors of a Landkreis elect provincial representatives. Properties who do not pay a rent of twenty thaler have no representation." For Schön, the value and size of a farm was a direct measure of political competence. Nevertheless he was influenced by Rehdiger's search for intellect and talent, for in the non-agricultural sector of the population he agreed to quite different criteria: "The academic and clerical classes should vote on a per capita basis."

Consistent with his position in the debate over earlier provincial Landtage, Schön was in agreement with an assembly of three houses, counterbalancing one another. But he predictably argued against an aristocratic composition of the upper house. Instead he advocated a simpler proposal, more deviant from Prussian tradition. "Elders of the land," men over the age of forty, should be eligible for election to the higher chamber. Schön argued, like Stein, that civil and military administrators should occupy no place in the National College, for they were already strongly represented in the third house. Schön anticipated the development of discord between

---

[47] Stein, Über den Entwurf einer Repräsentation, Königsberg, 7 Nov. 1808, Botzenhart, *Stein Briefe* 2/2: 920–23 (no. 885).

[48] For this and the following paragraphs: Schön, Gutachten, [n.d.], Pertz, *Gneisenau* 1: 412–15.

the two lower houses, and he viewed this as positive: "conflict of intellect" is healthier than "conflict of the Estates."

Rehdiger's second proposal and his colleagues' critiques of it were the Stein ministry's last formal memoranda on representation. Forced to leave office at a high point in this debate, Stein bequeathed the unfinished drafts to his successors with the urgent bidding that they pursue "the plans for national Estates which are still in a state of development."[49] They were never carried beyond this stage of discussion. Historians have tended to overlook them in part for this reason. However, for our purpose of probing the mentality and ideology of the reform movement, it is the debate itself which is important.

Stein and his co-workers were obviously working toward a consensus, even though they still represented divergent positions. It is clear that they would have endorsed no system which did not base representation on Estates, some type of established classes. But more striking is their insistence upon property as the measurement for political rights. To be sure, it is not the only standard they debated. Rehdiger added a new tone to the discussion with his search for ways to recognize talent, service and prestige, and his colleagues enthusiastically accepted his criteria. Qualities such as education, intellectual achievement, religious leadership, social distinction, business experience, and even age played an important part in the early liberals' deliberations on how to establish the best electorate. But when they sought practical means to measure these distinctions, they fell back upon property, the common denominator in the discussion. Stein, who stressed the value of a reformed noble class, saw wealth, especially in the form of real estate, as the best means of defining the new aristocracy. Vincke, who hoped to see the nobility eventually wither away as a hereditary class, argued that property was a more ancient test of civic responsibility than the status of one's ancestors, and the most valid one he could devise. And Schön, who wanted to eliminate aristocracy as an Estate in national representation, considered property essential as a criterion for determining the state's best citizens.

PRUSSIAN CONSTITUTIONAL GOALS AND CHANGING EUROPEAN SOCIETY

In the emerging European middle-class society, economic considerations were becoming more and more intertwined with political life. The old regime understood birth—a balance between aristocracy and royal monarchy—as the key to political prestige. Early capitalist society commonly equated property holding in the private sphere with an interest in public welfare. The wealthy were qualified to sit in legislative bodies because it was in their interest to protect and nurture the new economic system.[50]

Eighteenth-century England, the conscious model of several Prussian

[49] Stein to Beyme, [Berlin], 2 Jan. 1809, Botzenhart, *Stein Briefe* 3: 8–9 (no. 8).

[50] Jürgen Habermas, *Strukturwandel der Öffentlichkeit: Untersuchungen zu einer Kategorie der bürgerlichen Gesellschaft*, Politica, 4 (Neuwied, 1962), 102–103.

reformers, was a society built around the primacy of land ownership. Real estate was at once the key to social, economic and political prestige. As early as the seventeenth-century Civil War, the political slogan "liberty" had often been used to mean rights of the propertied.[51] In Lockean political philosophy property formed the cornerstone of all social relations. In practice bourgeois property was coming to define individuals' social and political identity. It became the basis of suffrage in the nineteenth century.[52]

The American Revolution, especially its second phase, which established the order of the new society through state and federal constitutions, was a victory of the propertied—northern capitalists and southern planters—over the propertyless. Most of the state constitutions provided for a senate which had higher ownership qualifications than the lower houses, reflecting the conviction that large proprietors were politically more capable than small ones. Governors in several states had to belong to the economic elite, or they were elected by large property owners. The suffrage requirements in most states were tied to wealth and land, and the federal constitution accepted the state standards for national elections. Land was plentiful in North America, and it was easy for founders of a new political system to equate political rights, under their slogans of "freedom" and "democracy," with property ownership. The yeoman freeholder, the honest independent property owner, was a central element of American post-revolutionary political ideology.[53]

The French Revolution was an attempt to build a government of bourgeois property owners and taxpayers, a constitutional monarchy. The violent participation of urban lower classes brought more radical demands, but Jacobin leaders were able to make concessions to the sansculottes only insofar as they did not alienate property owners. And the Napoleonic settlement confirmed the middle-class striving for a constitutional system based on a propertied oligarchy. The social elite of post-revolutionary France was based on property and wealth, and immobile property played a dominant role.[54]

---

[51] Pauline Gregg, *A Social and Economic History of Britain 1760–1972* (London, 1973), 23–24, 148–57; Christopher Hill, *Puritanism and Revolution: Studies in Interpretation of the English Revolution of the Seventeenth Century* (London, 1958), 68.

[52] Elizabeth Fox-Genovese and Eugene D. Genovese, *Fruits of Merchant Capital: Slavery and Bourgeois Property in the Rise and Expansion of Capitalism* (New York and Oxford, 1983), 275–87; Louis Namier, *England in the Age of the American Revolution* (London, 1961), 24.

[53] Staughton Lynd, "Beyond Beard," in B. Bernstein, ed., *Towards a New Past,* 46–64; Wood, *Creation of the American Republic,* 202–22, 503–508. An excellent case study of the question of property and enfranchisement in America is Hans-Christoph Schröder, "Das Eigentumsproblem in den Auseinandersetzungen um die Verfassung von Massachusetts, 1775–1787," in Rudolf Vierhaus, ed., *Eigentum und Verfassung: Zur Eigentumsdiskussion im ausgehenden 18. Jahrhundert* Veröffentlichungen des Max-Planck-Instituts für Geschichte 37 (Göttingen, 1972): 11–67; Rowland Berthoff and John M. Murrin, "Feudalism, Communalism, and the Yeoman Freeholder: The American Revolution Considered as a Social Accident," in *Essays on the American Revolution* ed. Stephen G. Kurtz and James H. Hutson (Williamsburg, Chapel Hill and New York, 1973): 256–88.

[54] E. J. Hobsbawm, *The Age of Revolution 1789–1848* (New York: Mentor, 1962), 74–100. Georges Lefèbvre, *Napoléon,* Peuples et Civilisations 14 (Paris, 1953), 139–48; Jean Tulard,

Private property was a hallowed concept in the Germanies as in the rest of Europe. The Enlightenment tradition had established it as one of the Rights of Man. During the French revolutionary era, progressive Prussians had underlined civil government's responsibility to maintain property rights, which they equated with personal freedom. In the 1790s, political journalists reacted vehemently to what they saw as the French National Assembly's trespassing on the sacredness of private property.[55] Prussian officials of 1808 would consciously avoid this "mistake." Instead, with their program of reforms from above, they would elevate the role of property by assigning it political responsibility.

In tying their notion of political enfranchisement to property ownership, the Prussian reformers, like political philosophers in England and physiocrats in France, referred to property as if it were a timeless entity, something which had always existed.[56] However, they were using the idea of property in a new sense, that of the rising bourgeoisie. Private wealth, as always an identification of rank and status, was no longer a matter of family ties and inheritance. It was becoming a commodity to be actively used: bought, sold, traded and increased. Bourgeois property ownership and the market were becoming bases of human relationships and political identity. The Prussian reformers unselfconsciously reflected this profound transition while they purposefully abetted it.

Had the Stein ministry been successful in enacting its constitutional plans, it would have established a political corollary to the evolving society in Prussia. Under conditions of increasing commercialization, the middle class grew in importance. It sought freedom from semifeudal and mercantilistic restraints. The ideal of freedom and the corollary of political enfranchisement were to be enjoyed by those who shared a stake in society through their ownership of property. This theme was to become a familiar part of the political liberalism of the nineteenth century. The rhetoric of 1808 was echoed later in the revolutionary assemblies of 1848 and in the liberal party platforms of the 1860s.[57]

In their eagerness to bring the new society into being, the reformers did not recognize how they were establishing the possibility of perpetuation of the old aristocracy when they tied political privilege to property. After all, their position was an explicit rejection of the old measure of status, birth. The mobile wealth of the cities which every reformer emphasized as important, was a specifically non-aristocratic form of property. The re-

---

"Problèmes sociaux de la France impériale," *Revue d'histoire moderne et contemporaine* 17 (1970): 640–49.

[55] Günther Birtsch, "Freiheit und Eigentum: Zur Erörterung von Verfassungsfragen in der deutschen Publizistik im Zeichen der französischen Revolution," in Vierhaus, ed., *Eigentum und Verfassung*, 179–92.

[56] Fox-Genovese and Genovese, *Fruits of Merchant Capital*, 277.

[57] Theodore S. Hamerow, *Restoration, Revolution, Reaction: Economics and Politics in Germany 1815–1871* (Princeton, 1958), 61–62; Theodore S. Hamerow, *The Social Foundations of German Unification: Ideas and Institutions* (Princeton, 1969), 292–93.

formers justified their emphasis on landed property by stressing that agriculture was Prussia's major enterprise. Their expectation was that in a free real estate market urban capitalists would invest in land and thus change the complexion of rural society. The composition of the rural electorate would, of course, change as well.

Significantly, many Junkers themselves agreed to the principle that property entitles one to a political voice. The East Prussian Estates Committee composed two memoranda in response to the Stein government's constitutional plans. Above all the noble landowners feared possible excesses:

> Should one get the idea of including peasants too, then we would shortly be forced to accept all inhabitants: village laborers, tenants and cottagers, city house owners and gardeners. What confusion! What danger! Furthermore, even in the case of taxation, it is dangerous to allow petty owners a vote, or to allow theoreticians participation.[58]

The aristocratic Committee argued for reestablishment of three Estates: lords, noblemen, and middle class. The third, however, should form a separate political organization to prevent competition between city and country which would only result in disorder. The first Estate, lords, would be established as the very largest property owners, those with 100 hufen (1,730 ha. or 4,300 acres). "It is unmistakably evident that such an [element] is necessary. Large owners have more interest in the whole; they feel every pressure infinitely more; and they can be ruined by small owners." The second Estate should be composed of the aristocracy and the Kölmer, as was the practice "according to the ancient constitution." However, the qualifications "must not sink any lower, for otherwise the most dangerous anarchy would arise." East Prussian noblemen understood that self-government by property owners would work to their own interest.

Everyone agreed that the questions of who managed property and how it was managed held the answers to Prussia's future. All but the most reactionary elements of the populace were willing to endorse the new, capitalist definition of property, which would allow the bourgeoisie to prosper. For the near future, this would not jeopardize the position of the Junker class, which was already adapting to the conditions of the market economy.

---

[58] For this and the following paragraph: Korff, Promemoria, [April 1808], Rep. 2, Tit. 23, no. 1, Vol. 2, fols. 194–95, StA Königsberg; Scheltz, Bemerkungen zu den anliegenden P.M., 23 April 1808, ibid., fols. 196–97.

VI. ANCHORING THE FOUNDATIONS OF A CAPITALIST ECONOMY

PRIVATE PROPERTY AND A FREE REAL ESTATE MARKET

Prussian blueprints for economic reforms grew directly out of the crisis following the military disaster of 1806. By the spring of 1807, estates, villages and towns throughout Hohenzollern lands lay in ruins, due to the physical damage of war. While the reform party was fighting to gain footing, the populace was being forced to make tremendous sacrifices to support not only the invading French, but also the soldiers of Prussia's ally, Russia. When the foreign troops did not freely receive requisitioned supplies and animals, they plundered, leaving farmlands, grain stocks, and animal herds depleted. Napoleon's program of economic warfare damaged Prussia even more. The Peace of Tilsit obligated the Hohenzollern state to pay enormous "war contributions." The final sum of 120 million francs, or 32 million thaler, was higher than the entire prewar annual income of the monarchy. Although this figure was not established until some months after the reformers began their work, they anticipated from the beginning that it would be crippling. Moreover the peace terms gave the contributions a political as well as an economic overtone by stipulating that the French forces would occupy Prussian soil until payment was completed. The Peace of Tilsit, moreover, reduced Prussia's territory by half and its population by a greater degree, with a corresponding shrinkage of the tax base. The royal treasury, hastily taken from Berlin as the court fled Napoleon's armies, along with private capital held in government accounts, was quickly consumed by pressing military expenditures. On 21 November 1806, Napoleon triumphantly issued from Berlin the proclamation establishing the Continental System, barring all English trade from the continent. Though directed against Britain, this measure struck a disabling blow to Prussia's vital agricultural export business. Commerce stood still.[1]

As a result of these problems, there occurred a severe devaluation of Prussia's currencies; and this in turn stifled commerce even more and made

---

[1] Traité de paix entre la France et la Prusse, Tilsit, 9 July 1807, Alexandre de Clercq, ed., *Recueil des traités de la France* (Paris, 1864–1902) 2: 217–23; Convention entre la France et la Prusse, Königsberg, 12 July 1807, ibid., 270–73; Schmoller, "Epochen der preussischen Finanzpolitik," 112; Krause, *Der Provinzialminister Schroetter,* 60–66; Haussherr, *Erfüllung und Befreiung,* 15–17, 51–74, 228–41; Beguelin, *Denkwürdigkeiten,* 144–47, 169–74; Karl Borchard, *Staatsverbrauch und öffentliche Investitionen in Deutschland 1780–1850* (Diss., Göttingen, 1968), 22; Oswald Prentiss Backus III, *Stein and Russia's Prussian Policy from Tilsit to Vienna* (Diss. Yale, 1949; Microfilm Ann Arbor, 1980), 26–34.

the collection of taxes chaotic. Interest rates rose astronomically. Speculation in the form of payment of debts and purchases of property with inflated paper currency was rampant. Credit in Prussia, both that of the government and that of its merchants, plunged to a nadir at a time when foreign loans were essential.[2]

This combination of events produced severe anguish among the population. Far from being able to pay taxes to meet the state's obligations, many subjects were forced to concentrate on trying to rebuild destroyed property or merely obtain life-sustaining food. Requests came daily to the government for exemption from tax obligations due to inability to pay. Provincial officials predicted starvation if the government did not step in with relief. A Breslau newspaper's description in October 1807 is typical:

> Almost with certainty one can expect the greatest misery and a real famine . . . before spring arrives. The price of food has risen enormously, not to mention the general scarcity of money. For example, in some places a quart of butter costs fifteen silver groschen and an egg costs one silver groschen. If the already high grain prices have not yet risen to that degree, it is because the farmers must sell their stores in order to . . . defray the considerable costs of billeting soldiers.

Auerswald reported from his province that a major concern was the prevention of starvation:

> Our situation has become more critical. . . . Nothing has come out of the peace settlement which can abate our misery. . . . [We must receive from the government] grain, cattle and horses, . . . for presently the very *lives* of numerous people, as well as the possibility of continuation of agriculture, depend upon these things.[3]

Prussian leaders feared that such conditions would provoke revolutionary activity in the towns and countryside. Along with the appeals for assistance, numerous reports of unrest filled the files of the would-be reformers. When French troops entered the province of Silesia in the winter 1806–1807, many villagers had ceased to pay their feudal obligations. Some peasants in this region, who already had a history of protest and unruliness, believed the French had liberated them from their masters. In one area they staged a strike lasting nearly a year between the summers of 1807 and 1808. East Prussian officials worried, furthermore, that the news of peasant emancipations in the neighboring Grand Duchy of Warsaw and in the Kingdom of Westphalia would reach their province and prompt rural radicalism. Leopold von Gerlach described to his son the potentially explosive conditions in Berlin: "Due to the scarcity of bread, there occur daily small

---

[2] Borgstede to Stein, Stargard, 10 Dec. 1807, Nachlass Kehr, Kl. Erw. 508, fol. 112 (no. 63), Bundesarchiv, Koblenz; Brand to Staegemann, [Königsberg, mid-Dec. 1807], ibid., fols. 120–22 (no. 68); L'Abaye, Über den gesunkenen Wert . . . des Kredits der preussischen Staatspapiere, Berlin, 13 Dec. 1807, ibid., fols. 193–94 (no. 120).

[3] Aus dem schlesischen Hauptzeitungsbericht pro Oktober 1807, Breslau, 17 Nov. 1807, ibid., fol. 94 (no. 47); Auerswald to Schroetter, Königsberg, 14 July 1807, Auerswald Nachlass, Rep. 92, I, 2, Geheimes Staatsarchiv, Berlin-Dahlem; Carmer, Promemoria zur Abwendung der Hungersnot, Breslau, 29 March 1808, cited in Scheel, *Reformministerium* 2: 469, n. 1.

disturbances at the bakery shops. So far they have been insignificant, but on one occasion violence erupted, and the help of the [French] soldiers was necessary." Ironically, the occupying troops kept order in the cities and villages which allowed the reform government to prepare for orderly innovations rather than to confront distraught peasants and artisans.[4] The reform party concentrated on alleviating the immediate distress of the affected populace while at the same time laying plans for a new economic framework which would remove what they considered the underlying, long-term causes of the crisis.

Schroetter, the administrator responsible for the eastern provinces not under direct French jurisdiction, submitted on 20 July 1807 an urgent report, appealing for eight thousand head of livestock to be distributed among domain inhabitants to give them a new start. He requested money, lumber, and horses to rebuild damaged structures and replace missing draft animals.[5] The Immediate Commission, serving as the interim government in Memel, recognized the need for emergency aid by granting Schroetter fifty thousand thaler to be used to alleviate the distress of war victims. But the Immediate Commission criticized the basic principles underlying Schroetter's report, calling it "a temporary measure like that of the man who gives bread to a starving individual . . . in order to save his life." The fundamental causes of poverty were not even touched. The state could not fulfill its obligations by granting alms, for the people would only come to regard the government as an eternal source of charity. "In our opinion, the government can successfully act only by seeking out and destroying the long-range hindrances to prosperity."[6] Out of this critique grew the two sets of plans for economic reform.

Attempting to attack the problem at its roots, the Immediate Commission drew up its own proposal for relief and reform which it was able to present in a report dated 17 August. Following Schroetter's lead, the Immediate Commission focused upon agriculture. Business and commerce would be restored to a firm footing if prosperity were reestablished in rural areas. Essential to the plan were the steps proposed to eliminate feudal and mercantilistic limitations on the real estate market. Agriculturalists must have ready means of obtaining credit. Under existing conditions the laws of entail, which prohibited estate owners from burdening their lands with

---

[4] Ziekursch, *Hundert Jahre Agrargeschichte,* 278–79; Ernst Klein, *Von der Reform zur Restauration: Finanzpolitik und Reformgesetzgebung des preussischen Staatskanzlers Karl August von Hardenberg,* Veröffentlichungen der Historischen Kommission zu Berlin 16 (Berlin, 1965), 129; Leopold von Gerlach to Wilhelm von Gerlach, Berlin, 26 June 1808, in Schoeps, ed., *Aus den Jahren preussischer Not,* 356; Hans Mottek, *Wirtschaftsgeschichte Deutschlands: Ein Grundriss,* vol. 2, *Von der Zeit der französischen Revolution bis zur Zeit der bismarckschen Reichsgründung* (Berlin, 1976), 19; William W. Hagen, *Germans, Poles, and Jews: The Nationality Conflict in the Prussian East, 1772-1914* (Chicago, 1980), 67–70.

[5] Schroetter, Immediatbericht, 20 July 1807, R[ichard] Staberock, ed., *Stein und der Wiederaufbau des preussischen Staates,* Teubners Quellensammlung für den Geschichtsunterricht an höheren Schulen 2, 70 (Leipzig and Berlin, 1929), 3 (no. 3).

[6] Immediate Commission, Immediatbericht, Memel, 17 Aug. 1807, ibid., 4–8 (no. 5).

debt without the consent of future owners, restricted loans, mortgages, and sale of property. Entail should be abolished along with all other laws and traditions preventing the free exchange of real estate. This was an argument, in effect, for termination of the feudal notion of aristocratic property, as well as for elimination of the economic division between city and countryside. The Immediate Commission's proposal also implied the necessity of repealing the eighteenth-century peasant protection statutes (*Bauernschutz*). These measures, which strictly forbade the enclosure of peasant farms into noble estates or into larger non-aristocratic holdings, had been a favorite program of Frederick the Great who sought to preserve the three-class system by protecting the traditional status of the peasantry. Arguing by specific example, the Immediate Commission cited a case in which four peasant families tilled plots of one hufe (twenty acres) each, using four draft animals apiece. The land could be worked more efficiently, the Commission argued, if the four farms were combined under the proprietorship of one household which utilized hired laborers and six rather than sixteen animals.[7]

Finally, the Commission insisted that in order to restore prosperity to Prussia, serfdom, "a remnant of the dark ages," must be abolished. They proposed that within a maximum of six years all servile relationships be terminated. Their plan linked enlargement of farms and abrogation of serfdom in a single process: During the six-year transition period, estate owners who felt they could not (or did not wish to) maintain their existing number of peasant farms would report to their respective provincial administrative offices. Provincial officials would supervise the union of small farms into larger units of between four and ten hufen (eighty to two hundred acres). Every peasant family whose farm was eliminated through the enlargement process would be granted immediate freedom and would be compensated for its land. After six years, or after complete abolition of all serfdom, it would be expedient to allow "every estate owner to use his lands as he wished," renting it out to tenants or integrating it into his own estate and employing hired labor.

Anticipating objections from landlords, the Immediate Commission argued that abolition of feudal relationships would not cause a shortage of agricultural labor. Rather, it would relieve proprietors from having to support an uneconomical number of workers. A free labor market, like a free real estate market, was essential to the healthy restoration of economic prosperity:

> The number of people presently seeking work is disproportionately larger than the demand for labor. Therefore, no one will be . . . unable to locate workers on account of abolition of serfdom. If one [landlord] in a hundred does face this situation, this just demonstrates that he treats his people badly. . . . It is an advantage to [society] if such an owner is forced to sell his estate on this account.

[7] For this and following paragraphs: Ibid. On the Bauernschutz legislation see Schissler, *Preussische Agrargesellschaft*, 55, 115.

Schroetter's response was quick. Aware of the Immediate Commission's criticism of his request for help in the provinces, the provincial minister presented by 17 August—the same day as the Immediate Commission's report—his own program for long-term recovery. Schroetter and his staff, like the Immediate Commission, called for elimination of restrictions on free disposition of land, including the feudal limitations on incurring debts upon entailed estates. But they proposed even more far-reaching changes in the economy, including the abolition of all governmental restrictions on foreign commerce and regulations of manufacture. Asserting that state proprietorship of domain lands was uneconomical, Schroetter advocated perpetual leasing of the royal farms. He argued that every profession should be open to all citizens, regardless of social class. Furthermore he emphatically demanded the abrogation of serfdom, for which, he asserted, "the general voice of the times and a sound economy have long cried." He did not, however, address the question of peasant land ownership or suggest a change in the Bauernschutz legislation.[8]

Still awaiting Stein's arrival, King Frederick William was faced with two far-reaching proposals for agrarian reform. Predictably, the king preferred to put his trust in the minister from whom he had received advice for many years, rather than the impatient young bureaucrats of the Immediate Commission. Beyme addressed a cabinet order to Schroetter requesting the preparation of an edict which would make the proposed reforms applicable to all Hohenzollern territories, rather than to just East and West Prussia. He recommended that Schroetter take the Immediate Commission's report into consideration, especially the provisions abolishing the Bauernschutz and providing for enlarging peasant farms.[9]

Schroetter's staff in Königsberg revised and expanded their proposal. Their report, "Regulation . . . for Reestablishment of East and West Prussia," of 9 September 1807, was in its final draft upon Stein's arrival later that month. It included a proposal, adapted from the Immediate Commission's report, for the enlargement of some peasant farms. The most important innovation in the new document was a program for establishment of a strict laissez-faire economic policy in regard to peasant-landlord relationships. According to the Regulation, small farmers who owned their land would be emancipated immediately from feudal bonds. Those who tilled land by virtue of a hereditary or terminable lease, as well as nonfarming serfs, could receive freedom as early as 1810. Either the vassal or the master could initiate the process, and all ties would be dissolved within

[8] Schroetter, Immediatbericht, 17 Aug. 1807, Dep. Brünneck, no. 124, fols. 175–88, StA Königsberg. Excerpts from this lengthy document can be found in Knapp, *Bauern-Befreiung* 2: 155–56 and Staberock, *Stein und der Wiederaufbau*, 8–9 (no. 6). See also Pertz, *Stein* 2: 16–17; Georg Winter, "Zur Entstehungsgeschichte des Oktoberedikts und der Verordnung vom 14. Febr. 1808," *Forschungen zur brandenburgischen und preussischen Geschichte* 30 (1927), 11.

[9] Kabinettsordre to Schroetter, Memel, 23 Aug. 1807, [Ewald] *Zu Schutz und Trutz am Grabe Schön's: Bilder aus der Zeit der Schmach und der Erhebung Preussens* (Berlin, 1876), 214–16. The document is printed in abridged form in Staberock, *Stein und der Wiederaufbau*, 9–10 (no. 7).

two and one-half years. The lord would not pay an indemnity to the peasant family, nor would the latter have to purchase its freedom. Schroetter and his colleagues granted proprietors the right to dispose of vacated peasant land as they pleased. This meant, of course, that peasants forfeited their land as they gained their freedom.[10]

The question of disposition of peasant lands was the issue which sparked deep controversy between the Immediate Commission and the East Prussian office. The Commission in Memel presented Stein with a detailed response to Schroetter's proposal, arguing that an "aristocratic bias" colored the minister's recommendations. They argued for measures to protect peasant holdings from greedy landlords. Unable to solve this thorny debate, Stein postponed it for further consideration so that the other provisions of the reform could be speedily effected. Only ten days after his arrival in Memel, Stein was able to publish, over the king's signature, the momentous Edict of 9 October 1807.[11]

Contemporaries and historians alike have acknowledged this measure as the most significant legislative act of the Stein ministry. It is generally described as the decree which emancipated peasants from feudal servitude. The primary purpose of the measure, however, was the establishment of a free real estate market and a modern form of property ownership, as the measure's own title implies: "Edict Regarding [both] Facilitated Ownership and Free Use of Real Estate [and] Personal Conditions of the Rural Populace." Of twelve articles in the royal decree, eight deal with freedom of trade in land: "Every inhabitant of our states is entitled without any limitations to possess immobile properties of any kind." Nobles could henceforth purchase not only formerly "aristocratic" lands, but also "peasant farms," as well as properties within municipal boundaries. Aristocratic estates were no longer entailed family possessions. The middle class, urban dwellers with capital to invest, were now permitted to hold mortgages on or to purchase agricultural property. Finally, the act granted peasants the legal right to own landed property of any type. With regard to proprietorship of land all Prussian subjects were for the first time legally on equal footing.

Abolition of the servile relationship between landlords and peasants was a logical extension of the decree's major objective. A free land market could not exist if peasants held contracts binding them to farms and masters:

---

[10] Each paragraph of the Verordnung, wodurch die allgemeinen Mittel zum Retablissement der Provinzen Ost- und Westpreussen festgelegt werden, 9 Sept. 1807, is summarized in Knapp, *Bauern-Befreiung* 2: 162–64. The synopsis in Staberock, *Stein und der Wiederaufbau,* 14–15 (no. 13), is even shorter.

[11] Stein, Bemerkungen über die Aufhebung der Erbuntertänigkeit, [Memel], 8 Oct. [1807], Scheel, *Reformministerium* 1: 10–11 (no. 6); Stein to Immediate Commission, Memel, 8 Oct. 1807, in Botzenhart, *Stein Briefe* 2/2: 456 (no. 395); Edikt, den erleichterten Besitz und den freien Gebrauch des Grundeigentums sowie die persönlichen Verhältnisse der Landbewohner betreffend, Memel, 7 Oct. 1807, Scheel, *Reformministerium* 1: 11–16 (no. 7). See the useful discussion of historiographical terms employed to describe the measure in Schissler, "Bauernbefreiung," 136–42.

With the publication of this ordinance, the servile condition of those subjects and their wives and children who own their land or who hold perpetual leases ceases completely. . . . At the Feast of St. Martin 1810 [11 November, the traditional end of the agricultural year when peasant contracts were renewed], all serfdom is abolished. After Martinmas 1810, there will be only free people.[12]

Despite their differences about the best way to dispose of peasant properties, there was one primary underlying goal upon which the reformers agreed: profitable market-oriented agriculture. Their edict legalized modern forms of credit and mortgaging, as well as sale and transfer of property. Indeed, the act ordained and prescribed a capitalist form of ownership by abolishing the legal basis for entail, the institution which prohibited the alienation of aristocratic lands from family possession. Noble families might elect to continue practicing this custom, but only as a matter of private agreement. The state and its courts would no longer regulate such affairs. On the other hand, mortgages, two-party contracts central to the maintenance of a sound system of credit, were important to the state. Shortly after promulgation of the October Edict, the government decreed that mortgages would come under the jurisdiction of higher courts, rather than the customary local courts, to insure increased security and efficiency of state supervision.[13]

The reformers believed that with their edict they had abolished the economic limitations of hereditary aristocratic privilege in landownership. This had been one of their primary objectives from the beginning. In earlier times, when the only free men were noblemen, Theodor von Schön argued, it had been appropriate to grant privileges to the landowning class. But "the external and internal conditions of the state and of all Europe have changed so completely and so visibly . . . that the state no longer has an interest in supporting the nobility. Furthermore, the aristocracy can no longer find . . . security in purely agricultural pursuits." The "true nobility" of our land, Schön continued, has nothing to do with the "chance of birth." It is rather the middle class which can do the most for the welfare of the nation. If we remove the artificial limitations of land proprietorship, the middle class can provide Prussia with a genuine nobility. They will become "the supporters of order, the strongest pillar of the existing monarchy and the class with the greatest obligation to the state."[14]

Contemporaries, especially the educated middle classes, were jubilant over the publication of the agrarian edict. Hamburg's *Politisches Journal* reported that the news of the Prussian decree evoked an "immediate, elevating, uplifting sensation." On New Year's Day, 1808, the *Zeitung für die elegante Welt* described the great hopes awakened by the "magnificent Edict of 9 October [which] promises to destroy gradually feudal institutions,

---

[12] Edikt, Memel, 7 Oct. 1807, Scheel, *Reformministerium* 1: 11–16 (no. 7).

[13] Ibid. On mortgages, see Schroetter to Stein, Königsberg, 25 Dec. 1807, Kehr Nachlass, Kl. Erw. 508, fols. 125–26 (no. 72), Bundesarchiv, Koblenz.

[14] Schön to Altenstein, 14 Aug. 1807, Winter, *Reorganisation*, 263–64 (no. 207).

prerogatives of birth, and servile relationships. . . . Finally it has arrived, the beautiful tomorrow . . . when people and talents will gain [just] recognition and appropriate treatment." The periodical, *Volksfreund* (*Friend of the People*), proclaimed the agrarian legislation to be a victory of the "natural and inalienable rights of humanity." Typical of early liberal thinkers, the rejoicers did not distinguish between political and economic freedoms. Those who celebrated the morality and justice of emancipation saw it as a part of the process of establishing a modern economy. The Prussian administrator, Heinrich von Beguelin, viewed the agrarian reforms as the "surest means of fostering industry and the national well-being." "What do you think of the innovations?" he wrote a friend in October, 1807. "We are springing ahead by centuries!"[15] Beguelin was correct when he asserted that the land reform would ultimately provide a foundation for industry, for it was a significant step in the establishment of the mobility necessary for a modern labor force.

Consistent with their objective of establishing free trade in agriculture, the reformers moved ahead with plans to withdraw the state from the business of farming by placing the domain lands on an open market. Among the reform party there raged a debate about the effects such a step would have in the short run on the economy and on the state's ability to procure credit abroad.[16] However, all parties agreed with Vincke who drafted a memorandum arguing the long-term advantage of sale, lease or mortgage of the royal properties:

> Under the existing system the lands are of little value to the state [when compared] to the return they would yield if [managed privately] by judicious owners. . . . Furthermore, [the costs of state proprietorship] are increased by a whole bureaucracy of . . . administrators. Yet these disadvantages are small when compared to those [resulting from] the mass of unproductive workers, the overburdening of civil servants [and] the inefficient and highly ruinous [governmental] interference in private affairs.[17]

The reformers planned to issue mortgage notes on the domains which in the short run would provide a badly needed source of state revenue, but ultimately would facilitate a transfer of ownership to the private sector of the economy. The East Prussian Estates Assembly approved this plan in February 1808, as the Stein government was already undertaking measures to put it into effect.[18]

---

[15] Quoted newspapers and memoirs cited in Schmidt, *Freiherr vom und zum Stein: Schriften,* 136.

[16] Immediate Commission, Immediatbericht, Memel, 3 Dec. 1807, Kehr Nachlass, Kl. Erw. 508, fols. 108–109 (no. 57), Bundesarchiv, Koblenz; Wittgenstein to Stein, Hamburg, 22 Nov. 1808, ibid. listed, fol. 191.

[17] Vincke, Denkschrift betr. die bei Veräusserung der Domänen zu beobachenden Grundsätze, Memel, 6 Dec. 1807, Aktenzüge Kehrs für die Edition "Preussische Finanzpolitik," ibid., fol. 145 (no. 718).

[18] Plan zur Credit-Assoziation der königlichen Domainen mit dem ritterschaftlichen Credit-System [21 Dec. 1807], Rep. 2, Tit. 23, no. 1, Vol. 1, fols. 55–56, StA Königsberg; Mauer, *Das Landschaftliche Kreditwesen,* 207–10.

Land, the economy's most precious resource, the most promising type of investment and the most permanent form of asset, was to become available to those who could make it the most profitable: private capitalists. Henceforth the market, not arbitrary laws or antiquated customs, would determine who enjoyed the prestige of property ownership.

FREE CHOICE OF PROFESSION

In a brief section entitled "Free Choice of Occupation," the Edict of 9 October abolished the legal barriers which separated the three Estates of Prussia: "Every nobleman is entitled to pursue middle-class professions without detriment to his status; all middle-class citizens and peasants have the right to [alter their status and occupation]." This simple statement, low-keyed in its wording, was the legal foundation for a modern, mobile society in Prussia. The reformers intended that talent and resources establish a person's place in society. Freedom of choice would determine the geographical distribution and economic stratification of the population. This was Prussia's formal adoption of the new European-wide ideal of the career based on talent.[19]

Having made this sweeping provision of a constitutional nature, Stein's colleagues debated its application tirelessly for the remainder of the reform year. They were concerned first with establishing a process to facilitate the transition of peasants from serfdom to freedom and secondly with abolition of guild regulations, the legal basis of corporate society in urban areas.

The most complicated problem with regard to the peasants was the one whose solution was postponed by Stein in October: Who would gain title to peasants' land under the new system of social mobility? Once villagers were free to leave their lands—indeed free to go to cities to pursue "middle-class" professions—would they gain modern titles to their farms, or would their properties, being parts of noble estates, revert to the ownership of the aristocratic holders? The reform party was aware that a decision on this matter would have far-reaching implications. On the one hand, the measure could depopulate the countryside, transforming century-old peasant communities into ghost villages and leaving the rural population without economic resources. On the other hand, allowing traditional guarantees such as the Bauernschutz to remain intact would undermine the social mobility and the free land market sought by the reformers from the beginning.

There were also political implications. Since the reformers regarded political representation as based on property, the disposition of land would establish the state's pattern of enfranchisement. Emancipation of serfs meant in theory that the bureaucracy relinquished its minute regulation of peasant conditions. But Stein's government, while in favor of a free market

---

[19] Hobsbawn, *The Age of Revolution,* 218–37.

system, was hesitant about possible obliteration of the traditional lower Estate. The ministry thus faced a potential ironic choice of establishing a new set of bureaucratic rules and offices to govern the market and safeguard the peasantry.

One of several proposals to redefine the peasants' position was that of Minister von Schroetter who called for establishment of a laissez-faire system. He urged that peasant tenure contracts be silently terminated as a corollary to the abolition of personal servitude. A freed serf's land either would return to the lord's holdings or become purchasable by the estate owner, depending upon the particular type of contract. Schroetter's staff maintained that peasants and their heirs should be treated the same as aristocrats. Neither the status of birth, nor contracts held under an abolished system, should imply privilege, state protection, or guaranteed rights. The concept, "freedom" no longer conveyed privilege, but rather it meant that everyone was on equal footing. Possession of the necessary capital to purchase, maintain and improve real estate should determine who practiced agriculture. Members of the abolished peasant class would seek their own place in society.[20]

Schroetter was aware that this position was consistent with the wishes of noble proprietors in his province who pled their cause directly to the king. If the "difficult and dangerous" process of emancipation is to be carried out, wrote the Estates Committee, "the first and most essential prerequisite is that every estate owner be granted the right to free disposition of his peasant lands without interference from the government. [He should be permitted to] enclose peasant farms . . . at his convenience." In replying to the landlords, Schroetter urged them to notice that "the abolition of serfdom . . . is by no means being undertaken solely for the benefit of the lower classes, but also for the [advantage of] estate owners. The right to enclose or combine peasant farms . . . is contained in my draft of the new edict."[21]

Members of the Immediate Commission raised vehement criticism to this part of Schroetter's proposal, voicing the fear that the sudden establishment of a free market without at least temporary safeguards would obliterate Prussia's peasantry. They drew a distinction between servitude, which they described as a "purely personal" issue, and the right to possess land, which they argued was contractual in nature. The Immediate Commission advocated state protection of peasants' status during a transitional period following emancipation. Stein agreed. Committed to "freedom," he

[20] Verordnung, wodurch die allgemeinen Mittel zum Retablissement der Provinzen Ost- und Westpreussen festgelegt werden, 9 Sept. 1807, summarized in Knapp, *Die Bauern-Befreiung* 2: 162–64.

[21] Eingabe von 13 Mitgliedern des Adels in der Provinz Ostpreussens an den König, 29 Aug. 1807, Staberock, *Stein und der Wiederaufbau*, 11–13 (no. 10). Schreiben des Staatsministers von Schroetter und des Kanzlers von Schroetter an die ostpreussischen Gutsbesitzer [n.d.], ibid., 13–14 (no. 12).

and several of his staff members nevertheless held also an attachment to the notion of a prosperous class of yeoman farmers. They emotionally defended the state's responsibility to safeguard small proprietors, the backbone of healthy agrarian society. Pointing to the negative consequences of land reform both in Mecklenburg on the Baltic and in Scotland where peasant holdings had been almost completely sacrificed to latifundia, Stein commissioned Schön to draft a new regulation providing for transitional safeguards of the nonnoble agriculturalists. Schön's plan, promulgated as the Ordinance of 14 February 1808, laid down the specific conditions under which emancipation and enclosure were to occur. It was a compromise: one-half of all land which had been under peasant proprietorship at the census dates of 1752 in East Prussia and 1774 in West Prussia would remain perpetually in the hands of nonaristocrats, "so that a useful, respectable peasant class might arise." The remaining half might be enclosed into aristocratic estates "in order that larger holdings may be established whose owners can increase their capital." Property which retained its classification as "peasant land" must be arranged in farms with a minimum size of four to eight hufen (80–160 acres) depending upon local agricultural conditions.[22]

The February Ordinance provoked a flood of protests from estate owners who argued that it was an attack upon their traditional rights and a reversal of the principles established in the October Edict. Throughout the year the Estates Committees repeatedly appealed for its withdrawal or amendment: "The strict observance of this provision ruins the estate owner and his peasants, violates his property rights, and brings none of the projected advantages to the state." Stein and his colleagues energetically defended the measure, stressing the state's need to maintain a healthy peasantry. Stein even argued that the February Ordinance had been too generous to landlords and urged increasing the proportion of protected peasant land when the ordinance was extended to other provinces of the monarchy. Stein and his colleagues believed that they were establishing not only a new economic system, but a new moral order as well, in which individuals would gain self-reliance through freedom and property.[23]

---

[22] Report of the Immediate Commission, 17 Aug. 1807, Schön, *Aus den Papieren* 2: 101–29. The "introduction" printed with this document is unhistorical. It was written by Schön in the 1840s. Immediate Commission, Immediatbericht, Memel, 19 Dec. 1807, Scheel, *Reformministerium* 1: 233–37 (no. 70). The insignificant amount of land which peasants had acquired subsequent to the census dates of 1752 and 1774 would be placed in a completely free market, according to Schön's plan. Stein to Schroetter, Königsberg, 29 Jan. 1808, Botzenhart, *Stein Briefe* 2/2: 639 (no. 577). Verordnung wegen Zusammenziehung bäuerlicher Grundstücke *formministerium* 1: 369–73 (no. 116). For more detail see Gray, "Schroetter, Schön and Society," *Central European History* 6 (1973): 60–74. See also the discussion on the part of the East and West Prussian officials regarding the proposed ordinance: "Wegen des Oktoberedikts," Rep. 2, Tit. 24, no. 1, fols. 4–31, StA Königsberg. Bock, "Reform und Revolution," *Militärgeschichte* 19 (1980): pp. 604–606.

[23] Bujack, *Das erste Triennium*, 5, 11–13; Stein to the Committee of the East Prussian Estates, Königsberg, 1 July 1808, Botzenhart, *Stein Briefe* 2/2: 773–76 (no. 737); Stein to Committee of East Prussian Estates, Königsberg, 16 Aug. 1808, ibid., pp. 818–20 (no. 781); Stein to the deputies of the Silesian nobility, Königsberg, 24 Sept. 1808 (summarized), ibid., 874 (no. 829);

In spite of the acid debate between those who favored landlords' unlimited right to enclose and those who believed the state should foster and protect a peasant class, it is clear that the process of "emancipation" was a land reform which would dislodge great numbers of peasant families from their hereditary farmsteads and their place in society. Schön, who argued emphatically for protection of the peasant proprietor class, insisted upon a minimum of four hufen (eighty acres) for post-reform peasant tracts. He was thinking not of village families, but of economic enterprise. At the turn of the nineteenth century, with the exception of the Kölmer estates, very few nonaristocratic holdings approximated this size. Peasants were accustomed to supporting their families on a fraction of that amount of land. Most would be left propertyless when their farms were combined with others to attain the minimum size. Schön and his colleagues described emancipation as a moral cause. "There is no greater injustice than a fellow subject of the state being denied a reasonable existence merely because he was born on this or that piece of soil," they proclaimed. But the October Edict and the February Ordinance together established an official state policy of accelerating the previously spontaneous process that turned peasants into landless proletarians which had been underway for decades. What the population rise and the commercialization of farming had earlier accomplished, the government would now oversee. The reformers were explicit about their expectations for agriculture. Vincke, for example, argued that very small proprietors were a "burden to society," and looked forward to their elimination. His memoranda on political reform were filled with anticipation of the time when "the Edict of October 9 [will have] created a middle class of farmers."[24]

The reformers had little to say about the multitude of rural folk who would be displaced in the process of emancipation and land consolidation. It is striking that the memoranda of the Stein government so seldom mention

---

Darstellung der Gründe weshalb um eine nähere Declaration der Verordnung vom 14. Febr. 1808, §6 dringendst . . . gebeten werden muss, Königsberg, 11 Dec. 1809, Rep. 2, Tit. 23, no. 6, fols. 3–5, StA Königsberg. The quotation from this document, though dating from 1809, is typical of the statements issued throughout the year of Stein's tenure. Gagliardo, *From Pariah to Patriot*, 187–96.

[24] Immediate Commission report of 17 Aug. 1808, Schön, *Aus den Papieren* 2: 125; Vincke, Zwecke und Mittel der preussischen Staatsverwaltung, [Berlin], 3 Aug. 1808, Scheel, *Reformministerium* 3: 710 (no. 225); Vincke, Über die Organisation der Unterbehörden, 2. Für die Finanzverwaltung, [Berlin], 14 June 1808, ibid., 2: 614 (no. 188). The process of establishing freedom of property rights in an effort to establish middle-class proprietorship was not limited to Prussia. On this phenomenon in the Confederation of the Rhine, see Fehrenbach, *Der Kampf um die Einführung des Code Napoléon*, 22–27. See also Schlumbohm, *Freiheit*, 83, for a discussion of the ideological link between "freedom" and "property." On the size of turn-of-the-century land holdings, see Wilhelm Abel, *Geschichte der deutschen Landwirtschaft vom frühen Mittelalter bis zum 19. Jahrhundert*, Deutsche Agrargeschichte 2 (Stuttgart, 1962), 193–99; K. Böhme, *Gutsherrlich-bäuerliche Verhältnisse*, 8; Rudolf Berthold, "Einige Bemerkungen über den Entwicklungsstand des bäuerlichen Ackerbaus vor den Agrarreformen des 19. Jahrhunderts," *Beiträge zur deutschen Wirtschafts- und Sozialgeschichte des 18. und 19. Jahrhunderts*, Deutsche Akademie der Wissenschaften zu Berlin, Schriften des Instituts für Geschichte, Series 1, Vol. 10 (Berlin, 1962), 8.

these people who under the old regime were considered "classless." Their lack of status would present no problem after Estates themselves had been abolished and all people were free. The liberals' philosophy taught them that emancipated (and landless) villagers, along with everyone else, would benefit from the new prosperity brought by more efficient agriculture. However, as long as property was related to political rights, the reformers were creating a new, disenfranchised class. The difference between the old and the new systems was that now the freed peasants enjoyed the legal right to enter any profession and climb to any status. In the long run the emancipated families would form the mobile working class, basic to development of an industrial capitalism. Meanwhile the agriculturalists who enjoyed economic advantage—aristocrats, Kölmer, prosperous peasants, and middle-class entrepreneurs who turned to husbandry—would thrive under the new market conditions.

The reformers' debate over maintenance of a peasant class was complicated by the special situation of the "immediate peasants," the inhabitants of the royal domain farms. The October Edict and the February Ordinance dealt only with the land and people of private estates, so additional regulations were needed to determine the fate of the domain villagers and their lands. Abolition of serfdom was no problem in this circumstance. Hohenzollern monarchs had kept pace with enlightened economic thought and modern agricultural practices in managing their royal states. In 1805 Frederick William III had culminated a century of gradual reforms on the domains with the abolition of remaining vestiges of servitude for the fifty thousand domain peasants. After the opening of the reform year he declared "emphatically" that "as of 1 June 1808, my domain peasants are emancipated from servile bonds. . . . They are free persons. . . . They are released from obligations to pay indemnities and from compulsory labor or dues."[25]

Yet the reformers faced the same question they encountered following the promulgation of the October Edict: Does abolition of servile duties also mean cancellation of peasants' contracts to farm the land? Who had the greater claim to the land, the peasant who had been bound to cultivate it for centuries, or the state which had collected the rents? The issue was colored by the government's plans to sell the domains and by its lack of resources to support the peasants in the postwar crisis. The Immediate Commission had granted funds for temporary relief prior to Stein's arrival, but restoration of destroyed villages, crops and livestock, an obligation of the state as feudal lord under the old system, would require a capital outlay impossible for the bankrupt Prussian government. The peasants themselves,

---

[25] Kabinettsordre an den Geheimen Finanzrat und Kammerpräsidenten von Gerlach, Memel, 28 Oct. 1807, Scheel, *Reformministerium* 1: 55 (no. 24). On earlier domain reform, see Robert Stein, *Die Umwandlung der Agrarverfassung Ostpreussens durch die Reform des neunzehnten Jahrhunderts,* Schriften des königlichen Instituts für ostdeutsche Wirtschaft an der Universität Königsberg, 5, 1–5,3 (Königsberg, 1918–34) 1: 50–60, 292–300; Knapp, *Die Bauern-Befreiung* 1: 81–114.

obviously lacking the money to restore their properties, would have to forfeit their holdings if domain farms were simply placed in a free market.

The Immediate Commission's proposal for dealing with tenure rights of domain peasants was based upon the premise that the state was obliged to dispose of its properties in a profitable manner. In order to promote efficient agriculture, the Commission regarded it as the government's responsibility, furthermore, "to remove cultivation from the hands of the poor class of peasants who lack capital and to place it in the possession of prosperous land-dwellers." They advocated that domain peasants be placed entirely on their own resources. "Those who cannot continue to cultivate their lands . . . or to meet their obligations without support should forfeit their right to occupy their farms." The state should terminate the peasants' free use of royal commons. It should require those able to maintain their farms under the new conditions to purchase the property at a fair market price.[26]

Like his colleagues, Schroetter advocated the suspension of all forms of feudal support such as building materials, firewood, the use of commons, and reduced prices for supplies. However, he did not deem it wise to require a monetary payment for the land. This, he argued, would drive practically all the tillers away from the soil. The abolition of traditional supports should constitute the purchase price. The state, Schroetter pointed out, would gain considerable assets in deleting these traditional expenses from its budget. Furthermore, it would receive revenue both from the sale of supplies which previously had been given to the peasants and from leasing domain commons.[27]

In reviewing the two plans, Stein was struck with the fact that the Immediate Commission had abandoned their argument that the state should foster peasant proprietorship, whereas Schroetter had assumed an apparently greater concern for the small farmers' tenure rights. Stein pointed out that when the eastern Hohenzollern provinces had originally been settled in the thirteenth century, peasants had enjoyed ownership, and since then they had sunk gradually into a condition of servitude. The state should return the land to the peasants, the original owners, he maintained. Although he was one of the strongest advocates of procuring desperately needed revenue from sale of the domains, Stein favored Schroetter's position which would be less remunerative for the government. The leader of the reform government felt that it was vital to maintain peasant proprietorship in the modern age. At Stein's direction, Schroetter finalized his proposal which was promulgated as a royal decree on 27 July 1808.[28]

---

[26] Memorandum of the Immediate Commission quoted in Volkmar Gropp, *Der Einfluss der Agrarreformen des beginnenden 19. Jahrhunderts in Ostpreussen auf Höhe und Zusammensetzung der preussischen Staatseinkünfte*, Schriften zur Wirtschafts- und Sozialgeschichte 9 (Berlin, 1967), 100. Knapp, *Die Bauern-Befreiung* 2: 186–87.

[27] Ibid., 2: 181, 184–86.

[28] Stein, Denkschrift über Verleihung des Eigentumsrechts an die Immediatbauern, Königsberg, 14 June 1808, Scheel, *Reformministerium* 2: 604–10 (no. 187); Verordnung wegen

In the debate over rights of domain peasants versus those of the government, Schroetter maintained a modestly benevolent position toward the villagers. Where noble estate owners' prerogatives were not affected, Schroetter thought it prudent to foster small farmers' welfare. The Immediate Commission, who in other circumstances pled the cause of a yeoman class, was not interested in maintaining the peasant families of the domains. Of more importance to them was the state, which should maximize its benefit from transition of domains to post-feudal conditions. In their major thrust, however, both groups of planners agreed: Domain lands should be put into the hands of private entrepreneurs. The agrarian legislation of 1808 laid the foundation for a capitalist economy in the countryside.

Similar measures were called for in the cities. Although serfdom did not exist there, the guild system (*Zunftzwang*) had the same economic effect. So long as it remained intact, free market conditions were precluded, and the commodity of labor did not exist. By the time the reformers were at work in Prussia, guilds had been under criticism for at least a half a century. Adam Smith and adherents of his economic principles decried them. The eighteenth-century physiocratic school of economics, prevalent in France, favored the elimination of guilds. As early as the 1750s, German political writers such as Johann Heinrich Gottlob von Justi and G. F. Lamprecht attacked the medieval corporations for their inefficiency, corruption and restrictiveness in market freedom. By the time of the French Revolution, guilds were under outright assault. In 1791 the revolutionary government in Paris abolished them. Napoleon carried this tradition to Central Europe as he extended the French empire. By 1807 in much of northern and western Germany, guilds had been either abolished, restricted, or made nonobligatory in key facets of the economy. One of Prussia's most outspoken critics of the guild system was Professor Hoffman, whose book, *The Interest of People and Citizens with the Present Guild System* (1803), represented the guilds as serving only selfish interests and hence harming the general welfare of society.[29]

Some time before the Stein-Hardenberg party formed as a cohesive group, Prussian leaders had begun to chip away at local guild institutions. As early as May 1806—months before Prussia experienced the military consequences of the Napoleonic war—Stein, Schroetter, and other gov-

---

Verleihung des Eigentums von den Grundstücken der Immediateinsassen in den Domänen von Ostpreussen, Litauen und Westpreussen, Königsberg, 27 July 1808, Christian Jakob Kraus, *Staatswirthschaft*, ed. Hans von Auerswald (Königsberg, 1808–11) 5: appendix, 318–30. The document is severely abbreviated in Scheel, *Reformministerium* 2: 693–95 (no. 217).

[29] Kurt von Rohrscheidt, *Vom Zunftzwang zur Gewerbefreiheit: Eine Studie nach den Quellen* (Berlin, 1898), 183–96; J. H. Clapham, *The Economic Development of France and Germany 1815–1914* (Cambridge, 1966), 76–77, 83–85; Witt Bowden, Michael Karpovich, and Abbott Payson Usher, *An Economic History of Europe Since 1750* (New York, 1937), 28–30, 172–73, 185–87; Johann Gottfried Hoffmann, *Das Interesse des Menschen und Bürgers bei den bestehenden Zunftverfassungen* (Königsberg, 1803).

ernment leaders had effected a major transformation in the textile trade of the northeastern provinces. A royal decree of 4 May 1806 abolished regulations in the manufacture and sale of linen and cotton, making this a "completely free trade, bound to no guild or corporation." This applied expressly to textile works of both the cities and the countryside. This regional industry was suffering from the competition of Silesian weavers, and the government leaders viewed the establishment of a free market as the cure to its ills. In view of the centrality of the textile industry in spawning economic change in both Great Britain and on the continent, this can be viewed as a significant step.[30]

Another ordinance, similar in effect yet very local in its orientation, is also illustrative of the reformers' readiness to solve economic problems by the elimination of guild restrictions. A decree of 17 April 1806 freed the craft of stonecutting. Estate owners and foresters had complained that guild limitations prohibited their removing granite boulders from the land except under the supervision of master stonemasons. Furthermore, the ancient provisions limiting the actual hewing of stones to city and town locations caused unnecessary expense and delay in preparing building materials. The new ordinance made it possible to employ "common laborers" for the masonry craft, providing an impetus to both agriculture and the building trade.[31]

As the Stein government took shape, the long tradition of criticism of guilds, along with preliminary steps in specific trades, pointed to the possibility of an all-out assault on the corporate organizations. Of the reform party, Altenstein and Hardenberg were among the first to demand their unequivocal abrogation. "Guilds are harmful," Altenstein asserted in his Riga memorandum.

> They no longer belong in our age. . . . [They] make labor expensive. The entire guild system is disadvantageous to the . . . worker. . . . Everywhere it is regarded as the greatest gain when labor is employed in a factory system, free of guilds. . . . All guilds must be abolished as soon as possible.

Schroetter agreed. His reform proposal of 27 August 1807, an early draft of his plan for economic restoration after the war, explicitly advocated abrogating Prussia's guild system.[32]

However, the Stein administration of 1807–1808 did not follow up on this strong rhetoric. While the Prussian guilds were a focus of attention on the part of the reformers, they were not attacked with the same zeal, for example, as the institution of serfdom. Stein's colleagues merely perpetuated

---

[30] Verordnung wegen des freien Betriebes der Lein- und Baumwollen-Weberei in Ost-, West- und Neu-Ostpreussen, 4 May 1806, *Sammlungen der Gesetze und Verordnungen,* 85–87 (no. 5); Meier, *Französische Einflüsse,* 291; Rohrscheidt, *Vom Zunftzwang,* 204–20; Klaus Thiede, *Die Staats- und Wirtschaftsauffassung des Freiherrn vom Stein* (Jena, 1927), 115–16.

[31] Meier, *Französische Einflüsse* 2: 291; Rohrscheidt, *Vom Zunftzwang,* 216–20.

[32] Altenstein, Über die Leitung des preussischen Staats, Winter, *Reorganisation,* 409–11 (no. 262); Knapp, *Die Bauern-Befreiung* 2: 162–63.

patterns of change already in progress. They continued to eliminate specific abuses and arbitrary limitations in businesses which were apparently suffering, but they did not attempt to sweep away guild institutions as such. They worked to cast off restrictions both in trades which were encountering economic hardship and in those which dealt in the production and delivery of life necessities, including food and shelter.

In January 1808, the Stein ministry effected the dissolution of regulations in the crafting and sale of millstones, allowing the employment of unskilled laborers and permitting importation from abroad. Wartime conditions had aggravated a long-standing problem, the inability of millers to deliver an adequate supply of cereal products to an ever-increasing population. The reform measure was designed to alleviate this situation, by "foster[ing] the milling of flour and barley." An ordinance two months later confronted the issue in a more central way by abolishing the infamous *Mühlenzwang* which reserved the privilege of milling for the state, as well as for specific corporations, estate owners, and cities. The old system strictly forbade individuals to grind their own grain or to have it processed at any but prescribed mills. Subsequent to the reform, all landowners enjoyed the right to establish and operate mills of any type, a measure which the reformers thought would nurture a milling industry while making vital foodstuffs more available to the general public.[33]

The Stein government enacted its most extensive guild reform on 24 October 1808, shortly before Stein's forced departure. In the unoccupied provinces, this measure abolished completely the guilds of street vendors who in preindustrial times sold much of the foodstuffs consumed in towns. It also established the freedom of entry into the butcher and bakery trades. While not abrogating these particular guilds, the ordinance made membership voluntary rather than mandatory. Every inhabitant of a city, regardless of class or gender, gained the right to slaughter animals and to bake and sell food products of all types. The only qualification was a requirement to produce evidence of either training in the trade or a specified amount of property. The act also nullified previous restrictions on where flour and animals could be procured by bakers and butchers. Finally, it rescinded the old law requiring practitioners of the trade to provide daily fresh bread and meat. Henceforth, market demand was expected to insure that consumers received quality products.[34]

---

[33] Patent, wegen Aufhebung der bisherigen Einschränkungen bei dem Handel mit Mühlensteinen, rücksichtlich der Provinzen Ost- und Westpreussen, 23 Jan. 1808, *Sammlung der Gesetze und Verordnungen,* 189–93 (no. 27); Edikt für Ostpreussen, Litthauen, Ermeland und den Marienwerderschen landräthlichen Kreis, die Mühlengerechtigkeit und die durchgängige Aufhebung des Mühlenzwanges betreffend, 29 March 1808, ibid., 217–24; Thiede, *Die Staats- und Wirtschaftsauffassung,* 118; Rohrscheidt, *Vom Zunftzwang,* 248–72.

[34] Verordnung, wegen Aufhebung des Zunftzwanges und Verkaufmonopols der Bäcker-, Schlächter- und Höckergewerke in den Städten der Provinzen Ost-, Westpreussen und Litthauen, 24 Oct. 1808, *Sammlung der Gesetze und Verordnungen,* 315–17 (no. 53); Rohrscheidt, *Vom Zunftzwang,* 285–312.

An ordinance of 19 November 1808, prepared under Stein's direction, but not promulgated until after his departure, abolished a set of regulations which set the cities apart from the rural areas in terms of consumer trade. The new provision granted every individual the right to purchase and to sell products and crafted articles produced in the countryside, thus allowing the establishment of "industry" outside of city walls.[35]

The Stein ministry led Prussia in the direction of free markets and individual freedom of action. Wherever they encountered an economic or distribution problem, the reformers sought to solve it by removing guild restrictions, thus accelerating processes already underway. Their legislation altering guild privilege was corollary to the Municipal Ordinance of 1808 which removed the political functions of corporations by creating direct proportional political representation.

However, the reformers' responses to corporatism were as remarkable for what they did not do as for what they did. While the reform year saw the establishment of market freedom in the textile and non-luxury food trades, it left most guild institutions intact. The reformers effected no changes in the corporate regulation of brewing and the sale of beverages, the restaurant business, or confectionaries. Most Prussian artisans experienced no alteration in their economic orientation as a result of the Stein government's work. Clothing manufacture, shoe making, tailoring, tanning, hat and glove making, carpentry, cabinet making, locksmithery, roofing, plumbing, glazing, bookbinding, turnery, and dozens of other preindustrial crafts endured no loss of privilege. While guilds were becoming obsolete in Prussia, it is not accurate to credit the Stein government with their demise. Where they functioned smoothly, the colleagues of Stein were content to allow them to regulate craftsmanship, commerce, and social life.[36]

Theodor von Schön, known to contemporaries and historians alike as a resolute devotee of the principles of Adam Smith, summed up the equivocal position of the reform party in a lengthy essay written in July, 1808: "Further Considerations on the German Guild System." Schön composed his article in response to a newspaper discussion on the subject and intended it for public consumption. Schön believed that those who found guilds incompatible with a modern system of manufacture were misled. He maintained, rather, that the "natural order" of the guilds made them an ideal basis for "factory" organization. He emphasized that the guildmaster understood

---

[35] Ordnung für sämmtliche Städte der preussischen Monarchie, mit dazu gehöriger Instruktion, behufs der Geschäftsführung der Stadtverordneten bei ihren ordnungsmässigen Versammlungen, 19 Nov. 1808, *Sammlungen der Gesetze und Verordnungen,* 324–61 (no. 57).

[36] Many historians maintain that Stein resolutely opposed abolition of the guilds. See Hasek, *The Introduction of Adam Smith's Doctrines,* 142–43 and Hamerow, *Restoration, Revolution and Reaction,* 23–24. The documents reveal no such rigid position. Stein was often interestingly silent on the question of guilds during the reform year. See Beschluss der Generalkonferenz . . . wegen Aufhebung des Zunftzwanges und Verkauf-Monopols der Bäker- Schlächter- und Höckergewerke, Königsberg, 5 Oct. 1808, Scheel, *Reformministerium* 3: 894–95 (no. 271); Thiede, *Die Staats- und Wirtschaftsauffassung,* 106–34; Meier, *Französische Einflüsse* 2: 294.

the factory system, for he had long been doing on a small scale what industry would achieve on a large scale.[37]

Schön agreed with the guilds' critics that the existing system was inefficient and unjust. But reform of the guilds, rather than abolition, he contended, was the best manner in which to eradicate their liabilities. There was nothing inherently pernicious in the corporations. The system's two greatest deficiencies lay in its restriction of individual freedom and its prevention of competition. "Artisans who have capital and credit should be allowed to move without limitation into the class of manufacturers. A saddle maker, for example, should have the right to become owner of a wagon factory." He then should be allowed to employ the workers he needs, rather than those which some guild requires. He should have the privilege of selecting his own smiths, wheelwrights, leather workers and finishers, and these might be either guildsmen or nonguildsmen, according to the employer's choice. If such freedom existed, guilds could resume a positive social function, and they would lose their harmful, restrictive nature. Schön urged, furthermore, the abolition of guilds' monopolistic control of trades. Natural competition would be a healthier way to limit the number of master craftsmen. Moreover, guilds should not be tied to specific localities. Masters should be free to move to areas where their products were needed. Obsolete guilds should be allowed to die.

Schön's proposals amounted to an almost complete removal of the economic function of guilds. Yet, in contrast to Adam Smith and Professor Kraus, Schön was particularly insistent that guilds not be destroyed. He stressed the positive aspects of a stable, ordered society in which every member was guaranteed a place. He saw the corporate organization as security for those members of the community who were not endowed with great intelligence or a superior talent, but who possessed the virtues of "diligence and a skill." The latter, he feared, would go unrewarded in a system of raw competition. Furthermore the public would have no assurance that it would not be cheated by "unskilled and inept quacks," if it could not rely on the standards maintained by guilds.

Schön romanticized the communal organizations:

> In a guild system there is no slavish relationship between workers and masters. The ties are certainly milder and more humane than those which exist between a factory owner and his employees. The guildmaster is head of a family. He governs it and protects it; he distributes the work and he looks after the family's needs. His authority is terminated if he abuses his position.

In spite of the Stein government's municipal reforms to the contrary, Schön even discussed the possibilities that guilds might form the basis for com-

---

[37] For this and the following paragraphs: Schön, "Noch etwas vom deutschen Zunftwesen," 16 July 1808, Dep. Brünneck, no. 62, StA Königsberg. The essay was written in response to an article in issue no. 138 of *Der Allgemeine Anzeiger* of 1808 and was intended for publication in that periodical.

munity government. They could collect taxes, superintend their own local administration and provide a liaison among the individual, the community, and the higher levels of government. If they elected their leaders directly from their own members, this would establish "real civil freedom for the individual as well as for the community. Who, if he has any true feeling for civil government, would trade this for government [imposed through] fear and suppression?"

To critics of guilds who based their arguments on the writings of Adam Smith, Schön retorted that Smith's work was to be *used*, but not slavishly followed.

> [While] there are few educated Englishmen who have not ardently studied Smith, there are very few who would try to apply his system to practical life without greatest caution. There is a difference between mathematical principles and those of economics. . . . In certain circumstances . . . absolute application of economic doctrines can have a most harmful effect. . . . It is quite useful for economists to be acquainted with the [theoretical] system, but they must never lose sight of local conditions and the times.

PATTERNS OF CHANGE

Ever mindful of the "local conditions and the times," the reformers pursued a policy in 1807 and 1808 of accelerating social and economic change. They established an enduring principle that private profit and economic development would henceforth be primary objectives of governmental policy. They moved Prussia toward a free enterprise system and a modern mobile society. Yet the reformers were deliberate in failing to undermine institutions which did not seem at the time to present economic difficulties. Epitomizing the position of early nineteenth-century German liberalism, they believed in the principles of freedom and individualism, but they stopped short of assailing corporate organizations simply for the sake of ideological goals. Their ideal was that of gradual, orderly innovation. They were anchored in the eighteenth-century world which valued corporatism as well as individualism and growth. This combination of qualities contributed to Prussia's unique form of corporate capitalism.

In agricultural society, as in manufacture, the reformers established a working compromise which shaped the direction of economic transformation. Committed to the notion of private property and freedom of real estate markets, they nevertheless allowed inequities of the semi-feudal agrarian system to perpetuate themselves in the new market arrangement. The reform party even found an ideological spokesman for its position in the British economist, John Maitland, Earl of Lauderdale, whose book, *An Inquiry into the Nature and Origin of Public Wealth* appeared in 1804.[38] An

---

[38] James Maitland, Eighth Earl of Lauderdale, *An Inquiry into the Nature and Origin of Public Wealth and into the Means and Causes of its Increase* (1804), ed., Morton Paglin, Reprints of Economic Classics (New York, 1962).

advocate of free trade, yet a critic of Adam Smith, Lauderdale spoke with a double tongue which suited the needs of Prussian leaders. On the one hand, he was committed to supply and demand; yet on the other, he championed protection of agriculture against the harsh workings of a market system. Lauderdale maintained that of the two spheres in which labor-producing wealth are employed, agriculture and manufacturing, the former "maintains in all periods of society [a] pre-eminent relation to [the latter]." He campaigned vigorously in favor of the British corn laws which would not only maintain the preeminence of the rural economy but would also prevent severe disruption of the social order in the countryside. So impressed was Theodor von Schön with Lauderdale that he found time during the hectic reform year to translate and publish the English economist's tract, presumably as a guide for his colleagues. "To the present," he argued, "there has been no more worthy critic of Smith than Lauderdale."[39]

A goal of the Prussian reformers was to avoid the imbalance of agrarian wealth in the hands of a few. They found in Lauderdale a justification for their position. He attributed England's prosperity to the fact that British society had no unbridgeable gap between large and small farmers. Prerevolutionary France, in contrast, was relatively poor because of the vast fortunes controlled by noblemen and the abundance of penniless tenant peasants.

> Great inequality of fortune, by impoverishing the lower orders, has everywhere been the principal impediment to the increase of public wealth. We know from experience that no country of equal extent ever enjoyed so much wealth as what is diffused over this island [England]. We have a right, therefore, to conclude that the distribution of property has been more favourable to the growth of wealth in this than in any other country.[40]

It was precisely this prosperity which the Stein party hoped to bring to Prussia by promoting the growth of substantial nonnoble holdings.

Disagreeing with Adam Smith and other economists who posited labor as the primary *source* of wealth, Lauderdale nevertheless stressed the importance of labor as the single most important *means of increasing* riches: "In a civilized society . . . , with the exception of what he derives from the ocean, the wealth of a man can alone be increased by labour."[41] One

---

[39] Lauderdale, *Ueber National-Wohlstand* (Berlin, 1808). A handwritten inscription in the copy of this book in the Niedersächsische Universitäts- und Staatsbibliothek, Göttingen, reads: "Vornehmliches Andenken des Übersetzers Geh- Ober- Finanz- Rath v. Schön am 8. Obre. 1808." See also: Schön, draft of an essay, "Ueber National Wohlstand vom Grafen Lauderdale," [n.d.], Dep. Brünneck, no. 2, StA Königsberg. Lauderdale's critics emphasized his inconsistency in favoring both free trade and protection of agriculture. See the anonymous review article on his book in *The Edinburgh Review, or Critical Journal* 4 (1804): 343–77. See G. F. Russel Barker, "James Maitland, Eighth Earl of Lauderdale," *Dictionary of National Biography* 12 (1909): 798–801.

[40] Lauderdale, *Nature and Origin of Public Wealth,* 318–45, quotation from 345.

[41] Ibid., passim., esp. xii–xiii, 273–82; Mortin Paglin, *Malthus and Lauderdale: The Anti-Ricardian Tradition* (New York, 1961), 35–45.

of the major purposes of the Prussian reformers' plans for emancipating the serfs was the creation of a labor market. The peasants who had tilled their lords' fields, baked at their lords' ovens and ground grain at their estates' mills had not been laborers in modern economic terms because their toil had not been that of freely contracting agents selling their services. The October Edict and the February Ordinance were designed to transform serfs into laborers as well as to free the use of capital in the rural economy. Both human and capital labor could then be employed to increase production.

Stein and his colleagues were committed to reform without revolution. Their work expressed the ideology of the new universal freedom, and it paved the way for profound economic and social innovations. The reforms of 1808 helped establish the conditions which would allow Prussia to accelerate its accommodation to a capitalist economy. The type of capitalism the reformers fostered would make it possible for new elites to establish themselves alongside the old. The concepts of freedom and mobility, when applied to lower levels of rural society, would mean in large part dislocation and loss of status. Workers in the cities and towns would not suffer as greatly, so long as they were skilled in trades which were in no economic difficulty. The reformers, however, remained convinced that they were helping people when their work was designed to increase profit, production, growth and change.

VII. THE STEIN REFORM MINISTRY AND THE PROCESS OF CHANGE IN PRUSSIA

THE FALL OF THE STEIN GOVERNMENT

From the moment of Stein's appointment, his ministry had faced bitter opposition. Chief among its foes were angry estate owners who feared loss of their privileged status as a result of government-directed social and economic changes. They obstinately attempted to delay and subvert the agrarian reforms by failing to publicize the new legislation, by purposefully misconstruing the October Edict and the February Ordinance, and by ignoring certain provisions which they found objectionable. They repeatedly petitioned for repeal and revision of the new agricultural laws.

It was not until the summer of 1808, however, that partisans of the old regime began to raise a voice which constituted a genuine threat to the Stein government. After a pause in the reform work in March 1808, during which Stein traveled to Berlin to attempt a final settlement with the French, the ministry resumed its program of innovations with renewed vigor. Stein and his colleagues did not conceal their plans to abolish patrimonial jurisdiction, to establish institutions of representative government, to enforce the already enacted provisions of the agrarian legislation, and to reform the military in a way which would jeopardize the established prerogatives of the aristocracy. This intensified activity hardened the opposition toward Stein. Conservatives, who in October 1807 had agreed on the necessity of internal changes, now saw their own positions threatened. They reacted with a flood of complaints to Stein, to Minister Schroetter and to the king. They contended that defeat on the battlefield was no excuse for the "revolutionary measures" which the Stein government favored.[1]

In the late summer, an accident with international implications added fuel to the fire of Stein's detractors. On 25 August 1808, the French apprehended a Prussian courier named Koppe who had in his possession two highly damaging letters written by Stein. In one, to an Altona (Hamburg) banker, Stein acknowledged that Prussia could continue to pay "war contributions" to France until the end of the winter, even though Prussian emissaries in Paris had officially denied this possibility. The other, more ruinous, letter was to Baron Wilhelm Ludwig zu Sayn-Wittgenstein. It re-

---

[1] Raack, *Fall of Stein,* 1–2, 26–27, 42–43; Ständische Comité to Frederick William, 15 June 1808, Bujack, *Das erste Triennium,* 11; Sessions-Acta der ständischen Comité, Königsberg, 6 July 1808, ibid., 12.

vealed Stein's involvement in an anti-French insurrectionary plot which was being planned by Scharnhorst, Gneisenau and others high in the Prussian government. Stein encouraged Wittgenstein to help spread the spirit of rebellion. Not only did the seizure of these letters severely compromise Prussia's negotiating position with France, it also made Stein politically vulnerable.[2]

Public opinion in Prussia, in which Stein and his advisors put much faith, began to turn against the ministry. This was especially true among the nobility whose dominant position in the state had been only negligibly altered by the innovations of the Stein government. Although scattered groups hastened to express confidence in Stein, memoranda began to pour into the court demanding his dismissal. The nobility resented not only the "radical" reforms which the ministry was forcing on Prussia, but also the ministry's appeals for public confidence and support. One petition of November 1808 expressed apprehension about the practice of allowing petitions to circulate in published form. With specific reference to a document expressing support for Stein, a committee of noblemen pointed out that this dangerous practice would

> lead others to believe that they enjoy this right of circulating petitions and collecting signatures, even in cases which relate more directly to the privileges of the crown. This . . . action may remind the people of similar measures which in our times preceded the overthrow of a great empire [France]. . . . We are concerned, for the sake of the monarch and of our citizenry, that . . . people are being permitted to stir up popular feeling in any manner which they choose.[3]

By the autumn of 1808 a core of aristocratic opposition had solidified against Stein. In November the estate owners explained their position: We did not oppose abolition of serfdom, the first measures of Stein's "new system," but rather we accepted this and other royal edicts "with silent obedience." Even the military reforms, which touched upon our own prerogatives, we did not criticize. However, several newspaper articles, one of which seems to carry official government sanction, have recently come to our attention. They speak of introducing general conscription and abolishing patrimonial jurisdiction, two matters which relate directly to the interests of the aristocracy. "The nobility would have to hold itself in contempt if it remained silent any longer." The climax of the intolerable situation was the recent capture by the French of Stein's letter. Newspapers' publication of the affair

> with such insulting remarks has caused a great outcry in the country. Everyone is waiting with nervous anticipation to see whether the king will find it in accord

[2] Stein to Wittgenstein, Königsberg, 15 Aug. 1808, Botzenhart, *Stein Briefe* 2/2: 813–16 (no. 779); Raack, *Fall of Stein,* 49–51; Ritter, *Stein,* 346–49.

[3] Immediateingabe von ständischen Vertretern und Einwohnern der Städte Königsberg, Braunsberg und Kreuzberg, Königsberg, 29 Oct. 1808, Botzenhart, *Stein Briefe* 2/2: 913–14 (no. 875); Immediateingabe einiger ostpreussischer Adliger, Königsberg, 1 Nov. 1808, ibid., 2/2: 915 (no. 877).

with his interests [to continue] entrusting the leadership of the state's affairs to a minister whom the powerful Napoleon seems to have subjected to every type of abuse.

King Frederick William let himself be swayed by the arguments of his "true and obedient servants," the nobility. He began to turn against Stein, openly reprimanding those East Prussian subjects who had dared to circulate a petition supporting Stein's reforms. Stein's policies, he pointed out, were matters "unsuitable for public discussion."[4]

It is possible that Frederick William would have defended the Stein government against its aristocratic detractors, had he not been bombarded with stronger attacks on Stein from sources much nearer the court. The conservatives, Voss and Zastrow, two of the early casualties of the campaigns of the Stein-Hardenberg supporters, had not overcome their bitterness. Now in Berlin, they had involved themselves in a plan to quietly increase French suspicion of Stein, even before discovery of the compromising letter. Beyme, who had retired from the court in June and had taken up residence on his estate in Steglitz near Berlin, was a participant in this intrigue. To the king he forwarded Zastrow's dispatches, designed to undermine Frederick William's confidence in Stein by emphasizing the minister's inability to make terms with the French. Meanwhile Beyme and the conservatives had devised an elaborate plan involving mysterious secret envoys to convince the French that Beyme would be a favorable replacement for Stein. Also involved in this artifice was General Karl Leopold von Köckritz, who like Beyme had previously held an informal position very close to the monarch as a member of the cabinet government. Contemporaries described Köckritz as "without brains, education, talent [or] social qualities; an officer of the narrowest, most common class." Köckritz's sensitivity was undoubtedly as much pricked as Voss's, Zastrow's and Beyme's, for he too had been ousted from a high position upon Stein's assumption of office. It was Beyme who bore greatest responsibility for compliance in, indeed leadership of, this particular plot. He provided the link between the French, the ousted conservatives, and the court. While some members of the reform government continued to mistrust Beyme to the point of hostility, Stein seems to have softened his feelings toward his former adversary. Apparently not until he was out of office did Stein suspect that Beyme had been part of an intrigue against him.[5]

---

[4] Promemoria eines Vertreters des Adels [after 17 Nov. 1808], Scheel, *Reformministerium* 3: 1033–35 (no. 316); Kabinettsordre an einige Bewohner von Königsberg, Braunsberg und Kreuzberg auf ihre Petition, [Nov. 1808], ibid., 3: 981 (no. 298). See also Immediateingabe einiger Gutsbesitzer, Prassen bei Bartenstein, 15 Nov. 1808, ibid., 3: 1022 (no. 310).

[5] This episode has been thoroughly researched by Raack, *Fall of Stein,* 82–93. Since his work appeared a major document which Raack used in archival form has been published: Chasot, Immediatbericht, Berlin, 12 Oct. 1808, Scheel, *Reformministerium* 3: 900–02 (no. 276). On Köckritz see Wittichen, "Das Kabinett und Fr. von Gentz," *Historische Zeitschrift* 89 (1902): 255–56; Beguelin, *Denkwürdigkeiten,* 133; Hardenberg, Fragment einer Darstellung der Regierung Friedrich Wilhelms III., [ca. 1808], Winter, *Reorganisation,* appendix, 572–75.

The most surprising of the several intrigues was one involving Altenstein, a member of Stein's own government. Altenstein was encouraged by Nagler who suddenly reappeared on the political scene after a period of quiet following Hardenberg's dismissal. The two brothers-in-law schemed to poison Frederick William's mind toward Stein and to pave the way for Altenstein's succession to the post of chief minister. They were incidentally forced to campaign against Beyme who was working to have himself installed in this position. In part their strategy consisted of convincing Hardenberg that Stein was becoming dangerous for Prussia's future. The conspirators knew that Hardenberg's opinions carried considerable weight with the king. Since they supplied most of the news which the exiled minister received about the government, it was easy for them to play up both the affair of the intercepted letter and the resulting lack of rapport between Stein and the French. They supplied Hardenberg with copious details about Stein's involvement in the insurrectionary plot. They also echoed the arguments of conservatives, who portrayed Stein as a radical. Hardenberg began to warn Frederick William against Stein.[6]

Altenstein and Nagler attacked not only Stein but also his "tactless friends" in the administration who were "agitating among the so-called populace." Altenstein singled out Schön, with whom only a year earlier he had enjoyed a close relationship. Seeking to influence Frederick William, Altenstein wrote to Hardenberg in early November concerning the possibility that Schön might be named to replace Stein: "Your advice will be decisive. . . . Herr von Schön has grown worse. It is clear that no one can get along with him. He follows [a] dangerous system, and he is completely devoted to it. He has no attachment to the king, but is committed to [using] the force of the people." Elsewhere, Altenstein emphasized Schön's irrationality. "Schön is a powerful figure," he wrote in a memorandum which would surely reach the king. "But [he is] a man with a narrow, one-sided education. . . . [His] unlimited ambition and his extremely high opinion of himself negate his quite valuable characteristics. . . . He is feared and hated."[7]

Stein was aware of the fact that plotters were all around him, but he was apparently unsure of exactly who was involved, and he did not know the extent of the conspiratorial activity. He grew nervous and discouraged. In genuine embarrassment over capture of the compromising letter, he tendered his resignation with the proposal that the king place him under arrest to exonerate the Prussian government. Frederick William refused

[6] Raack, *Fall of Stein,* 108–17; Hardenberg to Altenstein, Tilsit, 8 Oct. 1808, Scheel, *Reformministerium* 3: 898–99 (no. 274).

[7] Nagler, Immediatbericht, Königsberg, 8 Nov. 1808, Botzenhart, *Stein Briefe* 2/2: 925–27 (no. 887); Altenstein to Hardenberg, Königsberg, [10 Nov. 1808], Scheel, *Reformministerium* 3: 992–94 (no. 303); Altenstein, Denkschrift über die Wahl des Regierungsystems für Preussen bei dem wahrscheinlichen Abgang Steins, [Königsberg, ca. 10 Nov. 1808], ibid., 3: 1002 (no. 304); Altenstein, Denkschrift, [16 Nov. 1808], ibid., 3: 1025-26 (no. 313).

this suggestion. Twice again within two months, as the plot thickened about him, Stein attempted to resign, both times unsuccessfully. The second offer of resignation on 7 November was prompted by Stein's reception of the news that the French were making his removal from office a condition for terminating their occupation of Berlin. Frederick William, though his confidence in Stein was in fact waning, was unable to see through the maze which led from accepting a resignation to appointing a new ministry. He clung steadfastly to Stein until all hope of saving the ministry had been eroded, or perhaps more importantly, until after a fateful secret meeting between the monarch and Hardenberg.[8]

On 10 November 1808, Altenstein and Nagler brought about a dramatic rendezvous of Hardenberg and Frederick William, to the surprise of both. During the previous two days the brothers-in-law had carefully tutored Hardenberg on the existing state of affairs at the court and had suggested a plan of action. Hardenberg, apparently unsuspecting of Altenstein's own ambitious plan to secure for himself the position of finance minister, followed Altenstein's prescription almost literally in relaying advice to the king, who was moved to tears when his eyes fell upon his trusted advisor. On the basis of Hardenberg's suggestion, Frederick William planned to accept Stein's resignation and to endorse a new list of ministers which he did not realize had been originally prepared by Altenstein and Nagler.[9]

Several men near Stein were aware that he had numerous enemies in Prussia, but they were appalled to discover that reformers who had been such close colleagues could participate in the vicious conspiracy. Sack, Staegemann, Scharnhorst and Schön expressed outrage when they discovered that their leader was falling victim to this vulgar handiwork. Schön's diary for the eventful days of November and December 1808 reveals how this close colleague of Stein discovered bit by bit the web of the plot directed against not only Stein, but also against himself and other coworkers. He was genuinely angered that men whom he had deeply trusted had been party to such a self-seeking intrigue. "Stein's great cause is dead," he concluded. "It is degrading to the great man to defend him against the attacks of such worms."[10]

---

[8] Raack, *Fall of Stein,* 68–69, 97–98, 105–06.

[9] Ibid., 117-27. Altenstein to Hardenberg, Königsberg, [10 Nov. 1808], Scheel, *Reformministerium* 3: 992–94 (no. 303). The advice which Frederick William received from Hardenberg on 10 Nov. must have corresponded to the latter's written report, Denkschrift, Braunsberg, 12 Nov. 1808, ibid., 3: 1004-11 (no. 305).

[10] Sack to Scheffner, Berlin, 20 Dec. 1808, Arthur Warda and Carl Diesch, eds., *Briefe von und an Johann Georg Scheffner* (Munich, Leipzig and Königsberg, 1918–38) 4: 152–54; Scharnhorst to Götzen, [Königsberg], 9 Feb. 1809, Karl Linnebach, ed., *Scharnhorsts Briefe* (Munich and Berlin, 1914) 1: 360–62 (no. 247); Schön, Tagebuch, 30 Nov. 1808, 6 Dec. 1808, 21–29 Dec. 1808, Schön, *Aus den Papieren* 2: 50, 54, 64. Raack has suggested that Schön was possibly among the opponents of Stein. See *Fall of Stein,* 38, n. 36, 45. See also Raack's article, "A New Schleiermacher Letter on the Conspiracy of 1808," *Zeitschrift für Religions- und Geistesgeschichte* 16 (1964): 218–20. I believe that this argument is refuted by Schön's private diary of November 1808 through January 1809. See Dep. Brünneck, no. 27, StA Königsberg. (The diary is edited with some serious alterations in Schön, *Papieren* 2: 47–95.)

If the internal plots against Stein's party had not already sealed the fate of the ministry, an incident sometimes called the "honeyed-pill affair" would have done so. Early in November Schön commissioned his former professor, Theodor von Schmalz, to compose a pamphlet encouraging abolition of patrimonial jurisdiction. Since the destiny of the ministry was already in doubt, Schön was perhaps hoping to excite public demand to push through a reorganization of the judiciary before Stein was forced to leave his office. Schön advised Schmalz to "sweeten the pill with honey," meaning that he was to describe the reform in such a way that it would not appear distasteful to conservative opponents.[11]

The French censor in Berlin took offense at the "revolutionary" tone of Schmalz's pamphlet, although it embodied no more radical goals than those which the Stein ministry had officially adopted. The French authorities seized the proofs and imprisoned Professor Schmalz. They charged that the booklet was evidence that the Stein ministry was attempting to incite insurrection. The French marshall Davout gave an incredible, damaging interpretation to the "honeyed pill" reference. He connected it with a counterfeit letter, allegedly written by Countess Sophie von Voss, a highly influential figure in the Prussian court. (She was related to the more genuine plotter, Otto von Voss.) In the fabricated letter, the countess was to have advised Wittgenstein, the addressee of Stein's indiscreet dispatch, that if Prussians wanted to imitate "the brave people of the south," they must utilize "the chocolate of health." Davout, by circuitous reasoning, arrived at the conclusion that Schön's "honeyed pill" and Countess Voss' spurious "chocolate of health" were references to a plot to poison the Emperor Napoleon! The countess was summoned to an official court hearing. Wittgenstein was imprisoned. Schön was fortunate that he was not more severely handled.[12] Faced with this kind of irrational opposition, it is a wonder that the Stein party remained in office as long as it did.

On 24 November 1808, the same day the king formally accepted Stein's resignation, the departing minister put forward his "Political Testament," drafted by Theodor von Schön who seems to have become his closest helper in the last months of the ministry. The document reviewed the

---

[11] Raack, *Fall of Stein,* 132–33. On Schmalz, see Friedrich Gause, "Theodor von Schmalz," *Altpreussische Biographie,* 619; Eicke, *Der ostpreussische Landtag von 1798,* 75. Schön's lecture notes from Schmalz's courses: Dep. Brünneck, nos. 80, 82, 83, 84, StA Königsberg.

[12] Raack, *Fall of Stein,* 133–36; Friedrich Delbrück, Tagebuch, 20 Nov. 1808, *Die Jugend des Königs Friedrich Wilhelm IV. und des Kaisers und Königs Wilhelm I.: Tagebuchblätter ihres Erziehers Friedrich Delbrück,* ed. Georg Schuster, *Monumenta Germaniae Pedagogica,* 36, 37, 40 (Berlin, 1907–08) 3: 101–103; Sack to Stein, Berlin, 23 Nov. 1808, Botzenhart, *Stein Briefe* 2/2: 984–86 (no. 906). On the countess Voss, see Schön, Tagebuch, 3 Dec. 1808, Dep. Brünneck, no. 27, StA Königsberg (edited with changes, Schön, *Aus den Papieren* 2: 52). On the relationship between the lady-in-waiting and Schön's wife, see Schön's Selbstbiographie 2, [Schön], *Weitere Beiträge und Nachträge zu den Papieren des Ministers und Burggrafen von Marienburg Theodor von Schön* (Berlin, 1881), 55; L. v. Gerlach to his son Leopold, Berlin, 9 Nov. 1808, Schoeps, *Aus den Jahren preussischer Not,* 362–63; Voss, Immediatbericht, Berlin, 14/15 Nov. 1808, Botzenhart, *Stein Briefe* 2/2: 939–44 (no. 898); Schön to Frederick William, 2 Dec. 1808, Schön, *Aus den Papieren* 1: appendix, 67; Schön, Tagebuch, 30 Nov. 1808, ibid., 2: 48–49.

already completed reforms and pled with the successors of the 1808 ministry to continue the interrupted work. "I set my goal as the perfection of the domestic conditions of society," proclaimed Stein. "[This required] the elimination of the disharmony among the people, the abolition of conflict between the Estates which has brought us misfortune, and the legal establishment of opportunity for all individuals to freely develop their talents." Much has already been accomplished:

> The last remains of slavery, hereditary serfdom, is abolished, and the will of free people, that unshakable pillar of every throne, has been established. The unlimited right to acquire property is proclaimed. The privilege of determining one's own [vocation] has been returned to the people. The cities have been granted their independence.[13]

Yet the catalog of uncompleted reforms was long. They included further establishment of the power of the central government, abolition of the master-servant code regulating work contracts; creation of a fully independent judiciary; formation of a genuine, national political representation; and reform of the nobility as a prerequisite to establishing equality among the Estates.

THE REFORM YEAR 1808 AND THE DIRECTION OF CHANGE IN PRUSSIA

It would be easy to conclude, as Schön and many others at the time did, that the efforts of 1808 were completely undermined by the discouraging turn of events culminating in Stein's resignation. "I visited Stein," Schön wrote on 30 November, a week after the new administration of Altenstein and Alexander von Dohna-Schlobitten had taken over. "He is completely resigned to the situation. He knows the men who were untrue to him. . . . The laughter over the new ministers . . . is becoming louder. They are widely mocked and correctly so." Four days later: "All circumstances demonstrate that a time of weakness is beginning." On 5 December, Stein departed from the Prussian capital. "I saw him off," Schön wrote. "He takes much with him, the devotion of all honest men."[14]

It is unquestionable that the brief Altenstein-Dohna government of November 1808 through June 1810 failed to manifest the spirit of urgency about reforms that had characterized the Stein administration. The same is true of the chancellorship of Hardenberg which lasted until 1822, although numerous significant reforms were enacted under Hardenberg's direction. These consisted primarily of economic measures such as taxation

---

[13] Stein, Politisches Testament, Königsberg, 24 Nov. 1808, Scheel, *Reformministerium* 3: 1136–39 (no. 330). There are widely conflicting assessments of Schön's role in the authorship of the document due to many distorted claims of Schön during his later years and to the counterarguments his detractors raised. See Gray, *Theodor von Schön and Prussian Reforms 1806–1808*, 290–91. On the relationship between Stein and Schön during the last weeks of the ministry, see passim, and especially 216–49.

[14] Schön, Tagebuch, 30 Nov., 4 Dec., 15 Dec. 1808, Schön, *Aus den Papieren* 2: 49–53.

and customs laws, designed to extend the free market system. They also included new agrarian legislation and steps to emancipate the Jews. On balance, however, Hardenberg's term as *Staatskanzler,* and succeeding ministries right up to the eve of the revolutions of 1848, were characterized by an atmosphere of heavy bureaucracy.[15]

While the four decades of government following 1808 in Prussia lacked the spirit of enthusiasm and urgency of the Stein ministry, the patterns of administration and the direction of socio-political change evident throughout the first half of the nineteenth century had firm roots in the reform year. The zealous individuals who took office following the military disasters of Jena and Auerstädt set their state on a path which it continued to follow long after they had been forced from office. The initiatives of 1808 were not snuffed out by the fall of Stein.

Schön, Schroetter and their colleagues had given priority to agrarian reforms because they believed that Prussia would continue to live from agriculture as it had in the past. They were correct, because it was not until well after the middle of the nineteenth century that manufacture and urban enterprise began to catch up with the rural economy. The agrarian edicts of 1808 were designed to allow middle-class capitalists to enter agricultural enterprise, and to facilitate the growth of the rural market economy.[16] Many of the conceptualizers of the October Edict and the February Ordinance believed themselves to be creating a more just society for all rural inhabitants—indeed for all subjects of the Prussian crown. But they formulated their work in such a manner as to deprive lower-class families of their places in society and to favor the propertied.

These two ordinances of the reform year, written for East Prussia, West Prussia and Lithuania, were applied in only slightly revised forms to the middle and western provinces of the monarchy after the French evacuated these areas. They were further "clarified" with two acts of 1811 and 1816. The law of 14 September 1811 pursued the tendency established in the February Ordinance of dividing the holdings of prosperous peasants between themselves and their masters, while denying the poorest farmers the right to possess land at all. Under the new provision, those village families who held their farms under long-term and secure contracts could dissolve manorial bonds and obtain modern titles to their property by ceding one-third or one-half to their respective landlords. Then after five years of

---

[15] Vogel, *Allgemeine Gewerbefreiheit,* 97–105, 135–41; Bock, "Reform und Revolution," *Militärgeschichte* 19 (1980): 611–14; Gillis, *The Prussian Bureaucracy,* 22–36, 67, 85; Bernd Ristau, "Studien zur Agrarwirtschaft und Agrargesellschaft," *Archiv für Sozialgeschichte* 20 (1980): 520–22. Ristau argues that after the fall of Stein, the reform movement was distorted and slowed down because of the Prussian state debt and the material losses to the agricultural economy.

[16] Hartmut Harnisch, "Die Bedeutung der kapitalistischen Agrarreform für die Herausbildung des inneren Marktes und die industrielle Revolution in den östlichen Provinzen Preussens in der ersten Hälfte des 19. Jahrhunderts," *Jahrbuch für Wirtschaftsgeschichte,* 1970/4: 63–82, 71–72.

strenuous protest from estate owners, the government "revised" the 1811 law with the Edict of 29 May 1816. This new provision reduced the number of peasants eligible to obtain "freedom" by adding the stipulation that they be *spannfähig*, that is, capable of supporting a team of animals to work the land. This decreased by nearly two-thirds the number entitled to gain ownership.[17] This legislation was consistent with the assumption underlying the Stein ministry's reforms: small farms that did not contain the resources to make them viable in the market economy should not be supported in the first place.

If the reformers hoped to establish a class of prosperous peasants, their goals were realized. Recent statistical research indicates that during the first half of the century a small, but very prosperous, class of peasants (Grossbauern) were able to gain footing following the reforms. Many of these were former domain peasants who obtained titles to their lands following a Dissolution Ordinance of 7 July 1821. There also developed a group of middle-sized farmers who were able to carry on market-oriented enterprises.[18]

In terms of rural social change, one of the most important processes of the early nineteenth century was the movement of middle-class entrepreneurs into agriculture. This did not result in a displacement of the aristocracy, for under the new conditions many noble proprietors maintained their favored positions. As an economist concluded in 1839:

> The number of noble estates is unchanged from that of 1805. Only a very few can have been destroyed or dismembered since then. All those which still exist have become significantly larger in the last twenty years. This is due in part to the [agrarian edicts] and in part to purchase and enclosure of peasant farms.

Furthermore, rather than assimilation of Junkers into the middle class, expected by the reformers in 1808, change was in the opposite direction: the new non-aristocratic owners strove to be accepted into aristocratic society, and they were to a certain degree successful. Even many Grossbauern, peasants who had been fortunate enough to emerge from the reforms with substantial holdings, had begun by 1848 to share the views of their aristocratic neighbors with regard to land ownership and social change.[19]

While the propertied classes among the rural population prospered, the

---

[17] Hartmut Harnisch, "Vom Oktoberedikt des Jahres 1807 zur Deklaration von 1816: Problematik und Charakter der preussischen Agrarreformgesetzgebung zwischen 1807 und 1816," *Studien zu den Agrarreformen des 19. Jahrhunderts in Preussen und Russland*, Sonderband des Jahrbuchs für Wirtschaftsgeschichte (Berlin, 1978), 229–93. Harnisch emphasizes the differences between the reforms of 1807–1808 and the subsequent ones.

[18] Rudolf Berthold, "Die Veränderungen im Bodeneigentum und in der Zahl der Bauernstellen, der Kleinstellen und der Rittergütter in den preussischen Provinzen Sachsen, Brandenburg und Pommern während der Durchführung der Agrarreformen des 19. Jahrhunderts," ibid., 7–116.

[19] Haxthausen, *Die Ländliche Verfassung*, 1: 180–83. Hartmut Harnisch, "Probleme junkerlicher Agrarpolitik im 19. Jahrhundert," *Wissenschaftliche Zeitschrift der Universität Rostock* 21 (1972), Gesellschafts- und Sprachwissenschaftliche Reihe 1,2: 99–108; Koselleck, *Preussen zwischen Reform und Revolution*, 487–518.

agrarian transition accelerated the dislocation of small landowners and facilitated the growth of a large rural proletariat. The enclosure of common lands in the early nineteenth century completely transformed the rural landscape, and many peasants who were not forced to forfeit their lands as a direct result of the agrarian reform edicts were hard pressed to make ends meet without use of common pastures and woodlands or other forms of traditional manorial support. During the decade of the 1820s, moreover, a serious agricultural depression struck the provinces east of the Elbe, dealing a severe blow to small proprietors. Under market conditions, lack of credit prevented many from utilizing capital to their advantage, or even from surviving hard times. Theodor von Schön, who had become the chief provincial administrator of East Prussia, facilitated loans to large landowners during the critical decade of the twenties, but he did not make this assistance available to the smaller farmers, whom he had passionately defended in 1808. As often happens, the process of land reform increased the prospects of agricultural output as small farmers lost their lands to the owners of large estates. During the "pre-March era," (Vormärz), the decades preceding the March revolutions of 1848, Prussia gained a large rural proletarian class. It was the fastest growing group in the society.[20]

Agriculture in Prussia, as in much of Europe at the time, completed its transition from a semifeudal, commercially oriented operation, to a capitalist system. One result of this was a long-term rise in agrarian productivity. The particular form of rural capitalism which developed in Prussia contained many remnants of precapitalist social, political, and economic institutions. Patrimonial courts and aristocratic police jurisdiction remained intact on noble estates until the revolutions of 1848. With regard to the rural labor market, a master-servant code (Gesindeordnung) of 8 November 1810, established a peculiar form of employer-employee relationship reminiscent of serfdom. Under this law, once a work contract was established, the laborer could be held in his or her position by force, and the police were obliged to return runaway workers if proprietors requested them to do so. The law of 1810 specifically granted the right of "limited corporal punishment" to rural employers. These harsh measures had their counterparts in other European states undergoing similar transitions. England possessed its own version of the master and servant laws. They were a common limitation on free labor markets, which worked to the advantage of employers.[21]

---

[20] Schissler, *Preussische Agrargesellschaft*, 168–73; William J. Orr, Jr., "East Prussia and the Revolutions of 1848," *Central European History*, 13 (1980): 304–06; Conze, "Vom 'Pöbel' zum 'Proletariat,' " *Vierteljahrsschrift für Soziaf- und Wirtschaftsgeschichte* 41 (1954): 334–38; Treue, *Wirtschafts- und Technikgeschichte*, 257; Robert A. Dickler, "Organization and Change in Productivity in Eastern Prussia," in *European Peasants and their Markets: Essays in Agrarian Economic History*, ed. William N. Parker and Eric L. Jones (Princeton, N. J., 1975), 269–92; Harnisch, "Die Bedeutung der kapitalistischen Agrarreform," 78–79.

[21] Ibid., 63–82; Heitz, "Varianten des preussischen Weges," 99–109; Helmut Bleiber, "Staat und bürgerliche Umwälzung in Deutschland: zum Charakter besonders des preussischen

As for urban laborers, a series of major governmental reforms of 1810 and 1811 furthered the Stein ministry's initiative by making guild membership voluntary in the practice of trades and crafts. The legislation left guilds with remnants of their former functions. They retained many of their social roles such as the maintenance of benefit funds and the care of widows and orphans. But their loss of mandatory membership deprived them in large measure of control over their trades. The guilds' political and religious functions were eliminated by the reforms.[22]

Typically, in certain exceptional cases the laws allowed restriction of free exercise of trade to continue, but they were enforced by police power rather than by the old corporations, furthering the process of bureaucratic control over society. Even the regulations of standards of craftsmanship became a matter of police jurisdiction. Guilds remained semicorporate groups in a society moving toward a free labor market. Economic circumstances eroded the artisan work-household as journeymen lost their former status within the guild system. Increasingly, their relationships to their trades were determined by factors extraneous to guild rules and practices. More and more the journeymen began to approximate the members of a modern labor force.[23]

A comparative lack of industry in Prussia, nevertheless, allowed little opportunity for the development of a prosperous modern working class. The more steady growth of industry in western Europe was beginning to undermine Prussian handicrafts at the same time governmental reforms had deprived them of their economic security. The number of artisans in Prussian cities almost doubled by the 1840s, but there was no corresponding increase in work for them.[24]

The social revolution fostered by the 1808 ministry and carried further by its successors was everywhere evident, but there were no clear winners. Even the established middle classes whom the reforms were designed to support, endured frustration in the first half of the century. The thriving eighteenth-century commerce of the Baltic seaports, which had been destroyed by the Napoleonic wars and the Continental Blockade, did not again attain its pre-1806 level for half a century. The British Corn Laws, protective legislation in Russia, and the agricultural depression at home contributed to the economic distress of the shippers of Königsberg, Danzig and Memel. It was Prussia's relative disadvantage in an international market

---

Staates in der ersten Hälfte des 19. Jahrhunderts," *Universalhistorische Aspekte und Dimensionen des Jakobinismus*, Sitzungsberichte der Akademie der Wissenschaften der DDR 10/G (Berlin, 1976), 213–14; Mottek, *Wirtschaftsgeschichte Deutschlands*, 2: 38–39; E. J. Hobsbawm, *The Pelican Economic History of Britain*, vol. 3, *From 1750 to the Present Day: Industry and Empire* (Middlesex, 1969), 86, 124. Vogel portrays the Gesindeordnung in a more positive light: *Gewerbefreiheit*, 184–87.

[22] Bergmann, *Das berliner Handwerk*, 35–54; Vogel, *Gewerbefreiheit*, 176–84.

[23] Bergmann, *Das berliner Handwerk*, 102–21.

[24] Rohrscheidt, *Vom Zunftzwang*, 371–84; Hamerow, *Restoration, Revolution and Reaction*, 24–30; Gillis, *Prussian Bureaucracy*, 8–10.

which hindered the growth and prosperity expected by Stein and his colleagues.[25]

As with economic and social change, the patterns of bureaucratic transformation conformed to the precedents of the reform year. Stein's and Altenstein's extensive administrative reorganization plan, dated 24 November 1808, was shelved, only to be rewritten in 1810 but never implemented. The structure of the bureaucracy, from the ministerial level down to the local plane, was shaped, not by reforms of a constitutional nature, but rather by the precedents set when officials found practical solutions to recurring problems. Its form was always dependent upon the personalities and circumstances of the moment.

One major administrative condition which prevailed as a legacy of 1807–1808 was the supremacy of the ministerial bureaucracy vis-à-vis the crown. By 1817, when the top level of government took the form of the State Council (Staatsrat), it was an accepted constitutional pattern that professional bureaucrats determined state policies. The kings appointed ministers, but they never again made the kinds of decisions that Frederick William III's predecessors had made. The Staatsrat assumed, moreover, what can only be called a legislative function, a role which the 1808 reform ministry would ideally have assigned to a national assembly.[26] But of course, Stein and his colleagues themselves foreshadowed the practice of assigning legislative responsibilities to bureaucratic institutions.

Discussion continued in Prussia about constitutional reforms and establishment of representative government, at least until the conclusion of the Congress of Vienna in 1815. For the purpose of broadening the taxation base and obtaining desperately needed revenue, Hardenberg experimented with a number of ideas including national representative assemblies and reform of older Estates institutions. His most concrete measure in this regard was the Assembly of Notables convened in January 1811 which, like the East Prussian Landtag of 1808, had a major function of obtaining revenue to pay the French war contributions debt. While it included delegates from all "Estates," these were over-balanced with a high representation of members of the professional bureaucracy, and it included a disproportional number of provincial nobles. It convened only once.[27]

---

[25] Orr, "East Prussia and the Revolution," 307–08.

[26] Henning Schrimpf, "Die Auseinandersetzung um die Neuordnung des individuellen Rechtschutzes gegenüber der staatlichen Verwaltung nach 1807," *Der Staat: Zeitschrift für Staatslehre, öffentliches Recht und Verfassungsgeschichte* 18 (1979), 59–60, 62–66, 71–75. Schrimpf puts forward the significant argument that the mentality of 1808 was perpetuated in the postreform era. However, he is imprecise when he implies that the administrative reform plans of 1808 were literally put into effect. Preuss, "Bildung und Burokratie," *Der Staat* 14 (1975): 378–79; Vogel, *Gewerbefreiheit*, 85–105; Koselleck, *Preussen zwischen Reform und Revolution*, 217–83.

[27] Vogel, *Gewerbefreiheit*, 120–32; Elisabeth Fehrenbach, "Verfassungs- und sozialpolitische Reformen und Reformprojekte in Deutschland unter dem Einfluss des napoleonischen Frankreich," *Historische Zeitschrift* 228 (1979), 312–13.

Working with vague constitutional or ideological guidelines, bureaucrats employed the notion of "general welfare and security" to justify practices which led in many cases to greatly increased control of subjects' daily activities. The broad absolutist concept of "Polizei" carried over into the postreform era, and it was a part of a mentality which justified extensive state supervision of personal and economic affairs. The notion of governmental authority (Polizei) pertained not only to the executive and legislative functions of government, but to the judicial as well. During the nineteenth century there arose many cases in which individuals' rights were pitted against those of the state. The bureaucratic government, accustomed to acting for the "common good," successfully claimed precedence in such cases, leading sometimes to oppression of the very citizens whose rights it had set out to secure. It is easy to see how this could happen, given the Stein government's willingness to use the power of the state in an absolutist but arbitrary manner to solve social, economic and political problems.[28]

Many provincial and local institutions of the nobility which had traditionally maintained the interests of the old Estate system continued to function in the era preceding the 1848 revolutions. Individual provinces maintained their own particular forms of credit institutions, Landtage, or county assemblies which strove to defend local interests against those of the increasingly centralized state government. Without abolishing these, the ministerial bureaucracy, first under Altenstein and Dohna, and then under Hardenberg, attempted to erode their influence. Hardenberg, resistant to a rebirth of political power of the old nobility, nevertheless relented during the war years of 1812 and 1815, at which time foreign affairs and military needs accommodated a rejuvenation of some provincial aristocratic institutions. Following the precedents of 1808, Hardenberg pursued an anti-aristocratic policy without, however, envisioning a disembodiment of noble institutions. Like Stein, he contributed to Prussia's eclectic brand of modern bureaucratic absolutism in which remnants of the Ständestaat system continued to function.[29]

A tension between aristocracy and bureaucracy continued to exist, and in fact, some contemporaries viewed this as the major political issue of the pre-March period. An observer close to the court, but also in touch with the provinicial nobility, made the observation that:

> opposition to the bureaucracy was always the watchword of the assembled Landtag [of the Electoral Mark]. . . . There was also aristocratic opposition where we were in Berlin and later in Saxony. . . . The criticism directed itself against the phenomenon of "too much government" that resulted from the paperwork and the practical activities of out-side agencies.[30]

---

[28] Lüdtke, *"Gemeinwohl," Polizei und "Festungspraxis,"* 62–82; Schrimpf, "Auseinandersetzung," *Der Staat* 18 (1979): 78–80.

[29] Botzenhardt, "Verfassungsproblematik," in *Ständetum und Staatsbildung in Brandenburg-Preussen,* Veröffentlichungen der Historischen Kommission zu Berlin, 55 (Berlin and New York, 1983), 440–49.

[30] Rochow, *Vom Leben am preussischen Hofe,* 214.

In the postreform era, the old provincial landowning class retained a significant degree of political hegemony, enabling it to rival the new, strengthened bureaucracy. This is not surprising, given the patterns established in 1806–1808.

The social and economic transformation which was already in process before 1806, and which the Stein government accelerated, continued apace during the subsequent decades, despite an increasingly conservative rhetoric. The difference between 1808 and the following years was that the incredible enthusiasm and optimism of the Stein party had turned into a disposition of bureaucratic resignation. The zeal for reform was missing in the Altenstein-Dohna ministry, in Hardenberg's chancellorship, and in subsequent ministries. After Stein's fall, Prussian leaders fostered change without, however, sharing in the idealism which convinced them that they were creating a better world for all. Nevertheless, the process of change fostered by the ideals and the practices of the reformers of 1808 could not be halted. It moved in an uneven but forceful pattern.

The tragedy of the reform movement is manifest through the disappointment of those colleagues of Stein who remained true to the original ideals of the years 1806 to 1808. The tragedy is not so much that they were prevented from carrying out their program but that their program produced quite unexpected results. They zealously sought a new society of economic growth, social justice, politically active citizens, and rewards for individual virtue. Their work paved the way for a capitalist society, and this they identified as a standard of progress. But their efforts also fostered a stifling atmosphere of heavy government, bureaucratic arbitrariness, and limitation of individual freedom. Their agrarian and economic reforms brought about increased agricultural output and at the same time social dislocation and downward mobility.

BIBLIOGRAPHY

Archival Sources

1. StA Königsberg-Staatsarchiv Königsberg: Geheimes Staatsarchiv Preussischer Kulturbesitz, formerly in Göttingen, currently in Berlin-Dahlem.
   A. Rep. 2: Oberpräsidium.
   B. Rep. 300 von Brünneck I: Schön Nachlass.
2. Geheimes Staatsarchiv Preussischer Kulturbesitz, Berlin-Dahlem:
   A. Rep. 92: Auerswald Nachlass.
   B. Rep. 92: Gneisenau.
3. Staatsarchiv Münster: Vincke Nachlass.
4. Bundesarchiv Koblenz: Eckart Kehr Nachlass.

Published Primary Sources

Allgemeines Landrecht für die preussischen Staaten von 1794. 2 vols. Edited with introduction by Hans Hattenhauer. Bibliography by Günther Bernert. Frankfurt/M, 1970.

[Bassewitz, M. F. von]. *Die Kurmark Brandenburg in Zusammenhang mit den Schicksalen des Gesammtstaats Preussen während der Zeit vom 22. Oktober 1806 bis zu Ende des Jahres 1808.* 2 vols. Leipzig, 1851–1852.

Beguelin, Heinrich von, and Amalie von Beguelin. *Denkwürdigkeiten aus den Jahren 1807–1813 nebst Briefen von Gneisenau und Hardenberg.* Edited by Adolf Ernst. Berlin, 1892.

Brinkmann, Carl. "Eine neue Quelle zur preussischen Geschichte nach dem Tilsiter Frieden." *Forschungen zur brandenburgischen und preussischen Geschichte* 24 (1911): 371–445.

[Buchholz, Friedrich]. *Gallerie preussischer Charaktere.* Germanien [sic], 1808.

Buchholz, Friedrich. *Untersuchungen über den Geburtsadel und über die Möglichkeit seiner Fortdauer im neunzehnten Jahrhundert.* Leipzig, 1807.

Clercq, Alexandre de, ed. *Recueil des traités de la France.* 22 vols. Paris, 1864–1902.

Conze, Werner, ed. *Die preussische Reform unter Stein und Hardenberg: Bauernbefreiung und Städteordnung.* Quellen- und Arbeitshefte zur Geschichte und Politik, vol. 4128. Stuttgart, 1973.

Conze, Werner, ed. *Quellen zur Geschichte der deutschen Bauernbefreiung.* Quellensammlung zur Kulturgeschichte, vol. 12. Göttingen, 1957.

Dehio, Ludwig, ed. "Eine Reformdenkschrift Beymes aus dem Sommer 1806." *Forschungen zur brandenburgischen und preussischen Geschichte* 38 (1926): 321–38.

Delbrück, Friedrich. *Die Jugend des Königs Friedrich Wilhelm IV. und des Kaisers und Königs Wilhelm I.: Tagebuchblätter ihres Erziehers Friedrich Delbrück.* 3 vols. Edited by Georg Schuster. Monumenta Germaniae Pedagogica, vols. 36, 37, 40. Berlin, 1907–1908.

[Ewald]. *Zu Schutz und Trutz am Grabe Schön's: Bilder aus der Zeit der Schmach und der Erhebung Preussens.* Berlin, 1876.

Gerhard, Dietrich and William Norvin, eds. *Die Briefe Barthold Georg Niebuhrs.* 2 vols. Veröffentlichungen der Literatur-Archiv-Gesellschaft in Berlin, vols. 1–2. Berlin, 1926–1929.

Handbuch über den königlichen preussischen Hof und Staat für das Jahr 1805. Berlin, 1805.

Haxthausen, August von. *Die ländliche Verfassung in den einzelnen Provinzen der preussischen Monarchie.* Königsberg, 1839.

Hoffmann, Johann Gottfried. *Das Interesse des Menschen und Bürgers bei den bestehenden Zunftverfassungen.* Königsberg, 1803.

Hoffmann, J[ohann] G[ottfried]. "Nekrolog des Staats-Sekretärs und Chef-Präsidenten der Königlichen Bank Friese." In *Nachlass kleiner Schriften staatswirthschaftlichen Inhalts,* 688–708. Berlin, 1847.

Kant, Immanuel. *Gesammelte Schriften.* 23 vols. Berlin and Leipzig, 1910–1955.

Klein, Ernst Ferdinand, ed. *Annalen der Gesetzgebung und Rechtsgelehrsamkeit in den preussischen Staaten.* 26 vols. Berlin and Stettin, 1788–1808.

Kraus, Christian Jakob. *Staatswirthschaft.* 5 vols. Edited by Hans von Auerswald. Königsberg, 1808–1811.

Kraus, Christian Jakob. *Vermischte Schriften über staatswirthschaftliche, philosophische und andere wissenschaftliche Gegenstände.* 8 vols. Edited by Hans von Auerswald. Königsberg, 1808–1817.

Krug, Leopold. *Über Leibeigenschaft oder Erbuntertänigkeit der Landbewohner der preussischen Staaten.* Halle, 1798.

Leonhardi, F. G. *Erdbeschreibung der preussischen Monarchie.* 3 vols. Halle, 1791–1799.

Linnebach, Karl, ed. *Scharnhorsts Briefe.* Only one of several planned volumes published. Munich and Berlin, 1914.

Maitland, James, Earl of Lauderdale. *An Inquiry into the Nature and Origin of Public Wealth and into the Means and Causes of its Increase.* Edinburgh, 1804. Reprint. Edited with an introduction by Morton Paglin. Reprints of Economic Classics. New York, 1962.

[Maitland, James], Earl of Lauderdale. *Ueber National-Wohlstand.* Translated by Theodor von Schön. Berlin, 1808.

Marwitz, Friedrich August Ludwig von der. *Ein märkischer Edelmann im Zeitalter der Befreiungskriege.* 2 vols. in 3. Edited by Friedrich Meusel. Berlin, 1908–1913.

[Morgenbesser, Ernst Gottlob]. *Beyträge zum republikanischen Gesetzbuche enthalten in Anmerkungen zum Allgemeinen Landrechte und zur Allgemeinen Gerichtsordnung für die preussischen Staaten.* Königsberg, 1800.

Müller, Adam. *Vermischte Schriften über Staat, Philosophie und Kunst.* Vienna, 1817.

Pertz, G. H., ed. *Denkschriften des Ministers Freiherrn vom Stein über deutsche Verfassungen.* Berlin, 1848.

Ranke, Leopold von, ed. *Denkwürdigkeiten des Staatskanzlers Fürsten von Hardenberg.* 5 vols. Leipzig, 1877.

Rehberg, August Wilhelm. *Ueber die Staatsverwaltung deutscher Länder und die Dienerschaft des Regenten.* Hanover, 1807.

"Review of Lauderdale's Nature and Origin of Public Wealth." In *The Edinburgh Review, or Critical Journal* 4 (1804): 343–77.

Rochow, Caroline von, and Marie de la Motte-Fouqué. *Vom Leben am preussischen Hofe 1815–1852.* Edited by Louise von der Marwitz. Berlin, 1908.

Rühl, Franz, ed. *Aus der Franzosenzeit: Ergänzungen zu den Briefen und Aktenstücken zur Geschichte Preussens unter Friedrich Wilhelm III., vorzugsweise aus dem Nachlass von F. A. von Stägemann.* Leipzig, 1904.

Rühl, Franz, ed. *Briefe und Aktenstücke zur Geschichte Preussens unter Friedrich Wilhelm III., vorzugsweise aus dem Nachlass von F. A. von Stägemann.* 3 vols. Leipzig, 1899–1902.

Sammlung der für die königlichen preussischen Staaten erschienenen Gesetze und Verordnungen von 1806 bis zum 27sten Oktober 1810, als Anhang zu der seit den Jahre 1810 edirten Gesetz-Sammlung für die königlichen preussischen Staaten. Berlin, 1822.

Scheel, Heinrich, ed. *Das Reformministerium Stein: Akten zur Verfassungs- und Verwaltungsgeschichte aus den Jahren 1807/08.* 3 vols. Compiled by Doris Schmidt. Deutsche Akademie der Wissenschaften zu Berlin. Schriften des Instituts für Geschichte, Series I: Allgemeine und Deutsche Geschichte, vols. 31a–31c. Berlin, 1966–1968.

Schissler, Hanna and Hans-Ulrich Wehler, eds. *Preussische Finanzpolitik 1806–1810: Quellen zur Verwaltung der Ministerien Stein und Altenstein.* Collected by Eckart Kehr. Göttingen, 1984.

Schmalz, Theodor. *Erklärung der Rechte des Menschen und des Bürgers: Ein Commentar über das reine Natur- und natürliche Staatsrecht.* Königsberg, 1798.

Schmalz, Theodor. *Das reine Naturrecht.* Königsberg, 1792.

Schmalz, [Theodor]. *Staatsverfassung Grossbritanniens.* Halle, 1806.

Schmidt, Günther, ed. *Freiherr vom und zum Stein: Schriften von und über Stein.* Berlin, 1955.

Schön, Theodor von. *Aus den Papieren des Ministers und Burggrafen von Marienburg Theodor von Schön.* 6 vols. Leipzig, Halle and Berlin, 1857–1883.

[Schön, Theodor von]. *Studienreise eines jungen Staatswirths in Deutschland am Schlusse des vorigen Jahrhunderts: Beiträge und Nachträge zu den Papieren des Ministers und Burggrafen von Marienburg Theodor von Schön.* Leipzig, 1879.

[Schön, Theodor von]. *Studienreisen eines jungen Staatsmanns in England am Schlusse des vorigen Jahrhunderts: Beiträge und Nachträge zu den Papieren des Ministers und Burggrafen von Marienburg Theodor von Schön.* [Edited by F. Ewald]. Berlin, 1891.

[Schön, Theodor von]. *Weitere Beiträge und Nachträge zu den Papieren des Ministers und Burggrafen von Marienburg Theodor von Schön.* Berlin, 1881.

Schoeps, Hans Joachim, ed. *Aus den Jahren preussischer Not und Erneuerung: Tagebücher und Briefe der Gebrüder Gerlach und ihres Kreises 1805–1820.* Berlin, 1963.

Schottmüller, Kurt, ed. *Der Polenaufstand 1806/07: Urkunden und Aktenstücke aus der Zeit zwischen Jena und Tilsit.* Sonder-Veröffentlichungen der Historischen Gesellschaft für die Provinz Posen, vol. 4. Lisa, 1907.

Staberock, R[ichard], ed. *Stein und der Wiederaufbau des preussischen Staates.* Teubners Quellensammlung für den Geschichtsunterricht an höheren Schulen, 2/70. Leipzig and Berlin, 1929.

Stadelmann, Rudolf. *Preussens Könige in ihrer Thätigkeit für die Landeskultur,* Part 4, *Friedrich Wilhelm III.* Publikationen aus den königlichen preussischen Staatsarchiven, vol. 30. Leipzig, 1887.

Steffens, Wilhelm, ed. *Briefwechsel Sacks mit Stein und Gneisenau (1807/17).* Veröffentlichungen der Historischen Kommission für Pommern, vol. 5. Stettin, 1931.

Thaer, Albrecht. *Einleitung zur Kenntniss der englischen Landwirtschaft und ihrer neuen praktischen und theoretischen Fortschritte in Rücksicht auf Vervollkommung deutscher Landwirtschaft für denkende Landwirthe und Cameralisten.* Hannover, 1798.

Varnhagen von Ense, K. A. *Denkwürdigkeiten des eigenen Lebens.* Edited by Joachim Kühn. Berlin, 1922.

Vincke, Ludwig von. *Darstellung der inneren Verwaltung Grossbritanniens.* Edited by B. G. Niebuhr. Berlin, 1815.

Voigt, Johannes. *Darstellung der ständischen Verhältnisse Ost-Preussens vorzüglich der neuestern Zeit.* Königsberg, 1822.

Warda, Arthur and Carl Diesch, eds. *Briefe von und an Johann Georg Scheffner.* 5 vols. Munich, Leipzig and Königsberg, 1918–1938.

Winter, Georg, ed. *Die Reorganisation des preussischen Staates unter Stein und Hardenberg.* Publikationen aus den preussischen Staatsarchiven, vol. 93, Part I: Allgemeine Verwaltungs- und Behördenreformen, vol. 1: Vom Beginn des Kampfs gegen die Kabinettsregierung bis zum Wiedereintritt des Ministers vom Stein. Only one of several planned volumes published. Leipzig, 1931.

Wittichen, Paul. "Das preussische Kabinett und Friedrich von Gentz: Eine Denkschrift aus dem Jahre 1800." *Historische Zeitschrift* 89 (1902): 239–73.

Secondary Sources

Abel, Wilhelm, *Agrarkrisen und Agrarkonjunktur: Eine Geschichte der Land- und Ernährungswirtschaft Mitteleuropas seit dem hohen Mittelalter.* Hamburg and Berlin, 1978.

Abel, Wilhelm. *Geschichte der deutschen Landwirtschaft vom frühen Mittelalter bis zum 19. Jahrhundert.* Deutsche Agrargeschichte, vol. 2. Stuttgart, 1962.

Adams, George Burton. *Constitutional History of England.* 1921; London, 1965.

Authorcollective. *Unterrichtshilfen: Geschichte. 7. Klasse.* Berlin, 1972.

Authorcollective. *Geschichte. Lehrbuch für Klasse 7.* Berlin, 1975.

Bach, Theodor. *Theodor Gottlieb von Hippel, der Verfasser des Ausrufs: "An mein Volk". Ein Gedenkenblatt zur fünfzigjährigen Feier der Erhebung Preussens.* Breslau, 1863.

Backus, Oswald Prentiss, III. "Stein and Russia's Prussian Policy from Tilsit to Vienna." Diss., Yale, 1949 (Ann Arbor, 1980).

Benecke, G. *Society and Politics in Germany 1500–1750.* London, 1974.

Berding, Helmut. "y Begriffsgeschichte und Sozialgeschichte." *Historische Zeitschrift* 223 (1976), 98–110.

Bergmann, Jürgen. *Das Berliner Handwerk in den frühphasen der Industrialisierung.* Einzelveröffentlichungen der Historischen Kommission zu Berlin, vol. 11: Publikationen zur Geschichte der Industrialisierung. Berlin, 1973.

Berthoff, Rowland and John M. Murrin. "Feudalism, Communalism, and the Yeoman Freeholder: The American Revolution Considered as a Social Accident." In *Essays on the American Revolution,* edited by Stephen G. Kurtz and James H. Hutson, 256–88. Williamsburg, Chapel Hill and New York, 1973.

Berthold, Rudolf. "Einige Bemerkungen über den Entwicklungsstand des bäuerlichen Ackerbaus vor den Agrarreformen des 19. Jahrhunderts." In *Beiträge zur deutschen Wirtschafts- und Sozialgeschichte des 18. und 19. Jahrhunderts,* 81–131. Deutsche Akademie der Wissenschaften zu Berlin, Schriften des Instituts für Geschichte, Series 1, vol. 10. Berlin, 1962.

Berthold, Rudolf. "Die Veränderungen im Bodeneigentum und in der Zahl der Bauernstellen, der Kleinstellen und der Rittergütter in den preussischen Provinzen Sachsen, Brandenburg und Pommern während der Durchführung der Agrarreformen des 19. Jahrhunderts." In *Studien zu den Agrarreformen des 19. Jahrhunderts in Preussen und Russland,* 7–116. Sonderband des Jahrbuchs für Wirtschaftsgeschichte. Berlin, 1978.

Berthold, Rudolf. "Zur Herausbildung der kapitalistischen Klassenschichtung des Dorfes in Preussen." *Zeitschrift für Geschichtswissenschaft* 25 (1977): 557–74.

Berthold, Rudolf, Hartmut Harnisch, and Hans-Heinrich Müller. "Der preussische Weg der Landwirtschaft und neuere westdeutsche Forschungen." *Jahrbuch für Wirtschaftsgeschichte,* 1970/74, 259–89.

Birtsch, Günther. "Freiheit und Eigentum: Zur Erörterung von Verfassungsfragen in der deutschen Publizistik im Zeichen der französischen Revolution." In *Eigentum und Verfassung: Zur Eigentumsdiskussion im ausgehenden 18. Jahrhundert,* edited by Rudolf Vierhaus, 179–192. Veröffentlichungen des Max-Planck-Instituts für Geschichte, vol. 37. Göttingen, 1972.

Birtsch, Günther. "Der preussische Hochabsolutismus und die Stände." In *Ständetum und Staatsbildung in Brandenburg-Preussen: Ergebnisse einer internationalen Fachtagung,* edited by Peter Baumgart. Veröffentlichungen der Historischen Kommission zu Berlin, vol. 55: Forschungen zur preussischen Geschichte, 389–408. Berlin and New York, 1983.

Birtsch, Günther. "Zum konstitutionellen Charakter des preussischen Allgemeinen Landrechts von 1794." In *Politische Ideologien und Nationalstaatliche Ordnung: Studien zur Geschichte des 19. und 20. Jahrhunderts: Festschrift für Theodor Schieder,* edited by Kurt Kluxen and Wolfgang J. Mommsen, 97–115. Munich and Vienna, 1968.

Black, C. E. *The Dynamics of Modernization: A Study in Comparative History.* New York, 1966.

Bleek, Wilhelm. *Von der Kameralausbildung zum Juristenprivileg: Studium, Prüfung und Ausbildung der höheren Beamten des allgemeinen Verwaltungsdienstes in Deutschland im 18. und 19. Jahrhundert.* Historische und Pädagogische Studien, vol. 3. Berlin, 1972.

Bleiber, Helmut. "Staat und bürgerliche Umwälzung in Preussen: Zum Charakter des Staates in der ersten Hälfte des 19. Jahrhunderts." In *Universalhistorische Aspekte und Dimensionen des Jakobinismus.* Sitzungsberichte der Akademie der Wissenschaften der DDR, vol. 10/G. Berlin, 1976.

Bock, Helmut. "Reform und Revolution: Zur Einordnung des preussischen Reformministeriums Stein in den Kampf zwischen Fortschritt und Reaktion." *Militärgeschichte* 19 (1980): 599–614.

Böhme, Karl. *Gutsherrlich-bäuerliche Verhältnisse in Ostpreussen während der Reformzeit von 1770 bis 1830.* Staats- und sozialwissenschaftliche Forschungen, vol. 20, No. 3. Leipzig, 1902.

Borchard, Karl. "Staatsverbrauch und öffentliche Investitionen in Deutschland 1780–1850." Diss., Göttingen, 1968.

Botzenhart, Erich. *Die Staats- und Reformideen des Freiherrn vom Stein: Ihre geistige Grundlagen und ihre praktischen Vorbilder.* Tübingen, 1927.

Botzenhardt, Manfred. "Verfassungsproblematik und Ständepolitik in der preussischen Reformzeit." In *Ständetum und Staatsbildung in Brandenburg-Preussen: Ergebnisse einer internationalen Fachtagung,* edited by Peter Baumgart. Veröffentlichungen der Historischen Kommission zu Berlin, vol. 55: Forschungen zur preussischen Geschichte, 431–55. Berlin and New York, 1983.

Bowden, Witt, Michael Karpovich, and Abbott Payson Usher. *An Economic History of Europe Since 1750.* New York, 1937.

Braunschwig, Henri. *Enlightenment and Romanticism in Eighteenth-Century Prussia.* Translated by Frank Jellinek. Chicago and London, 1974.

Brünneck, Wilhelm von. *Die Pfandbriefsysteme der preussischen Landschaften.* Berlin, 1910.

Brünneck, Wilhelm von. *Zur Geschichte des Grundeigentums in Ost- und Westpreussen.* 2 vols. Berlin, 1891–1896.

Bruford, W. H. *Germany in the Eighteenth Century: The Social Background of the Literary Revival.* Cambridge, 1935.

Buchheim, Karl. "The *Via Dolorosa* of the Civilian Spirit in Germany." In *German History: Some New German Views,* edited by Hans Kohn, 44–64. London, 1954.

Bues, Adelheid, "Adelskritik—Adelsreform: Ein Versuch zur Kritik der öffentlichen Meinung in den letzten beiden Jahrzehnten des 18. Jahrhunderts an Hand der politischen Journale und der Auseinandersetzungen des Freiherrn vom Stein." Diss., Göttingen, 1948.

Büsch, Otto. *Militärsystem und Sozialleben im alten Preussen 1713–1807: Die Anfänge der sozialen Militarisierung der preussisch-deutschen Gesellschaft.* Veröffentlichungen der Berliner Historischen Kommission beim Friedrich-Meinecke-Institut, vol. 7. Berlin, 1962.

Bujack, [Georg]. *Das erste Triennium des Comités der ostpreussischen und littauischen Stände.* Königsberg, 1887.
Capelle, Richard. "Beiträge zur Geschichte der Erbentage, namentlich derjenigen in der Grafschaft Mark." *Beiträge zur Geschichte Dortmunds und der Grafschaft Mark* 23 (1914): 75–169.
Clapham, J. H. *The Economic Development of France and Germany 1815–1914.* Cambridge, 1966.
Conrad, Hermann. *Staatsgedanke und Staatspraxis des aufgeklärten Absolutismus.* Rheinisch-Westfälische Akademie der Wissenschaften, Geisteswissenschaften, Vorträge, vol. 173. Opladen, 1971.
Conze, Werner. "Nation und Gesellschaft: Zwei Grundbegriffe der revolutionären Epoche." *Historische Zeitschrift* 198 (1964): 1–43.
Conze, Werner. "Vom 'Pöbel' zum 'Proletariat': Sozialgeschichtliche Voraussetzungen für den Sozialismus in Deutschland." *Vierteljahrsschrift für Sozial- und Wirtschaftsgeschichte* 41 (1954): 333–64.
Craton, Michael, James Walvin, and David Wright, eds. *Slavery, Abolition and Emancipation: Black Slaves and the British Empire.* London and New York, 1976.
Czybulka, Gerhard. *Die Lage der ländlichen Klassen Ostdeutschlands im 18. Jahrhundert.* Beiträge zum Geschichtsunterricht, vol. 15. Braunschweig, 1949.
Dann, Otto. "Gleichheit." In *Geschichtliche Grundbegriffe: Historisches Lexikon zur politisch-sozialen Sprache in Deutschland,* edited by Otto Brunner, Werner Conze, and Reinhard Koselleck, 2: 997–1046. 4 vols. to present; publication in progress. Stuttgart, 1972–.
de Bertier de Sauvigny, G. "Liberalism, Nationalism, Socialism: The Birth of Three Words." *Review of Politics* 32 (1970): 147–66.
Dickler, Robert A. "Organization and Change in Productivity in Eastern Prussia." In *European Peasants and their Markets: Essays in Agrarian Economic History,* edited by William N. Parker and Eric L. Jones, 269–92. Princeton, 1975.
Disch, Karl. "Der Kabinettsrat Beyme und die auswärtige Politik Preussens in den Jahren 1805/06." *Foschungen zur brandenburgischen und preussischen Geschichte* 41 (1928): 331–66; 42 (1929): 93–134.
Dorn, Walter E. "The Prussian Bureaucracy in the Eighteenth Century." *Political Science Quarterly* 46 (1931): 403–23; 47 (1932), 75–94, 259–73.
Droz, Jacques. "Europa-Ideen der deutschen Demokraten und Antidemokraten am Ende des 18. und zu Beginn des 19. Jahrhunderts." In *Die demokratische Bewegung in Mitteleuropa im ausgehenden 18. und frühen 19. Jahrhundert: Ein Tagungsbericht,* edited by Otto Büsch und Walter Grab, 353–59. Einzelveröffentlichungen der Historischen Kommission zu Berlin, vol. 29. Berlin, 1980.
Eicke, Hermann. *Der ostpreussische Landtag von 1798.* Göttingen, 1910.
Eisenstadt, S. N. *Modernization: Protest and Change.* Englewood Cliffs, N.J., 1966.
Epstein, Klaus. *The Genesis of German Conservatism.* Princeton, 1966.
Epstein, Klaus. "Stein in German Historiography." *History and Theory: Studies in the Philosophy of History* 5 (1966): 241–74.
Eulen, Foko. *Vom Gewerbefleiss zur Industrie: Ein Beitrag zur Wirtschaftsgeschichte des 18. Jahrhunderts.* Schriften zur Wirtschafts- und Sozialgeschichte, vol. 12. Berlin, 1967.
Fann, Willerd R. "The Rise of the Prussian Ministry, 1806–1827." In *Sozialgeschichte heute. Festschrift für Hans Rosenberg,* edited by Hans-Ulrich Wehler, 119–29. Kritische Studien zur Geschichtswissenschaft, vol. 11. Göttingen, 1974.
Faulenbach, Bernd. "Deutsche Geschichtswissenschaft zwischen Kaiserreich und NS-Diktatur." In *Geschichtswissenschaft in Deutschland,* edited by Bernd Faulenbach, 66–85. Beck'sche Schwarze Reihe, vol. 111. Munich, 1974.
Fehrenbach, Elisabeth. *Der Kampf um die Einführung des Code Napoléon in den Rheinbundstaaten.* Institut für europäische Geschichte, Vorträge, no. 56. Wiesbaden, 1973.
Fehrenbach, Elisabeth. *Traditionale Gesellschaft und revolutionäres Recht: Die Einführung des Code Napoléon in den Rheinbundstaaten.* Kritische Studien zur Geschichtswissenschaft, vol. 13. 2d ed. Göttingen, 1978.
Fehrenbach, Elisabeth. "Verfassungs- und Sozialpolitische Reformen und Reformprojekte in Deutschland unter dem Einfluss des Napoleonischen Frankreich." *Historische Zeitschrift* 228 (1979): 288–316.
Fisher, Herbert A. L. *Studies in Napoleonic Statesmanship: Germany.* Oxford, 1903.
Fox-Genovese, Elizabeth and Eugene Genovese. *Fruits of Merchant Capital: Slavery and Bourgeois Property in the Rise and Expansion of Capitalism.* New York and Oxford, 1983.
Friedrich, Carl J. "The Continental Tradition of Training Administrators in Law and Jurisprudence." *Journal of Modern History* 11 (1939): 129–48.

Gagliardo, John G. *From Pariah to Patriot: The Changing Image of the German Peasant 1770–1840.* Lexington, Ky., 1969.

Gall, Lothar. "Liberalismus und 'bürgerliche Gesellschaft': Zu Charakter und Entwicklung der liberalen Bewegung in Deutschland." *Historische Zeitschrift* 220 (1975): 324–56.

Gause, Fritz. *Die Geschichte der Stadt Königsberg in Preussen.* 3 vols. Osteuropa in Vergangenheit und Gegenwart, vol. 10. Köln, 1968.

Gerold, Heinz. "Militärisches Debakel eines überlebten Systems: Zum 175. Jahrestag der Schlacht von Jena und Auerstedt." *Militärgeschichte* 20 (1981): 587–89.

Gillis, John R. *The Prussian Bureaucracy in Crisis 1840–1860: Origins of an Administrative Ethos.* Stanford, 1971.

Görlitz, Walter. *Die Junker: Adel und Bauern im deutschen Osten. Geschichtliche Bilanz von 7 Jahrhunderten.* Glücksburg/Ostsee, 1957.

Gooch, G. P. *History and Historians in the Nineteenth Century.* London, 1954.

Gray, Marion W. "Government by Property Owners: Prussian Plans for Constitutional Reform on the County, Provincial and National Levels in 1808." *Journal of Modern History* 48 (1976): on-demand reprint, 1–51.

Gray, Marion W. "Der ostpreussische Landtag des Jahres 1808 und das Reformministerium Stein: Eine Fallstudie politischer Modernisation." *Jahrbuch für die Geschichte Mittel- und Ostdeutschlands* 26 (1977): 129–45.

Gray, Marion W. "The Rise of German Nationalism and the Wars of Liberation (1803–1814)." In *Napoleonic Military History: A Bibliography,* edited by Donald D. Horward, 435–78. Military History Bibliographies, vol. 9. Garland Reference Library of Social Science, vol. 194. New York and London, 1986.

Gray, Marion W. "Schroetter, Schön and Society: Aristocratic Liberalism versus Middle-Class Liberalism in Prussia, 1808." *Central European History* 6 (1973): 60–82.

Gray, Marion Wilson, Jr. "Theodor von Schön and Prussian Reforms 1806–1808." Diss., Univ. Wisconsin, 1971.

Gregg, Pauline. *A Social and Economic History of Britain 1760–1972.* London, 1973.

Gropp, Volkmar. *Der Einfluss der Agrarreformen des beginnenden 19. Jahrhunderts in Ostpreussen auf Höhe und Zusammensetzung der preussischen Staatseinkünfte.* Schriften zur Wirtschafts- und Sozialgeschichte, vol. 9. Berlin, 1967.

Habermas, Jürgen. *Strukturwandel der Öffentlichkeit: Untersuchungen zu einer Kategorie der bürgerlichen Gesellschaft.* Politica, vol. 4. Neuwied, 1962.

Hagen, William W. *Germans, Poles, and Jews: The Nationality Conflict in the Prussian East, 1772-1914.* Chicago, 1980.

Hamerow, Theodore S. *Restoration, Revolution, Reaction: Economics and Politics in Germany 1815-1871.* Princeton, 1958.

Hamerow, Theodore S. *The Social Foundations of German Unification: Ideas and Institutions.* Princeton, 1969.

Harnisch, Hartmut. "Die Bedeutung der kapitalistischen Agrarreform für die Herausbildung des inneren Marktes und die industrielle Revolution in den östlichen Provinzen Preussens in der ersten Hälfte des 19. Jahrhunderts." *Jahrbuch für Wirtschaftsgeschichte* 1977/4: 63–82.

Harnisch, Hartmut. "Probleme junkerlicher Agrarpolitik im 19. Jahrhundert." *Wissenschaftliche Zeitschrift der Universität Rostock* 21 (1972). Gesellschafts- und Sprachwissenschaftliche Reihe 1, 2: 99–117.

Harnisch, Hartmut. "Vom Oktoberedikt des Jahres 1807 zur Deklaration von 1816: Problematik und Charakter der preussischen Agrarreformgesetzgebung zwischen 1807 und 1816." In *Studien zu den Agrarreformen des 19. Jahrhunderts in Preussen and Russland,* 229–93. Sonderband des Jahrbuchs für Wirtschaftsgeschichte. Berlin, 1978.

Hartung, Fritz. *Deutsche Verfassungsgeschichte vom 15. Jahrhundert bis zur Gegenwart.* Stuttgart, 1965.

Hartung, Fritz. *Hardenberg und die preussische Verwaltung in Ansbach-Bayreuth von 1792 bis 1806.* Tübingen, 1906.

Hasek, Carl William. *The Introduction of Adam Smith's Doctrines into Germany.* Studies in History, Economics and Public Law, vol. 117/2. New York, 1925.

Hasse, Gustav. "Theodor von Schön und die steinsche Wirtschaftsreform, zugleich ein Beitrag zu einer Biographie Th. von Schöns." Diss., Leipzig, 1915.

Haussherr, Hans. *Erfüllung und Befreiung: Der Kampf um die Durchführung des Tilsiter Friedens 1807/1808.* Hamburg, 1935.

Haussherr, Hans. "Hardenbergs Reformdenkschrift Riga, 1807." *Historische Zeitschrift* 157 (1938): 267–308.

Heike, Otto. *Die Provinz Südpreussen: preussische Aufbau- und Verwaltungsarbeit im Warthe- und Weichselgebiet 1793–1806.* Wissenschaftliche Beiträge zur Geschichte und Landeskunde Mitteleuropas, vol. 12. Marburg/Lahn, 1953.

Heitz, Gerhard. "Varianten des preussischen Weges." *Jahrbuch für Wirtschaftsgeschichte* 1969/3: 99–109.

Henning, Friedrich-Wilhelm. *Bauernwirtschaft und Bauerneinkommen in Ostpreussen im 18. Jahrhundert.* Beihefte zum Jahrbuch der Albertus-Universität Königsberg/Pr., vol. 30. Würzburg, 1969.

Henning, Friedrich-Wilhelm. *Herrschaft und Bauernuntertänigkeit: Beiträge zur Geschichte der Herrschaftsverhältnisse in den ländlichen Bereichen Ostpreussens und des Fürstentums Paderborn vor 1800.* Beihefte zum Jahrbuch der Albertus-Universität Königsberg/Pr., vol. 25. Würzburg, 1964.

Heuer, Uwe-Jens. *Allgemeines Landrecht und Klassenkampf: Die Auseinandersetzungen um die Prinzipien des Allgemeinen Landrechts Ende des 18. Jahrhunderts als Ausdruck der Krise des Feudalsystems in Preussen.* Berlin, 1960.

Heumann, Hans. *Unser Weg durch die Geschichte* (Ausgabe für Realschulen). Vol. 3, *Die Grundlagen unserer Gesellschaft.* Frankfurt am Main, 1975.

Hill, Christopher. *Puritanism and Revolution: Studies in Interpretation of the English Revolution of the Seventeenth Century.* London, 1958.

Hintze, Otto. "Preussische Reformbestrebungen vor 1806." In *Gesammelte Abhandlungen zur Staats-, Rechts- und Sozialgeschichte Preussens,* vol. 3 *Regierung und Verwaltung,* edited by Gerhard Oestreich, 504–29. Göttingen, 1967.

Hintze, Otto. "Das preussische Staatsministerium im 19. Jahrhundert." In *Gesammelte Abhandlungen zur Staats-, Rechts- und Sozialgeschichte Preussens,* vol. 3. *Regierung und Verwaltung,* edited by Gerhard Oestreich, 530–619. Göttingen, 1967.

Hobsbawm, E. J. *The Age of Revolution 1789–1848.* Mentor ed. New York, 1962.

Hobsbawm, E. J. "From Social History to the History of Society." In *Historical Studies Today,* edited by Felix Gilbert and Stephen R. Graubard, 1–26. New York, 1972.

Hobsbawm, E. J. *The Pelican Economic History of Britain.* Vol. 3, *From 1750 to the Present Day: Industry and Empire.* Middlesex, 1969.

Hubatsch, Walter. *Frederick the Great of Prussia: Absolutism and Administration.* Translated by Patrick Doran. London, 1973.

Hubatsch, Walther. *Die Stein-Hardenbergschen Reformen.* Erträge der Forschung, vol. 65. Darmstadt, 1977.

Hüffer, Hermann. *Die Kabinetsregierung in Preussen und Johann Wilhelm Lombard: Ein Beitrag zur Geschichte des preussischen Staates, vornehmlich in den Jahren 1797 bis 1810.* Leipzig, 1891.

Ipsen, Gunther. "Staat aus dem Volk: Scheitern, Wollen, Vollbringen des Freiherrn vom Stein in der preussischen Reform." *Der Staat: Zeitschrift für Staatslehre, öffentliches Recht und Verfassungsgeschichte* 12 (1973): 153–64.

Isenberg, Wilhelm. *Das Staatsdenken des Freiherrn vom Stein.* Schriften zur Rechtslehre und Politik, vol. 58. Bonn, 1968.

Just, Leo, ed. *Handbuch der deutschen Geschichte.* Vol. 3, Kurt von Raumer. *Deutschland um 1800: Krise und Neugestaltung 1789–1815.* Konstanz, 1965.

Kaufhold, Karl Heinrich. "Umfang und Gliederung des deutschen Handwerks um 1800." In *Handwerksgeschichte in neuer Sicht,* edited by Wilhelm Abel. Göttinger Beiträge zur Wirtschafts- und Sozialgeschichte, vol. 1. Göttingen, 1978.

Kehr, Eckart. "Zur Genesis der preussischen Bürokratie und des Rechtsstaats: Ein Beitrag zum Diktaturproblem." In *Der Primat der Innenpolitik: Gesammelte Aufsätze zur preussisch-deutschen Sozialgeschichte im 19. und 20. Jahrhundert,* edited by Hans-Ulrich Wehler, 31–52. Veröffentlichungen der Historischen Kommission zu Berlin, vol. 19. Berlin, 1970.

Kirsten, Ernst, Ernst Wolfgang Buchholz, and Wolfgang Köllmann. *Raum und Bevölkerung in der Weltgeschichte: Bevölkerungs-Ploetz.* 2 vols. Würzburg, 1955–1956.

Kisch, Herbert D. "The Textile Industries in Silesia and the Rhineland: A Comparative Study in Industrialization." *Journal of Economic History* 19 (1959): 541–64.

Klein, Ernst. *Von der Reform zur Restauration: Finanzpolitik und Reformgesetzgebung des preussischen Staatskanzlers Karl August von Hardenberg.* Veröffentlichungen der Historischen Kommission zu Berlin, vol. 16. Berlin, 1965.

Knapp, Georg Friedrich. *Die Bauern-Befreiung und der Ursprung der Landarbeiter in den älteren Theilen Preussens.* Leipzig, 1887.

Knemeyer, Franz-Ludwig. "Polizei." In *Geschichtliche Grundbegriffe: Historisches Lexikon zur politisch-sozialen Sprache in Deutschland,* edited by Otto Brunner, Werner Conze, and Reinhard Koselleck, vol. 4, 875–97. 4 vols. to present; publication in progress. Stuttgart, 1972–.

Kochendörffer, [Heinrich]. *Vincke.* 2 vols. Soest in Westfalen, 1932–1933.

Kocka, Jürgen. "Theoretical Approaches to Social and Economic History of Modern Germany: Some Recent Trends, Concepts, and Problems in Western and Eastern Germany." *Journal of Modern History* 47 (1975): 101–19.

Koselleck, Reinhard. *Preussen zwischen Reform und Revolution: Allgemeines Landrecht, Verwaltung und soziale Bewegung von 1791 bis 1848.* Industrielle Welt, vol. 7. Stuttgart, 1967.

Krause, Gottlieb. *Der preussische Provinzialminister Freiherr von Schroetter und sein Anteil an der steinschen Reformgesetzgebung.* Königsberg, 1898.

Kriedte, Peter, Hans Medick, and Jürgen Schlumbohm. *Industrialisierung vor der Industrialisierung: Gewerbliche Warenproduktion auf dem Land in der Formationsperiode des Kapitalismus.* Veröffentlichungen des Max-Planck-Instituts für Geschichte, vol. 53. Göttingen, 1977.

Krieger, Leonard. *The German Idea of Freedom: History of a Political Tradition from the Reformation to 1871.* Chicago, 1957.

Krollmann, Christian, Kurt Forstreuter, and Fritz Gause, eds. *Altpreussische Biographie.* 3 vols. Königsberg and Marburg, 1941–1975. Reprint of vol. 1. Marburg, 1978.

Krüger, Horst. *Zur Geschichte der Manufakturen und der Manufakturarbeiter in Preussen: Die mittleren Provinzen in der zweiten Hälfte des 18. Jahrhunderts.* Schriftenreihe des Instituts für Allgemeine Geschichte an der Humboldt-Universität Berlin, vol. 3. Berlin, 1958.

LaVopa, Anthony J. *Prussian Schoolteachers: Profession and Office, 1763–1848.* Chapel Hill, 1980.

Lefèbvre, Georges. *The Coming of the French Revolution: 1789.* Translated by R. R. Palmer. Princeton, 1947.

Lefèbvre, Georges. *Napoléon.* Peuples et Civilisations, vol. 14. Paris, 1953.

Lehmann, Max. *Freiherr vom Stein.* 3 vols. Leipzig, 1902–1905.

Lehmann, Max. *Knesebeck und Schön: Beiträge zur Geschichte der Freiheitskriege.* Leipzig, 1875.

Lemisch, Jesse. "The American Revolution Seen from the Bottom Up." In *Towards a New Past: Dissenting Essays in American History,* edited by Barton J. Bernstein, 3–45. New York, 1968.

Lippold, Hans. "Die Kriegs- und Domänenkammer zu Bialystock in ihrer Arbeit und Bedeutung für die preussische Geschichte." Diss., Königsberg, 1914.

Lüdtke, Alf. *"Gemeinwohl," Polizei und "Festungspraxis": Staatliche Gewaltsamkeit und innere Verwaltung in Preussen, 1815–1850.* Veröffentlichungen des Max-Planck-Instituts für Geschichte, vol. 73. Göttingen, 1982.

Lütge, Friedrich. *Deutsche Sozial- und Wirtschaftsgeschichte.* Berlin and Heidelberg, 1966.

Lütge, Friedrich. *Geschichte der deutschen Agrarverfassung vom frühen Mittelalter bis zum 19. Jahrhundert.* Deutsche Agrargeschichte, vol. 3. Edited by Günther Franz. Stuttgart, 1967.

Lundgreen, Peter. "Gegensatz und Verschmelzung von 'alter' und 'neuer' Bürokratie im Ançien Régime: Ein Vergleich von Frankreich und Preussen." In *Sozialgeschichte heute. Festschrift für Hans Rosenberg,* edited by Hans-Ulrich Wehler, 104–18. Kritische Studien zur Geschichtswissenschaft, vol. 11. Göttingen, 1974.

Lynd, Staughton. "Beyond Beard." In *Towards a New Past: Dissenting Essays in American History,* edited by Barton J. Bernstein, 46–64. New York, 1968.

Mann, Golo. *Deutsche Geschichte des 19. und 20. Jahrhunderts.* Frankfurt, 1969.

Mauer, Hermann. *Das Landschaftliche Kreditwesen Preussens agrargeschichtlich und volkswirtschaftlich betrachtet: Ein Beitrag zur Geschichte der Bodenkreditspolitik des preussischen Staates.* Abhandlungen aus dem Staatswirtschaftlichen Seminar zu Strassburg, vol. 22. Strassburg, 1907.

Mehring, Franz. *Gesammelte Schriften und Aufsätze.* Vol. 4, *Zur preussischen Geschichte von Tilsit bis zur Reichsgründung.* Edited by Eduard Fuchs. Berlin, 1930.

Meier, Ernst von. *Französische Einflüsse auf die Staats- und Rechtsentwicklung Preussens im 19. Jahrhundert.* 2 vols. Leipzig, 1907–1908.

Meier, Ernst von. *Der Minister vom Stein, die französische Revolution und der preussische Adel: Eine Streitschrift gegen Max Lehmann.* Leipzig, 1908.

Meier, Ernst von. *Die Reform der Verwaltungsorganisation unter Stein und Hardenberg.* Leipzig, 1881.

Meinecke, Friedrich. *Das Zeitalter der deutschen Erhebung (1795–1815).* 1906; Göttingen, 1963.

Melton, James Van Horn. "From Enlightenment to Revolution: Hertzberg, Schlözer, and the Problem of Despotism in the Late *Aufklärung.*" *Central European History* 12 (1979): 103–23.

Mendels, Franklin F. "Proto-Industrialization: The First Phase of the Industrialization Process." *Journal of Economic History* 32 (1972): 241–61.
Menne, Dieter. "Die Mitarbeit des Freiherrn von Vincke an den preussischen Reformbestrebungen 1806 bis 1808." Staatsexamenarbeit, Bochum, 1967.
Meyers, Peter. "Unterrichtsversuche zum Thema." In *Der Freiherr vom Stein in unserer Zeit: Gedanken und Versuche zur politischen Bildung.* Cappenberger Gespräche der Freiherr-vom-Stein Gesellschaft, vol. 5, 35–42. Cologne and Berlin, 1971.
Milkowski, Fritz. "Christian Jacob Kraus: Eine längst fällige Korrektur zur Geschichte der Volkswirtschaftlehre." *Schmollers Jahrbuch für Wirtschafts- und Sozialwissenschaften* 88 (1968): 257–97.
Mommsen, Hans. "Haupttendenzen nach 1945 und in der Ära des Kalten Krieges." In *Geschichtswissenschaft in Deutschland,* edited by Bernd Faulenbach, 112–20. Beck'sche Schwarze Reihe, vol. 111. Munich, 1974.
Mommsen, Wolfgang J. "Der deutsche Liberalismus zwischen 'klassenloser Bürgergesellschaft' und 'organisiertem Kapitalismus': Zu einigen neueren Liberalismusinterpretationen." *Geschichte und Gesellschaft: Zeitschrift für Historische Sozialwissenschaft* 4 (1978): 77–90.
Moore, Barrington, Jr. *Social Origins of Dictatorship and Democracy: Lord and Peasant in the Making of the Modern World.* Boston, 1967.
Mottek, Hans. *Wirtschaftsgeschichte Deutschlands: Ein Grundriss.* Vol. 2, *Von der Zeit der französischen Revolution bis zur Zeit der bismarckschen Reichsgründung.* Berlin, 1976.
Müller, Hans-Heinrich. "Der agrarische Fortschritt und die Bauern in Brandenburg vor den Reformen von 1807." *Zeitschrift für Geschichtswissenschaft* 12 (1964), 629–48.
Müller, Hans-Heinrich. "Bauern, Pächter und Adel im alten Preussen." *Jahrbuch für Wirtschaftsgeschichte* 1966/1: 259–77.
Müller, Hans-Heinrich. "Domänen und Domänenpächter in Brandenburg-Preussen im 18. Jahrhundert." *Jahrbuch für Wirtschaftsgeschichte* 1954/4: 152–92.
Myers, A. R. *Parliaments and Estates in Europe to 1789.* London, 1975.
Namier, Louis. *England in the Age of the American Revolution.* London, 1961.
Obenaus, Herbert. "Verwaltung und ständische Repräsentation in den Reformen des Freiherrn vom Stein." *Jahrbuch für die Geschichte Mittel- und Ostdeutschlands* 18 (1969): 130–79.
Obermann, Karl. "Bemerkungen über die soziale und nationale Bedeutung der preussischen Reformbewegung unter dem Ministerium des Freiherrn vom Stein." In *Die Volksmassen: Gestalter der Geschichte. Festgabe für Leo Stern,* edited by Hans Joachim Bartmuss et al., 127–53. Berlin, 1962.
Orr, William J., Jr. "East Prussia and the Revolution of 1848." *Central European History* 13 (1980): 303–31.
Paglin, Mortin. *Malthus and Lauderdale: The Anti-Ricardian Tradition.* New York, 1961.
Pertz, G. H. *Das Leben des Feldmarschalls Grafen Neithart von Gneisenau.* 6 vols. Berlin, 1864–1880.
Pertz, G. H. *Das Leben des Ministers Freiherr vom Stein.* 6 vols. Berlin, 1849–1855.
Pollock, James. "What Shall We Do With Germany?" *Current History* 2 (1942): 1–5.
Poole, J. R. *Political Representation in England and the Origins of the American Republic.* New York, 1966.
Postan, M. M. *Fact and Relevance: Essays on Historical Method.* Cambridge, 1971.
Preuss, Ulrich K. "Bildung und Büreaukratie: Sozialhistorische Bedingungen in der ersten Hälfte des 19. Jahrhunderts." *Der Staat: Zeitschrift für Staatslehre, öffentliches Recht und Verfassungsgeschichte* 14 (1975): 371–96.
Raack, R. C. *The Fall of Stein.* Harvard Historical Monographs, vol. 58. Cambridge, Mass., 1965.
Raack, R. C. "A New Schleiermacher Letter on the Conspiracy of 1808." *Zeitschrift für Religions- und Geistesgeschichte* 16 (1964): 209–23.
Ranke, Leopold von. *Sämmtliche Werke.* Vols. 46–48, *Hardenberg und die Geschichte des preussischen Staates von 1793–1813.* Leipzig, 1879–1881.
Reill, Peter Hanns. "Barthold Georg Niebuhr and the Enlightenment Tradition." *German Studies Review* 3 (1980): 9–26.
Ritter, Gerhard. *Das deutsche Problem: Grundfragen deutschen Staatslebens gestern und heute.* Munich, 1962.
Ritter, Gerhard. *Stein: Eine politische Biographie.* 2 vols. Stuttgart and Berlin, 1931; 3rd ed., Stuttgart, 1958.
Roeder, Veronika. "Preussische Geschichte in der sozialistischen Schule: Die preussischen Reformen und die Befreiungskriege im Geschichtsunterricht der DDR." *Geschichte in Wissenschaft und Unterricht* 32 (1981): 400–23.

Rohrscheidt, Kurt von. *Vom Zunftzwang zur Gewerbefreiheit: Eine Studie nach den Quellen.* Berlin, 1898.

Rosenberg, Hans. *Bureaucracy, Aristocracy and Autocracy: The Prussian Experience 1660–1815.* 1958; Boston, 1968.

Rosenberg, Hans. "The Rise of the Junkers in Brandenburg-Prussia, 1410–1653." *American Historical Review* 49 (1943–44): 1–22; 228–42.

Rosenberg, Hans. "Theologischer Rationalismus und vormärzlicher Vulgarliberalismus." In *Politische Denkströmungen im deutschen Vormärz,* 18–50. Kritische Studien zur Geschichtswissenschaft, vol. 3. Göttingen, 1972.

Ross, Günther. "Das Leben des Freiherrn von Altenstein bis zum Jahre 1807." Edited by Hans Haussherr. *Forschungen zur brandenburgischen und preussischen Geschichte* 53 (1941): 91–128.

Rudé, George. *Revolutionary Europe 1783–1815.* Meridian Histories of Modern Europe. Cleveland and New York, 1964.

Rumler, Marie. "Die Bestrebungen zur Befreiung der Privatbauern in Preussen, 1797–1806." *Forschungen zur brandenburgischen und preussischen Geschichte* 33 (1921): 179–92; 34 (1922): 1–24, 256–96; 37 (1925): 31–76.

Rytkönnen, Seppo. *Barthold Georg Niebuhr als Politiker und Historiker: Zeitgeschehen und Zeitgeist in den geschichtlichen Beurteilungen von B. G. Niebuhr.* Helsinki, 1968.

Salewski, Michael. "Der Freiherr vom Stein und die französische Revolution." In *Preussen, Deutschland und der Westen: Auseinandersetzungen und Beziehungen seit 1789. Zum 60. Geburtstag von Oswald Hauser,* edited by Heinrich Bodensieck, 3–22. Göttingen, 1980.

Salvadori, Massimo, ed. *European Liberalism.* Major Issues in History. New York, 1972.

Scheel, Heinrich. "Eine notwendige Polemik in Sachen Stein." In *Preussische Reformen—Wirklichkeit und Grenzen. Aus Anlass des 150. Todestages des Freiherrn vom und zum Stein,* edited by Heinrich Scheel, 75–83. Sitzungsberichte der Akademie der Wissenschaften der DDR: Gesellschaftswissenschaften 1982 1G. Berlin, 1982.

Scheel, Heinrich. "Probleme der deutsch-französischen Beziehungen 1789–1830." *Zeitschrift für Geschichtswissenschaft* 18 (1970): 163–71.

Schinkel, Harald. "Polizei und Stadtverfassung im frühen 19. Jahrhundert: Eine historisch-kritische Interpretation der preussischen Städteordnung von 1808." *Der Staat: Zeitschrift für Staatslehre, öffentliches Recht und Verfassungsgeschichte* 3 (1964): 315–34.

Schissler, Hanna. " 'Bauernbefreiung' oder Entwicklung zur agrarkapitalistischen Gesellschaft?" *Sozialwissenschaftliche Informationen für Unterricht und Studium* 8 (1979): 136–42.

Schissler, Hanna. *Preussische Agrargesellschaft im Wandel: Wirtschaftliche, gesellschaftliche und politische Transformationsprozesse von 1763 bis 1847.* Kritische Studien zur Geschichtswissenschaft, vol. 33. Göttingen, 1978.

Schleier, Hans. *Die bürgerliche deutsche Geschichtesschreibung der Weimarer Republik.* Akademie der Wissenschaften der DDR, Schriften des Zentralinstituts für Geschichte, vol. 40. Berlin, 1975.

Schlumbohm, Jürgen. *Freiheit: Die Anfänge der bürgerlichen Emanzipationsbewegung in Deutschland im Spiegel ihres Leitwortes.* Geschichte und Gesellschaft: Bochumer Historische Studien, vol. 12. Düsseldorf, 1975.

Schmidt, Walter. "Marx und Engels über den historischen Platz der preussischen Reformen." In *Preussische Reformen—Wirklichkeit und Grenzen. Aus Anlass des Todestages des Freiherrn vom und zum Stein,* edited by Heinrich Scheel, 54–74. Sitzungsberichte der Akademie der Wissenschaften der DDR: Gesellschaftswissenschaften 1982 1G. Berlin, 1982.

Schmoller, Gustav. "Die Epochen der preussischen Finanzpolitik bis zur Gründung des deutschen Reiches." In *Umrisse und Untersuchungen zur Verfassungs- Verwaltungs- und Wirtschaftsgeschichte besonders des preussischen Staates im 17. und 18. Jahrhundert,* 104–246. Leipzig, 1898.

Schönbeck, Otto. "Der kurmärkische Landtag vom Frühjahr 1809." *Forschungen zur brandenburgischen und preussischen Geschichte* 20 (1907): 1–103.

Schrimpf, Henning. "Die Auseinandersetzung um die Neuordnung des Individuellen Rechtschutzes gegenüber der staatlichen Verwaltung nach 1807." *Der Staat: Zeitschrift für Staatslehre, öffentliches Recht und Verfassungsgeschichte* 18 (1979): 59–80.

Schrimpf, Henning. *Herrschaft, Individualinteresse und Richtermacht im Übergang zur bürgerlichen Gesellschaft: Studien zum Rechtschutz gegenüber der Ausübung öffentlicher Gewalt in Preussen 1782–1821.* Minerva-Fachserie, Rechts- und Staatswissenschaften. Munich, 1979.

Schröder, Hans-Christoph. "Das Eigentumsproblem in den Auseinandersetzungen um die Verfassung von Massachusetts, 1775–1787." In *Eigentum und Verfassung: Zur Eigentums-*

diskussion im ausgehenden 18. Jahrhundert, edited by Rudolf Vierhaus, 11–67. Veröffentlichungen des Max-Planck-Instituts für Geschichte, vol. 37. Göttingen, 1972.
Schulze-Marmeling, Wilhelm. "Schön und Vincke: Englische Verfassungs- Verwaltungs- und Wirtschaftseinflüsse in Preussen um 1800." Diss., Münster, 1950.
Schumacher, Bruno. *Geschichte Ost- und Westpreussens.* Würzburg, 1959.
Schwab, Dieter. *Die "Selbstverwaltungsidee" des Freiherrn vom Stein und ihre geistigen Grundlagen, zugleich ein Beitrag zur Geschichte der politischen Ethik im 18. Jahrhundert.* Giessener Beiträge zur Rechtswissenschaft, vol. 3. Frankfurt am Main, 1971.
Selle, Götz von. *Die Georg-August Universität zu Göttingen 1737-1937.* Göttingen, 1937.
Sheehan, James J. *German Liberalism in the Nineteenth Century.* Chicago and London, 1978.
Sheehan, James J. "Partei, Volk und Staat: Some Reflections on the Relationship between Liberal Thought and Action in Vormärz." In *Sozialgeschichte heute. Festschrift für Hans Rosenberg*, edited by Hans-Ulrich Wehler, 162–74. Kritische Studien zur Geschichtswissenschaft, vol. 11. Göttingen, 1974.
Simon, Walter M. *The Failure of the Prussian Reform Movement, 1807-1819.* 1955. Reprint. New York, 1971.
Skinner, Quentin. "Taking Off." *New York Review of Books* 26, No. 4 (22 March 1979): 15–16.
Spies, Hans-Bernd, ed. *Die Erhebung gegen Napoleon 1806–1814/15.* Quellen zum politischen Denken der Deutschen im 19. und 20. Jahrhundert: Freiherr vom Stein Gedächtnisausgabe, vol. 2. Darmstadt, 1981.
Spranger, Eduard. "Altensteins Denkschrift von 1807 und ihre Beziehung zur Philosophie." *Forschungen zur brandenburgischen und preussischen Geschichte* 18 (1905): 471–517.
Stein, Robert. *Die Umwandlung der Agrarverfassung Ostpreussens durch die Reform des neunzehnten Jahrhunderts.* 3 vols. Schriften des königlichen Instituts für ostdeutsche Wirtschaft an der Universität Königsberg, vols. 5/1–5/3. Königsberg, 1918–1934.
Stern, Alfred, ed. "Beiträge zur Biographie des preussischen Staatsrats von Rehdiger. Aus dem Nachlass von Paul Lenel." *Historische Zeitschrift* 124 (1921): 220–49.
Streisand, Joachim. "Deutschland von 1789 bis 1915." In *Deutsche Geschichte*, edited by Authorcollective, vol. 2, 78–82. Berlin, 1967.
Suchenwirth, Richard. *Deutsche Geschichte von der germanischen Vorzeit bis zur Gegenwart.* Leipzig, 1938.
Sugenheim, Samuel. *Geschichte der Aufhebung der Leibeigenschaft und Hörigkeit in Europa um die Mitte des neunzehnten Jahrhunderts.* St. Petersburg, 1861.
Thiede, Klaus. *Die Staats- und Wirtschaftsauffassung des Freiherrn vom Stein.* Jena, 1927.
Thielen, Peter G. *Karl August von Hardenberg 1750-1822: Eine Biographie.* Köln and Berlin, 1967.
Tilly, Charles, and Richard Tilly. "An Agenda for European Economic History in the 1970's." *Journal of Economic History* 31 (1971): 184–98.
Tipps, Dean C. "Modernization Theory and the Comparative Study of Societies: A Critical Perspective." *Comparative Studies in Society and History* 15 (1973): 199–226.
Treue, Wilhelm. "Adam Smith in Deutschland: Zum Problem des 'politischen Professors' zwischen 1776 und 1810." In *Deutschland und Europa: Historische Studien zur Völker- und Staatenordnung des Abenlandes. Festschrift für Hans Rothfels*, edited by Werner Conze, 101–33. Düsseldorf, 1951.
Treue, Wilhelm. *Wirtschafts- und Technikgeschichte Preussens.* Veröffentlichungen der Historischen Kommission zu Berlin, vol. 56. Berlin and New York, 1984.
Tschirch, Otto. *Geschichte der öffentlichen Meinung in Preussen im Friedensjahrzehnt vom baseler Frieden bis zum Zusammenbruch des Staates.* 2 vols. Weimar, 1933–1934.
Tulard, Jean. "Problèmes sociaux de la France impériale." *Revue d'histoire moderne et contemporaine* 17 (1970): 640–49.
Unruh, Georg Christoph von. *Der Landrat: Mittler zwischen Staatsverwaltung und kommunaler Selbstverwaltung.* Köln and Berlin, 1966.
Vellen, Hildegard. "Bericht über eine Unterrichtsstunde." In *Der Freiherr vom Stein in unserer Zeit: Gedanken und Versuche zur politischen Bildung.* Cappenberger Gespräche der Freiherr-vom-Stein Gesellschaft, vol. 5, 43–49. Cologne and Berlin, 1971.
Vierhaus, Rudolf. "Politisches Bewusstsein in Deutschland vor 1789." In *Deutschland zwischen Revolution und Restauration*, edited by Helmut Berding und Hans-Peter Ullmann, 161–83. Athenäum/Droste Taschenbücher Geschichte, no. 7240. Königstein/Ts., 1981.
Voegelin, Eric. "Liberalism and Its History." *The Review of Politics* 36 (1974): 504–20.
Vogel, Barbara. "Die 'allgemeine Gewerbefreiheit' als bürokratische Modernisierungsstrategie in Preussen: Eine Problemskizze zur Reformpolitik Hardenbergs." In *Industrielle Gesellschaft*

und politisches System: Beiträge zur politischen Sozialgeschichte. Festschrift für Fritz Fischer, edited by Dirk Stegmann et al., 59–78. Schriftenreihe des Forschungsinstituts der Friedrich-Ebert-Stiftung, vol. 137. Bonn, 1978.

Vogel, Barbara. *Allgemeine Gewerbefreibeit: Die Reformpolitik des preussischen Staatskanzlers Hardenberg (1810–1820)*. Kritische Studien zur Geschichtswissenschaft, vol. 57. Göttingen, 1983.

Vogel, Barbara, ed. *Preussische Reformen 1807–1820*. Neue Wissenschaftliche Bibliothek, vol. 96, Geschichte. Königstein/Ts., 1980.

Vogel, Ursula. *Konservative Kritik an der bürgerlichen Revolution: August Wilhelm Rehberg*. Politica, vol. 35. Darmstadt-Neuwied, 1972.

Walker, Mack. *German Home Towns: Community, State and General Estates 1648–1871*. Ithaca, 1971.

Wallthor, Alfred Hartlieb von. *Die landschaftliche Selbstverwaltung Westfalens in ihrer Entwicklung seit dem 18. Jahrhundert*. Veröffentlichungen des Provinzialinstituts für westfälische Landes-und Volkskunde, Series 2, Book 14. Münster, Westfalen, 1965.

Warner, Karl-Friedrich and Bernd Januschke. "Freiherr vom Stein und der preussische Staat." In *Der Freiherr vom Stein im Unterricht: Versuche zur historisch-politischen Bildung*. Veröffentlichungen der Freiherr-vom-Stein Gesellschaft, vol. 5a, 9–41. Cologne and Berlin, 1971.

Webb, Sidney and Beatrice Webb. *English Local Government*. 11 vols. 1906. Reprint. Hamden, Conn., 1963.

Weber, Max. *Essays in Sociology*. Edited by H. H. Gerth and C. Wright Mills. New York, 1970.

Wehler, Hans-Ulrich. *Geschichte als historische Sozialwissenschaft*. Frankfurt am Main, 1973.

Wehler, Hans-Ulrich. *Modernisierungstheorie und Geschichte*. Kleine Vandenhoeck-Reihe, vol. 1407. Göttingen, 1975.

Winkler, Theodor. *Johann Gottfried Frey und die Entstehung der preussischen Selbstverwaltung*. Einzelschriften des Kommunalwissenschaftlichen Instituts an der Universität Berlin, vol. 3. Stuttgart and Berlin, 1936.

Winter, Georg. "Zur Entstehungsgeschichte des Oktoberedikts und der Verordnung vom 14. Febr. 1808." *Forschungen zur brandenburgischen und preussischen Geschichte* 30 (1927): 1–33.

Wood, Gordon S. *The Creation of the American Republic 1776–1787*. Chapel Hill, N.C., 1969.

Wunder, Bernd. *Privilegierung und Disziplinierung: Die Entstehung des Berufsbeamtentums in Bayern und Württemberg (1780–1825)*. Studien zur modernen Geschichte, vol. 21. Munich and Vienna, 1978.

Zeeden, Ernst Walter. *Hardenberg und der Gedanke einer Volksvertretung in Preussen 1807–1812*. Historische Studien, vol. 365. Berlin, 1940. Reprint. Vaduz, 1965.

Ziekursch, Johannes. *Das Ergebnis der friderizianischen Städteverwaltung und die Städteordnung Steins, am Beispiel der schlesischen Städte dargestellt*. Jena, 1908.

Ziekursch, Johannes. *Hundert Jahre schlesische Agrargeschichte, vom Hubertusburger Frieden bis zum Abschluss der Bauernbefreiung*. Verein für Geschichte und Altertum Schlesiens. Darstellungen und Quellen zur schlesischen Geschichte, vol. 20. Breslau, 1915.

INDEX

PUBLICATIONS

OF

The American Philosophical Society

The publications of the American Philosophical Society consist of PROCEEDINGS, TRANSACTIONS, MEMOIRS, and YEAR BOOK.

THE PROCEEDINGS contains papers which have been read before the Society in addition to other papers which have been accepted for publication by the Committee on Publications. In accordance with the present policy one volume is issued each year, consisting of four numbers, and the price is $20.00 net per volume. Individual copies of the PROCEEDINGS are $10.00.

THE TRANSACTIONS, the oldest scholarly journal in America, was started in 1769. In accordance with the present policy each annual volume is a collection of monographs, each issued as a part. The current annual subscription price is $60.00 net per volume. Individual copies of the TRANSACTIONS are offered for sale.

Each volume of the MEMOIRS is published as a book. The titles cover the various fields of learning; most of the recent volumes have been historical. The price of each volume is determined by its size and character, but subscribers are offered a 20 per cent discount.

The YEAR BOOK is of considerable interest to scholars because of the reports on grants for research and to libraries for this reason and because of the section dealing with the acquisitions of the Library. In addition it contains the Charter and Laws, and lists of members, and reports of committees and meetings. The YEAR BOOK is published about April 1 for the preceding calendar year. The current price is $8.50.

An author desiring to submit a manuscript for publication should send it to the Editor, American Philosophical Society, 104 South Fifth Street, Philadelphia, Pa. 19106.

www.ingramcontent.com/pod-product-compliance
Lightning Source LLC
LaVergne TN
LVHW081602100826
845153LV00004B/438

* 9 7 8 1 4 2 2 3 7 4 4 5 0 *